Writing Scientific Programs Under the OS/2 Presentation Manager

Writing Scientific Programs Under the OS/2 Presentation Manager

JAMES W. COOPER

IBM Thomas J. Watson Research Center
Yorktown Heights, New York

A Wiley-Interscience Publication
John Wiley & Sons, Inc.
New York / Chichester / Brisbane / Toronto / Singapore

Cooper, James William, 1943-
    Writing scientific programs under the OS/2 presentation manager /
James W. Cooper.
        p. cm.

    Includes bibliographical references.
    ISBN 0-471-51928-6
    1. OS/2 (Computer operating system)   2. Presentation manager
(Computer program)   3. IBM microcomputers — Programming.   I. Title.

QA76.76.063C665   1990
005.265--dc20   90-35921
                                                                    CIP

Printed in the United States of America

10 9 8 7 6 5 4 3 2 1

Contents

Preface

The introduction of OS/2 provides users of PC's and PS/2's with a DOS-like environment where they can actually perform multitasking and break through the barrier of 640K imposed by DOS. OS/2 also provides a friendly "point-and-shoot" user interface featuring mouse interaction, menus and device-independent graphics.

This sort of operating system provides an ideal platform for scientific programs, where data are often large arrays, and where slow data acquisition and processing should not lock a system up so that it can't be used for other tasks simultaneously. Thus, the thrust of this book is a series of explanations and examples of the parts of OS/2 that are most significant in the display, plotting, and acquisition of scientific data using interface cards.

In this book, we begin by showing how to write programs in C, and then explain how to write programs for the Presentation Manager so that you can get the most out of your system. Throughout, I have tried to include copious comments in every program listing so that you can read the comments for a quicker understanding of the intent of each program.

A number of people have made significant contributions to my understanding of OS/2 and the Presentation Manager and I would particularly like to acknowledge the help of Gennaro Cuomo, Jason Crawford, and Bryan Lewis of the Workstation Projects group at IBM Yorktown, Wolfgang Segmuller of the NSF-Net group, Rudy Dobransky in Lab Automation, Kaushal Amin from IBM Atlanta, Richard Redpath and Keith

Purcell at IBM in Cary, N.C., and David Reich and Marty Klos from IBM Boca Raton.

I particularly wish to acknowledge the clear explanations of device driver design that I received from Oleg Vishnepolsky at IBM Research. Much of the approach I describe here is derived from his explanation, and much of my first device driver was based on the model of a program he provided to me.

The clever method of linking a small amount of assembly code with a small model C program to produce a device driver was outlined to me by Dennis Rowe of IBM Boulder, who in turn has acknowledged help from Tom Rechtshaffen at IBM Yorktown. I also want to thank Marty Klos of IBM Boca Raton for explaining the details of DMA device drivers.

I also would like to acknowledge helpful comments on my manuscript from Frank Novak, David Bolen, Jean-Christophe Simon, Joe Hellerstein and Soren Peter Nielsen. Finally, I want to thank Beth McAuliffe and Joan Dunkin of the Yorktown text processing group for assistance in preparation of the camera ready copy.

James W. Cooper
April, 1990
Yorktown Heights, New York

Trademarks

OS/2™, C/2™, Personal System/2™ and Proprinter™ are trademarks of International Business Machines Corporation. Personal Computer AT® is a registered trademark of International Business Machines Corporation. HP™ is a trademark of the Hewlett-Packard Corporation. CodeView® is a registered trademark of the Microsoft Corporation. Turbo™ C is a trademark of Borland International.

Writing Scientific Programs Under the OS/2 Presentation Manager

1 Protected Mode Programs

OS/2 provides you with the ability to use and write programs using the Protected Mode of the 80286 and 80386 microprocessors. This means that you are free from the 640K barrier imposed by DOS and the Real Mode of the 8086 series of microprocessors, and can write programs that address and use up to 16 megabytes of memory, even if your machine does not actually contain this much physical memory.

More important the Protected Mode actually *protects* your program from accidentally accessing memory that belongs to some other program or even changing program code when you really meant to change program *data*. Because of this protection it is possible to write rather complex multitasking operating systems and assure the user that one task will not interfere with another task because of errors in programming or use. If such an error occurs, it is trapped by the microprocessor as an *exception* and usually dealt with by the operating system. OS/2 therefore provides you with the ability to perform multitasking on your personal computer.

MULTITASKING

OS/2 defines two types of multitasking: multiple *processes* and multiple *threads*.

Processes refer to separate programs that are running simultaneously in your computer, each receiving some slice of time. From the user's point of view, he must initiate each independent process by starting a program or running a program that starts other programs. Processes may share devices, files, or even memory, but can only communicate through *semaphores:* memory locations that can be set or cleared.

Threads are independent routines within a single program or process that run simultaneously. They are able to share data and open files. They are started and terminated within a single program, and are used to execute time-consuming background activities. For example, you might spin off a thread if a long computation is about to commence or if some plotting or printing task will take a long time to execute because the printing device is relatively slow. In general, threads are used to keep the main program "active" to the user, so that he doesn't have to wait for a job to complete.

OS/2 also has the ability to run multiple *sessions*. Each session can have its own command prompt and/or screen window. If you start more than one OS/2 full screen session, each will have its own full screen and each can run its own programs, which can each start several processes and threads. If you start OS/2 windowed sessions, they all appear on the Presentation Manager (PM) windowed screen at once. There is only one PM screen, but each window can represent a session containing one or more processes, or can represent part of a process or thread.

OS/2 PROGRAMMING STYLE

When you write OS/2 programs, you write them rather differently than you would DOS programs, because in a multitasking system you cannot be sure whether someone else is also using some of the system's resources such as the screen, disk files, or special-purpose cards. Therefore, in OS/2 you cannot:

1. Write to screen memory.

2. Write to I/O ports using IN and OUT instructions.

3. Make references to physical memory locations.

4. Write terminate and stay resident programs of the usual sort.

Instead, you must execute these functions through OS/2 calls.

PROTECTION RINGS

OS/2 1.2 is designed to work on the 80286 microprocessor operating in protected mode. The 80386 and 80486 processors run more rapidly than the 80286 but under OS/2 they operate in 80286 mode rather than in the more sophisticated memory modes provided by the 80386.

The 80286 processor defines four rings of protection, each with increasing privilege:

Ring 3	User programs
Ring 2	I/O Privileges
Ring 1	Not used by OS/2
Ring 0	Kernel code and device drivers: interrupt handling

Most programs that you write will run at ring 3, with no privileges. If you want to write a program that can access I/O ports and execute IN and OUT instructions, you must write it to run at ring 2. This is done through a special IOPL segment and is discussed later.

If you wish to control a device and set and acknowledge interrupts, this must be done at ring 0. The only kind of program that you can write to run at ring 0 is a *device driver*. Device drivers are programs loaded when the system is booted, and are always resident to handle device requests. It is through these device drivers that we will see how to control data acquisition boards.

TOOLS NEEDED TO WRITE OS/2 PRESENTATION MANAGER PROGRAMS

To write programs in this operating system, you will need a good programmer's text editor, such as the one provided with OS/2 or any of a number of commercial editors, a C compiler such as IBM C/2 1.1 or Micro-soft C 5.1 that will produce protected mode code, and the OS/2 1.2 Programmer's Toolkit. In addition to the manuals provided with the Toolkit, you should also have the set of OS/2 1.2 Technical Reference manuals. Finally, if you are going to write any device drivers, which require some assembly language programming, you will need an assembler that can produce protected mode code, such as IBM Assembler/2 or Microsoft's MASM 5.1. Additional vendors are planning to provide equivalent assem-blers and compilers as this book is being written.

ON LINE HELP

The syntax of all of the OS/2 PM functions is available on line when you load the OS/2 1.2 toolkit disks. The manual can be selected as an OS/2 program, and you can look up the syntax of any OS/2 programming call on line. This is somewhat easier than carrying around all of the OS/2 manuals needed for programming.

2 A Brief Introduction to the C Language

The C language was developed at Bell Laboratories for research use and is characterized by a number of features that make it ideal for scientific use. In particular, all floating point calculations are automatically carried out in double precision. Because of the early slow teletypewriter terminals, C also has a penchant for terseness that does not make it easy for the beginner to read some C code. In the examples here, we will try to help the reader new to C overcome these problems by carefully commenting our code and trying to make it as readable as possible.

This chapter is not a complete tutorial on the C language, but only an outline of its high points. If you need to learn the entire language, there are a number of excellent texts available.

ADVANTAGES OF C

Structure

One of the great advantages of the C language is that it gives the programmer the ability to write *structured* programs. In particular, you can write loops that have clear entry and exit conditions and can write functions whose arguments are always checked for correctness.

Bit Manipulations

C provides functions for setting and clearing bits and rotating them in words, which is a particularly useful concept for setting and clearing registers on add-in data acquisition and control cards in your PC.

Compactness

C is actually a fairly simple language: a number of the features that have been embedded in other computer languages are relegated to library routines in C, making the base language quite compact and easy to learn.

THE C COMPILER

A large number of compilers have been written for the C language, that compile code for virtually any computer system you can name. In this text, we will be considering compilers that can produce protected mode code for the 80286 and 80386 microprocessors and interact with OS/2. As of this writing, two compilers that fill these requirements are IBM C/2 1.1 and Microsoft C 5.1. Others will no doubt become available.

The C compilers are programs that translate the source code written with the help of a text editor program and into code for the specific computer on which you wish to run your program. The compilers generally produce *object modules* that typically have the .OBJ extension to their filename. This object module is linked with standard library routines using a linker program to produce an executable code file, having the .EXE extension.

There are a few compilers available now that have an integrated editing and compiling environment, in which you can type in your program, check it for errors, compile it, and run it without ever leaving the compiler's editing screen environment. At the moment these compilers, which include Microsoft's Quick-C and Borland's Turbo-C, do not work in the OS/2 environment, and in particular do not produce code that will run with the OS/2 Presentation Manager. However, you should look for such products to appear.

DATA TYPES IN C

C allows you to manipulate data as various types that are handled and checked for consistency by the C compiler. The data types that C handles are

int   The integer data type. In PCs, this is generally a 16-bit integer, but this will certainly vary with the computer's architecture.

char   The basic character type. In some machines, this may be the same as an integer, and in others it may be an 8-bit byte. In all cases, the char type is automatically converted to an integer where needed during calculation without warning the user of this conversion.

long   A long integer. In PCs this is a 32-bit integer.

float   This is the shortest floating point representation in your computer. In the PC, this is a 32-bit number in IEEE standard floating point format. A floating point number allows you to represent scientific data from about 1.0E-38 to 1.0E38, where the "E" means that the number is multiplied by **10** (not e) raised to that power.

double   The double precision floating point representation for that computer. It allows you to represent numbers to greater precision and, usually, to higher dynamic range as well. In the PC environment, double precision allows variables from -1.797E308 to -4.94E-324 and 4.94E-324 to 1.797E308.

NUMBERS IN C

All numbers without a decimal point in C programs are treated as integers and all numbers with a decimal point are considered to be double precision floating point. If you want to represent base-16 (hexadecimal) or base-8 (octal) numbers you precede the number with '0x' for hexadecimal and just

'0' for octal. If you want to specify that an integral value is to be stored as a long integer, you must follow it with an "L."

```
015              /*octal 15 or 13 decimal*/
0x15             /*hex 15 or 21 decimal  */
152L             /*long integer 152      */
```

WRITING A SIMPLE C PROGRAM

For our first C program, let us write a program to add together two floating point numbers and print out the result. Initially, we won't bother to read the numbers in, but instead will simply use values stored in the program.

```
/******************** ADD2 ****************************/
/** A C program to print out the sum of two numbers ******/
#include <stdio.h>      /* contains definitions of printf */
/*-----------------------------------------------------*/
void main()             /* main has no return value       */
{                       /* beginning of routine           */
    double a, b, c;     /* declare the variables used     */

a = 2.3;                /* assign values to the variables */
b = 4.5;

c = a + b;              /* add them together              */
                        /* print out the result           */
printf ("The sum is %f \n", c);

}                       /* end of the program             */
```

Observations on the ADD2 Program

There are a number of simple observations we can make about this simple program that hold for all C programs.

1. Comments begin with a /* and end with a */. Comments in this program are all less than a line long, but may, in fact, be many lines long.

2. The **#include** statement describes a file that is to be read in and used as if it were part of the program at this point. The file "stdio.h" contains function definitions for standard input and output routines, which in this case include the **printf** statement used in the program. IBM C/2 and Microsoft C 5.1 require these include files to describe the number and types of variables that may be put in any functions called by your program.

3. The main routine of any C program is always called **main().** This is where the program starts, regardless of how many routines the program contains.

4. The actual program code begins with a left brace "{" and ends with a right brace "}."

5. Every statement ends with a semicolon (;). Complex mathematical expressions or any other kind of statement may run on for several lines if necessary. The statement only stops when the semicolon is found.

6. All variable names must be declared in advance by name and type. In this program, the three variables are all of type **double.**

7. The equals sign is used to assign values to variables. Thus

   ```
   a = 4.3;
   ```

   means "put the value 4.3 in the location where the variable a is stored."

8. You can print out results using the **printf** statement. This statement consists of a *format string* and a list of variables.

9. The backslash character "\" in C has a special meaning. In the **printf** statement, it is used to represent the non-printing character that causes a new line to start. This is written as "\n."

Strings and Characters in C

A single character that is used as a constant **char** is enclosed in *single quotes*:

```
    char letter;        /* "letter" is of type char */

letter = 'a';           /* assign it the value      */
                        /* of the character a        */
```

A series of characters, however, becomes a quoted *string* and is enclosed in *double quotes*:

```
    printf("hello there");
```

A string is simply an array of characters terminated with a NULL byte. It is this NULL byte that determines the length of the string.

There are a series of special non-printing characters that are represented by preceding them with a backslash. The backslash itself is printed by preceding it with a backslash:

\n	New line character (carriage return)
\t	Tab character
\b	Backspace
\0	The null character (usually a zero byte).
\"	Double quote
\'	Single quote
****	Backslash

ARRAYS IN C

In C, all arrays start at an index of 0 and have a final index one less than the array's dimensions.   You can declare an array of values in C by simply enclosing the number of elements in the array in brackets following the variable name:

```
    float freq[500];            /*array of 500 values*/
```

In this case the first element is

```
freq[0]
```

and the last element

`freq[499].`

Two-dimensional arrays are represented as arrays of arrays as follows:

`float xmatrix[100][100];   /* 100 x 100 matrix */`

Elements in these arrays are stored by rows, and the rightmost subscript varies the fastest. As we will see later, this somewhat awkward construction is seldom used because of the common use of pointers in C.

CHARACTERS AND STRINGS IN C

An individual character variable of type **char** is generally one byte long in C. A *string* of characters is simply an array of characters.

`char name[80];          /*80-character string*/`

However, unlike some other languages, C does not allow you to operate directly on strings and assign them to variables. Thus, to copy a string into a string variable, you use the common string library function **strcpy.**

`strcpy(name, "Anastasia");`

VARIABLE NAMES IN C

Variable names in C can consist of letters, numbers, and the underscore character. They can be uppercase or lowercase or a mixture of cases. Unlike most other languages, the case of the characters is significant! Thus the variables

`Temperature = TEMPERATURE + temperature;`

are all *different*! There are no real restrictions on the length of variable names, but various compilers may restrict the number of characters they actually compare to see if two names are identical. In the case of IBM C/2 and Microsoft C, only 31 characters are significant.

You can use the case sensitivity and the underscore to improve the readability of variable names. Some examples include

```
SumOfPairs
sum_of_pairs
WinMessageBox
```

ARITHMETIC OPERATIONS

In C, you can perform the usual arithmetic operations on variables and constants using the usual operators.

+   addition

-    subtraction

*   multiplication

/   division

%   modulo (remainder after integer division)

C also has a number of bit operators for performing operations on words:

>>   shift right

<<   shift left

&   bit AND

| bit OR

^   bit XOR

~   ones complement

Note that there is no exponentiation operator. You can call library routines for these less common functions.

The Bit Operations

You can AND, OR, or XOR together two computer words using the above operators. Remember that AND means that a bit is 1 if both of the input bits are ones, and OR means that a bit is 1 if *either* of the input bits is a one. The XOR operation turns on the resulting bits if the two input bits are *different*.

THE #DEFINE DECLARATION

C allows you to define a symbolic name for any expression. At the most basic level this allows you to make use of named constants that can be changed by changing only their definition.

```
#define PI 3.1416

y = 2 * PI * r;          /*circumference*/
```

Note that the use of the symbol PI actually improves the readability of the expression and makes it clear what the constant means. By convention, C programmers usually make the names of constants all uppercase letters.

The **#define** declaration is actually a directive to a C *preprocessor* program that simply scans the code and substitutes the second expression for the first. Thus, you are not limited to numerical values, but can in fact substitute whole expressions for particular symbols.

Note that the **#define** directive does *not* end with a semicolon, since it is not a statement. If you put a semicolon on the line with a **#define** directive it becomes part of the expression that is to be substituted.

THE PRINTF FUNCTION

In our first C program, ADD2, we introduced the **printf** function, which consists of a format string and a list of variables. This format string is quite powerful and versatile: we will only summarize the more common features here:

```
char formatstring[nn];

printf("quotedstring", var1, var2, ...,var_n);

/* OR */

printf( formatstring, var1, var2, ...,var_n);
```

The format string can contain

- text to be printed out

- control characters as part of the text

- format specifiers for variables

All of the format specifiers start with a % sign. The most common of these are

%f floating point value

%d integer value

%c character

%s character string

You can specify a desired field width in these specifiers, by preceding the format character with a number:

```
    %6d      /* 6 digit integer            */
    %20s     /* 20-character string        */
```

and can add a precision field for floating point numbers:

```
    %8.2f    /* width of 8, 2 decimal places */
```

There is no distinction between floating point and double precision numbers because all such operations are carried out in double precision.

```
    float a;                 /* define types */
    int j;

    a =  4.26;
    j = 12;

    printf("The %dth value is %10.4f \n",j, a);
```

will print out

```
    The 12th value is       4.2600
```

The sprintf Function

The **sprintf** function performs exactly the same operations as the **printf** function, except that the characters are written into the character array (or string) you specify. The function

```
char buf[80];
float sum;

sprintf(buf, "The sum is %8.2f", sum);
```

writes the string "The sum is " followed by the current value of **sum** into the string **buf.**

Within the OS/2 Presentation Manager, we never use the **printf** function, but often will write to a text buffer using **sprintf** and then call a function to display the result.

MAKING DECISIONS IN C

The **if-else** statement is the most common way to make decisions in C.

```
if (KelvinTemp >= 273.16)
    printf("Water is liquid \n");
else
    printf("Water is solid \n");
```

This statement says that if the condition in the parentheses is true, execute the first statement, and if the condition is false, execute the second statement. It is also possible to write if statements without else clauses:

```
if (Denom <= 1.0e-30)
    printf("Can't divide by 0! \n");
```

There is, of course, no requirement that the statements under the if and else be indented, but it makes reading them somewhat easier.

BLOCKS OF STATEMENTS IN C

The C language is considerably more powerful than might be indicated by
the above simple example. You can write entire *blocks* of statements that
are to be executed when a condition is true or false. These blocks are
enclosed in the same braces used to begin and end the C program:

```
r = b*b - 4.0 * a * c;              /* value to take root of */

if (r >= 0 )                        /* if >0 calc. the roots */
   {
   x1 = (-b + sqrt(r))/(2.0 * a);
   x2 = (-b - sqrt(r))/(2.0 * a);
   printf("The roots are: %f and %f \n", x1, x2);
   }
else
                                    /*or print error message */
   printf("The roots are imaginary\n");
```

COMPARISON OPERATORS IN C

In C, most of the symbols used to compare two numbers with each other are
two characters long. A couple of them are different than in other languages,
as you note from the table.

>	Greater than
<	Less than
>=	Greater than or equal to
<=	Less than or equal to
==	Equal to
!=	Not equal to

Note in particular that if you wish to see if two variables are equal you must
write *two* equals signs:

```
if (a == b)
   printf("they are equal \n");
```

In C, nearly anything you write is a legal expression, and the expression

```
if (a = b)              /*mistake ! */
```

returns the value of **a** after assigning the value in **b** to it. This is the single most common programming mistake in the C language, and often difficult to spot because the compiler regards it as a perfectly legal statement! Note also that the "not equal" symbol is "!=" rather than the "<>" used in most other computer languages.

Combining Comparisons

If you want to perform some action based on two or more comparisons, you will need to combine their results. This is done using the logical operators for AND, OR, and NOT.

& &   AND

|| OR

!   NOT

These represent the most commonly confused symbols in C. The *single* "&" and "|" represent bitwise operations on a number. The *double* "&&" and "||" are operators used in combining two logical expressions:

```
if ( ( a == b ) && ( c == d))
    printf("both are equal \n");
```

Note the distinction C makes between the NOT operator and the one's complement operator. The "!" operator negates a logical value: so a TRUE value becomes FALSE and vice versa. The "~" operator inverts all the bits in an integer: all ones become zeroes and all zeroes become ones.

THE SWITCH STATEMENT

The **switch** statement provides a succinct way of making multiple choices when a variable might have one of a number of possible values. It has the general form

```
switch (variable)
  {
  case CON1:
        statements; /*execute if variable == CON1        */
        break;
  case CON2:
  case CON3:
        statements; /*execute if variable = CON2 or CON3*/
        break;
  default:
        statements; /*execute if none of the above       */
        break;
  }
```

The variable must be an integer or character variable, and the case selection values must be constants. The default case is optional and no statement is executed if the variable does not match any constant and there is not any **default** statement.

Note carefully the **break** statement after every case. If it is not included, the statements on the lines that follow will be executed. For example, suppose we wish to convert certain characters to their Greek equivalents.

```
    char c;        /* variable containing a character */

    switch (c)
      {
      case 'a':
        c = 224; /* ASCII value for alpha in PC font */
        break;
      case 'b':
        c = 225; /* ASCII value for beta in PC font */
        break;
      }
```

In this case, we do nothing to **c** if there is no match, so no default statement is needed.

You can also use the **break** statement to jump out of the current block or loop, but this leads to code that can be very hard to follow, and this is not recommended.

THE ORNERY TERNARY OPERATOR

The statement

```
if (a > b)
    z = a;
else
    z = b;
```

can be more compactly written using the "?:" ternary operator:

```
z = (a > b) ? a : b;      /* z is a if a >b, else z is b*/
```

Actually modern compilers generate the same code for either expression and the only criterion for choice between them is readability. On this basis, the ternary operator will not be used further in this text.

INCREMENT AND DECREMENT OPERATORS

Because C was developed when compilers weren't as "smart" as they are today, a number of C's constructions are designed to tell the compiler the simplest way to compile the code. Many of these terse operations are surprising to scientists used to working in other languages.

You can increment or decrement any integer or long integer variable in the same expression that uses it in a calculation by either preceding or following it with "++" or "--." If the symbols precede the variable, it is incremented or decremented before it is used, and if they follow, the variable is changed after it is used.

```
i++;            /* same as i = i + 1                    */
x[i++] = 12;    /* put 12 in x[i] and increment i       */
y[--j] = i;     /* decrement j and put the value        */
                /* of i in y[j]                         */
```

These auto-increment functions can be rather dangerous, since it is possible to write expressions containing several instances of a variable, and become confused about when the variable is incremented.

Whenever you want to perform any of the simple arithmetic operations on a variable and put the result back into that variable, you can do that with the combination operations that simply say perform the operation on that variable:

```
j += 2;        /* j = j + 2                           */
x *= 5;        /* multiply x by 5                     */
i -= j;        /* subtract j from i                   */
k /= 4;        /* divide k by 4                       */
reg >>= 2;     /* shift reg 2 places to the right     */
word <<=1;     /* shift word 1 place left             */
```

Note that modern compilers would probably generate the same code from the longer expressions for the same operations, but these have a certain succinctness that makes them appealing when involved in complex expressions as we will see in the following section on looping.

LOOPING STATEMENTS

For Loops

You can write loops in C using three different constructions. For loops where the lower and upper bounds are known in advance, the **for** loop is the simplest:

```
for (i = 0;  i < count; i++)
    x[i] = i;        /* put the value of i in each element*/
```

Note that since arrays always start at zero and end one before the final dimension size, we start our **for** loop at zero and loop while the index is *less than* the final count. These for-loops can contain more complex operations, and are not limited to incrementing the index by 1:

```
for (i = 0; i < (count / 2); i += 2)
    x[i] *= i;
```

The **for** loop can also operate on a block of statements:

```
for (i = 0; i < count; i++)
   {
   x[i] = y[i];
   y[i] = y[i] / 3;
   }
```

In summary, the three statements in the **for** loop consist of the starting condition, the ending condition, and what to do at the end of each pass through the loop. Since the loop conditions are checked before the loop is executed, it is possible that in some cases the loop will not be executed at all.

While Loops

The **while** loop performs operations in the loop until the condition specified becomes true. As with the **for** loop, the condition is checked before the loop is executed, and the loop might not be executed at all. The while-loop has the general form:

```
while (condition)
   {
   statements;
   }
```

It is generally used when a loop is to be executed an unknown number of times but will exit when some computed condition is fulfilled.

```
factorial = 1;          /*initialize factorial        */
while (num > 0)
   {
   factorial *= num;    /*multiply by current number */
   num-- ;              /*reduce num by 1             */
   }
```

You should note that a common programming error is forgetting that the variables you are testing must have initial values before you begin the **while** loop. In the fragment above, **num** must have a positive, non-zero value for the loop to be executed.

The do-while Loop

The **do-while** loop looks rather like the **while** loop:

```
do
    {
    statements;
    }
while (condition);
```

It differs only in that the loop is always executed *at least once* since the test for the termination condition takes place at the end of the loop. You should only use it when you are sure that there can never be conditions when the loop should not be executed. As you might expect, you can usually write programs to use either type of **while** loop, and the first type seems to be favored.

POINTERS IN C

The most unusual feature of C compared to other high-level languages is its use of *pointers*. A pointer is simply the *address* of a variable or of the beginning of an array. In C, the "&" operator means take the address of a variable, and the "*" operator means get the value pointed to by the pointer:

```
float x, y, *p;  /* p is a pointer to a            */
                 /* floating point number          */

p = &x;          /* get the address of x           */

y = *p;          /* y is assigned the same value as x */
                 /* and pointed to by p            */
```

Pointers are very commonly used instead of array variables, since they can be incremented as you pass through a loop, without the overhead of calculating the base of an array and adding an index to it each time.

```
#define MAX 100
float x[MAX], *p;
int i;

p = x;           /* p points to beginning of array  */
```

```
for (i = 0; i < MAX; i++)
    *p++ = 0;   /* zero out the array            */
```

C automatically increments pointers by the amount suitable for the size of variable they represent: 1 byte for char, 2 for integer, 4 for float, and 8 for double on the PC, so you needn't have any knowledge of these relative sizes. Note that this is entirely equivalent logically to

```
    for (i=0; i < MAX; i++)
        x[i] = 0;
```

but is likely to execute more rapidly, since there is no array-indexing calculation in each loop.

Pointers are also used to point to memory that is allocated and deallocated within a module using memory management functions such as **malloc.**

```
#include <malloc.h>
int i;
float *x, *p;
                    /* allocate 1000 floating pt numbers */
x = malloc(1000 * sizeof(float));
p = x;              /* use p as variable ptr             */
for (i=0; i < 1000; i++)
    *p++ = i;       /* convert i to float and store      */
```

Strings as Pointers

Since strings are arrays of characters and since the name of an array is in fact a pointer to its first element, you should recognize that string variable names are in fact always pointers to the strings.

```
char string[80], *ch;

ch = string;   /* set pointer to start of string   */
```

CONVERTING BETWEEN DATA TYPES IN C

C will automatically convert between type **char** and integers. It will make all other conversions, as well, but will warn you that it is making them. Thus, in the above example, we could have written

```
*p++ = (float)i;         /*convert integer to float*/
```

and would have avoided an error message from the compiler. The conversion of variables from one type to another in C is called *casting* and is accomplished by preceding the variable with the new type name in parentheses.

Pointers have types associated with them as well. For example, the **malloc** function returns a pointer to variables of type **void** (a pointer to no type), and it must be cast to point to type float. This casting is important, since incrementing a pointer of the wrong type may increment it by the wrong number of bytes:

```
float *x;
                      /* x is a pointer to 1000 floats */
x = (float *)malloc(4000);
```

FUNCTIONS IN C

While many languages provide both subroutines and functions, the C language provides only functions. A C function can have many variables and can return a single value of any simple type as an answer. All functions are assumed to return a value of type **int** unless another type is specifically declared:

```
float xsum( float a, float b)
/* returns the sum of a and b */
{
    float sum;              /* local variable   */
  sum = a + b;
  return(sum);
}
/*----- main routine starts below---------- */
void main()
{
```

```
        float x, y, tsum;
   x = 5.0;
   y = 6.3;

   tsum = xsum(x, y);        /*call the function */
   }
```

When you want to write subroutines that do not return values, you simply write functions of type **void** that return no value.

Unlike many other languages, all arguments to a function are passed *by value*. In other words, a *copy* of the variable's value is passed to the function, leaving the original in tact. This does not turn out to be much of a problem, however, because you can always pass a *pointer* to any variable to the function, and it will then have access to the original data. This is particularly useful when you want to pass a whole array to a function.

```
   /* Function to sum up an array */
   float arraysum(float *x, int count)
   {
           float sum;
           int i;
   sum = 0.0;                 /* initialize sum     */
   for (i=0; i<count; i++)
      sum += *x++;
   return(sum);
   }
   /*------main routine starts below--------------*/
   main()
   {
           float x[100], sum;
   /** code to put something in array must go here**/
   sum = arraysum(x, 100);   /* add it all together */
   }
```

Note that an array name is actually exactly the same thing as a pointer. The address of the beginning of the array **x** is the same as the value of the pointer **x**.

Static and Automatic Variables

Variables declared for use within a function usually exist only while the function is being called. Thus, if you call the function again later, a new space is created for this variable and the previous value will not be remembered. Such variables are called *automatic variables*. Since you usually are done with such variables when you exit from a function, you usually don't care if the values are remembered.

There are occasions, however, when you may call a function once to initialize some variables, and again later to perform some calculations. In this case you want these variables to be remembered. In C these are called *static variables* and are denoted by preceding the variable type with the keyword **static**.

```
void statfunc(int a, float x)
{
        double gronch;      /* automatic variable */
        static int brunch; /* static variable    */
```

Such static variables turn out to be useful in the Presentation Manager where window procedures are called many times during the life of the window.

Function Prototypes

When you write a function that is called from within a module or, more important, from another module, the C compiler must know the number and type of arguments and the return type of the function. You provide these by simply declaring the function at the top of each module using the same declaration as you used at the beginning of the function, except that you follow it with a *semicolon*.

If your function starts with this statement:

```
void statfunc(int a, float x)
```

you would put the following statement at the top of all modules that call that function:

```
void statfunc(int a, float x);
```

Since this can lead to errors very quickly as you change functions, it is more common to put these declarations in an *include file* that you reference at the beginning of each module:

```
#include "statf.h"
```

where this file may include declarations for a number of related functions.

A large number of include files are provided with your C compiler, which are typically kept in the subdirectory

```
\include
```

These define the variable types and return types for all of the C library routines. The C library manual for your compiler will tell you which ones to include. A number of similar files having slightly different calling conventions are also stored in the directory

```
\include\mt
```

which allow C library functions to be called from multitasking programs.

If you enclose the filename for the include file in *angle brackets*, C will look in the \include directory or that directory list defined by the DOS or OS/2 **include** environment variable. If you enclose the filenames in quotes, C will only look for them in the current directory.

THE SCANF FUNCTION

Until now, we have avoided explaining how to read in data from the keyboard. This is because the **scanf** function requires the use of pointers. It has the form

```
scanf("%f %d", &x, &j);
```

where the format strings have the same meaning as they did for **printf** but the values passed to the routine are *pointers* to the actual variables. There is also an analogous routine **sscanf** that operates on a character buffer:

```
sscanf(buf, "%f %d", &x, &j); /*convert from buffer*/
```

As we noted above, *strings* are always pointers, so that if you are reading in data to a string, the name of the string array is *not* preceded with the "&" sysmbol:

```
char st[80];
int i;

scanf( "%d %s", &i, st);   /* read integer and string */
```

FILE HANDLING IN C

There are two sets of file handling calls in C: **open, close, read, write** and **fopen, fclose, fread, fgets, fputs, fputc, fgetc.** The first group uses an integer called a *file handle,* and the second a pointer to a structure **FILE**. Since the latter group operates at a higher level, allowing the reading of strings of varying length from a text file, we will used it in our examples. The former group is sometimes used when individual bytes of unknown type must be read.

```
#include <stdio.h>
FILE *f;
char string[80];

f = fopen("filename.ext", "r"); /*open a file -read only */
if (f != NULL)
    begin
    fgets(string, 80, f);   /*read a string from the file*/
    fclose(f);              /*close the file            */
    end
```

You should note that the pointer **f** will be NULL if the file can't be found, and that performing an **fclose** on a null pointer will crash your program. Further, the **fgets** function reads a string to first end of line or end of file mark, and *includes* this new line character (\n) in the string that is read. Often you must write code to remove that character from the string.

GENERAL C LIBRARY FUNCTIONS

There are a large number of functions provided with the compiler for many types of operations. These are described in the C Library Reference manuals provided with your compiler. When you call these functions, be sure to add the **#include** header files specified for that function in the reference manuals.

STRUCTURES IN C

The last topic in our survey of C is the *structure*. A structure is a group of related variables of various types that are kept together. This turns out to be a very important concept in OS/2, because descriptions of files, windows, and other internals are all kept as structures. To define a structure you simply begin by writing it out following the **struct** keyword, with all of the variables enclosed in braces:

```
struct fblock
   {
   float x, y;          /*two fp variables*/
   int i, j;            /*two integers   */
   char name[80];       /*and a string   */
   };
```

The name **fblock** is the name of this structure and can be used to represent it without listing its elements again when we define actual variables of this structure type. Note particularly that the structure definition ends, like all statements, with a semicolon. Omission of this semicolon is a common programming error that leads to untold confusion by many compilers.

Then to declare variables of this structure type, we simply write

```
struct fblock f1, f2;    /*two structure variables   */
```

Elements within a structure are accessed by adding a period to the structure variable name and following it with the name of the element.

```
f1.x = 4.32;             /*floating element        */
f1.j = 12;               /*integer element         */
strcpy(f1.name, "foo");  /*put string into structure */
```

Pointers to Structures

You can allocate space for structures dynamically in your C program using the **malloc** function. Since we don't know the size of a structure in general, we can use the C **sizeof** function to calculate it for us.

```
struct fblock *pf;        /*pointer to structure */

/*allocate space for a structure*/
pf = (struct fblock *)malloc(sizeof(struct fblock));
```

This returns a pointer to a memory space where the structure is to be located. A special character pair "->" has been defined in C to get the value of a structure element where the base name is a pointer to the structure rather than the structure itself.

```
/*allocate space for a structure*/
pf = (struct fblock *)malloc(sizeof(struct fblock));

pf->x = 4.5;              /*assign value to element    */
strcpy(pf->name, "fred"); /*copy string into structure */
```

THE TYPEDEF DECLARATION

The **typedef** declaration provides a way for you to declare names for new data types. You could write

```
typedef struct fblock
    {
    float x, y;           /*two fp variables */
    int i, j;             /*two integers      */
    char name[80];        /*and a string      */
    } FBLOCK, *PFBLOCK;
```

Now you have defined the type FBLOCK as the type

```
struct fblock
```

and PFBLOCK as a pointer to that structure type. Then you can declare your variables and allocate structures more simply:

```
PFBLOCK pf;          /*pointer to structure */

/*allocate space for a structure*/
pf = (PFBLOCK)malloc(sizeof(struct fblock));
```

COMMENTS IN C

Since C can be so terse, comments are absolutely required to make C programs readable. As we noted earlier, a comment starts with "/*" and ends
with "*/." You can continue a comment for several lines, but this can lead
to lost beginnings and endings of comments. If a comment describing a
program's purpose or function will carry on for a number of lines, it is customary to start each line with "/*" and end each line with "*/" to make the
comment stand out for the reader. Contrast the two examples below:

```
/* This is a comment at the beginning of a program
This program is used to read in columns of scientific
data and display them on the screen as xy plots. Each
successive column is displayed in a distinct color. */


/*       or see the second way below....                     */
/*----------------------------------------------------------*/
/* This is a comment at the beginning of a program           */
/* This program is used to read in columns of scientific     */
/* data and display them on the screen as xy plots. Each     */
/* successive column is displayed in a distinct color.       */
/*----------------------------------------------------------*/
```

Since it is often useful to be able to "comment out" single lines of code in
a program under development, recent C standards have also added the
double slash ("//") as the beginning of a single line comment. Any line that
starts with two slashes is treated as a comment

```
c = a + b;         /* This line is compiled */
//c = a + b;       /* This line is skipped  */
```

THE C READABILITY DEFINITIONS

The C language tends to be terse and either elegant or so compact as to be unreadable. To make programs more readable and maintainable, particularly to those who may have started in other languages, we introduce the following "readability" definitions to replace some of the symbols that either do not print well or are hard to remember. The C preprocessor will automatically insert the correct C symbols before the compiler begins scanning the code, so there is no loss of generality in these symbol choices.

```
/****** C Readability definitions **************/
#define     begin       {
#define     end         }
#define     endif       }
#define     endfor      }
#define     endwhile    }
#define     OR          ||
#define     AND         &&
#define     BitAND      &
#define     BitOR       |
#define     MOD         %
#define     NOT         !
#define     OnesComp    ~
#define     then        /*then*/
```

These definitions are in our file **cdefs.h**, which we include in the code in the following chapters.

MACROS IN C

The **#define** statement in C can also be used to make some complex expressions appear simpler to the reader. Define statements that make use of arguments are called *macros*. For example, we could define a macro to get the upper 16 bits of a 32-bit word by

```
#define UPPERWORD(a) (((a) >> 16) & 0xffff)
```

and the **max** function is often implemented as a macro

```
#define max(a, b) ((a) > (b) ? (a) : (b))
```

STRUCTURED PROGRAMMING IN C

A structured program is one that follows a few simple rules that make it easy to read and maintain. Some of these are:

1. **Each function or routine must have a clearly distinguishable purpose.** You should set off each function within a module with a line of asterisks or dashes and start it with a comment explaining its purpose.

2. **Every routine should have only one entry and exit point.** You should be able to start at the beginning of a routine and know that code will be executed starting there, and be sure that code at the end of a routine will be executed last. This precludes the use of **goto** statements that disturb linear program flow. Use **if-then-else** and **while** statements to control program flow.

3. **A loop or block should only exit at the bottom.** While the **goto** and **break** statements could be used to exit prematurely from a loop, it is better to use flags and **if** statements instead. The same amount of code is generated in either case and the code is easier to read.

4. **Loops should be indented, so their meaning is clear.** Whether you choose to use braces or "begin" and "end" to replace the braces, you should align the block of code under these delimiters and indent the whole block. Be sure to put spaces between all variable names and their operators.

```
/*---good indentation and spacing --------------*/
max = 0;                        /*initialize max           */
for (i = 0; i < 10; i++)
    begin
    if ( x[i] > max) then /*look for largest value*/
        begin
        max = x[i];        /*save the new maximum    */
        isave = i;         /*and save its index      */
        end
    end

/*---another common indentation style-----------*/
max = 0;                        /*initialize max           */
for (i = 0; i < 10; i++) {
```

```
        if ( x[i] > max) {      /*look for largest value*/
            max = x[i];         /*save the new maximum  */
            isave = i;          /*and save its index    */
            }
        }


/*----harder-to-read indentation and spacing---*/
max=0;
for(i=0;i<10;i++){          /*no comments either*/
if (x[i]>max)
{max=x[i];
isave=i; }
}
```

5. **Avoid program "gullibility."** Be sure that you do not make any unwar-
   ranted assumptions about the validity of the variables you will be
   working with. Don't assume that the file exists, that the value is non-
   zero, or greater than zero, or that it is initialized. For example, the code
   below may not find the correct max:

```
for (i = 0;  i < 10;  i++)
    begin
    if ( x[i] > max) then /*look for largest value*/
        max = x[i];
    end
```

because **max** is never initialized before the search begins.

DEBUGGING A PROGRAM WITH CODEVIEW

You can debug any C program compiled with IBM C/2 1.1 or Microsoft C
5.1 with the protected mode CodeView debugger: CVP. To run CodeView,
you must have the statement:

```
IOPL=YES
```

in your CONFIG.SYS file. You should have the sources of all the C
modules in the same directory as the program you are debugging, and you
must compile the code with the /**Zi** switch to generate debugging information. Then, you must use the /**CO** linker switch to tell it to include line
number and symbolic information in the executable file. During develop-

ment, you commonly use both these switches all the time. When the program is complete, recompiling and relinking without them will make a much smaller program, which will run without IOPL=YES being set.

To debug the program HELLO.EXE, simply type

```
CVP HELLO
```

CodeView will start and display the first lines of C code. It will also display the menu items:

```
File  View  Search  Run  Watch  Options Language Calls Help
```

You can select any of these items with the mouse, or by holding down the Alt key and pressing the first letter of the menu item. For example, Alt-F pulls down the File menu.

You can then step through the program, insert and remove breakpoints, and examine values of variables.

PgUp   Move up a page in the code.

PgDn   Move down a page in the code.

F2   Toggle the display of registers on and off.

F3   Switch between C, assembler, and mixed C-assembler displays.

F4   Switch to the output screen. This will switch to PM screens when you debug PM programs. The CodeView screen returns in 4 seconds.

F5   Begin or continue executing the program.

F6   Move the cursor back and forth between the code window and an immediate window at the bottom.

F8   Step through the code.

F9   Set or clear a breakpoint.

F10   Step through the code without jumping to any called subroutines.

The key to using CodeView is to place a breakpoint at the first place where you wish to see what is happening. Then, start your program using F5 and when the breakpoint occurs, you will have a display of the C language code with the current instruction line highlighted. You can then watch the contents of any variable by name by pressing Ctrl-W and typing in the name of the variable. You can watch up to 10 variables at once and see how each changes as you step through the code. You can set additional breakpoints with F9 and remove old ones by putting the cursor on that line and pressing F9 again. You can also insert watchpoint expressions and have the program break when that expression becomes true. This does slow down the program execution significantly, however.

If your program has a number of modules, you can open another C module specifically by pressing Alt-F and then pressing "O" for Open and typing in the filename including the C extension. You can also go directly to that routine by pressing F6 to go to the command line at the bottom and typing the command "V" followed by the name of that function.

To exit at any time, simply press Alt-F followed by "X."

REFERENCES

1. Brian W. Kernighan and Dennis M. Ritchie, *The C Programming Language, 2nd edition.* Prentice - Hall: Englewood Cliffs, NJ, 1988.

2. Mitchell Waite, Stephen Prata, and Donald Martin, *C Primer Plus*, Howard W. Sams: Indianapolis, 1987.

3. Andrew Koenig, *C Traps and Pitfalls*, Addison- Wesley: Reading, MA, 1989.

3 Memory Management Under OS/2

Memory management in IBM C/2 and OS/2 is tied closely to the architecture of the 80286 microprocessor. While the 80286 can address up to 16 megabytes of memory, it is limited to addressing 64K segments at a time. This is because addressing is done through two 16-bit registers called the *segment register* and the *offset register*. Since the offset is limited to 16 bits, you can only refer to 65536 different bytes without changing the segment register. This leads to the concept of different *memory models* where different restrictions are placed on the amount of memory you can access. In addition, the 80x86 microprocessors specifically distinguish between memory for code and memory for data by using different segment registers to point to *code segments* and *data segments*.

MEMORY MODELS

There are five memory models supported by most C compilers using switches invoked at compile time:

small   The code and the data are limited to 64K bytes each.

medium   Has multiple code segments but only one data segment.

compact   Has a single code segment but multiple data segments.

large   Has multiple code and data segments, but each data segment is still limited to 64K bytes.

huge   Has multiple code and data segments, and data segments may be larger than 64K bytes. This is useful for handling large linear data arrays.

In scientific programming we will be concerned only with the large and huge memory models. In the large model, no single data element may be larger that 64K bytes or 16K floating point numbers, but there can be many such arrays, while in the huge model, there are no limits on data size. There is, of course, a small difference in performance between the two models, since the compiler must generate code to increment both the offset and the segment register in huge model programs. It turns out, however, that in most modern workstations this difference is not noticable.

NEAR AND FAR POINTERS

Most C compilers for the PC add the special keywords **near** and **far** to the language to define the characteristics of data pointers. A **near** pointer is a short or 16-bit pointer and can only point to a variable or array in the current data segment. A **far** pointer can point to data in another segment and those data can be as large as 64K bytes. In addition, a **huge** pointer is a special far pointer that the compiler can use to point to data arrays larger than 64K bytes by manipulating the segment and offset registers. These keywords can be used to modify data types regardless of which overall memory model you are using:

```
near int *c;      /* a near integer pointer */
float far *p;     /* a far floating pointer */
huge double *d;   /* a huge double  pointer */
```

COMPILER SWITCHES

The following uppercase switches can be used to generate code in the various memory models:

/AS small model

/AM medium model

/AC compact model

/AL large model

/AH huge model

In addition, the IBM and Microsoft compilers recognize lowercase character switches that you can use to generate customized memory models. There must be three lower case characters in such switches, one for code pointer size, one for data pointer size, and one for segment setup when the program starts. The three letters can come in any order, but to simplify the examples we will list them in the order code-data-segment:

code	data	segment
s	n	d
l	f	u
	h	w

Code Pointers: s and l. The **s** option means produce small code pointers and the **l** option means produce large code pointers.

Data Pointers: n, f, or h. The **n** option produces near data pointers (small) the **f** option produces far data pointers (64K limit) and the **h** option produces huge data pointers.

Segment setup: d, u, or w. The **d** option indicates that the stack segment (SS) equals the data segment (DS) on entry. This is the default for all normal programs. The **u** option tells the compiler to reserve different segments for the stack and data segments. This is the usual case for Presentation Manager programs. The **w** option sets up separate data and stack segments but does not load the data segment register on entry to the program. This is the usual case for dynamic link libraries.

PROTECTED MODE PROGRAMMING

OS/2 uses the *protected mode* of the 80286 and 80386 microprocessors. In this mode, the data segment registers are not loaded with a memory pointer, but with a *selector value* that is an offset into a selector table. The table contains the actual physical address of the code or data. This additional step is used so that the register contents do not have to change during memory management operations, which may result in the data being moved around in memory. This takes place completely transparently to the program.

The other main advantage of protected mode is that you cannot accidently address or change data outside the data area reserved for you, because data area limit registers are also set when you obtain memory from the system. If you attempt to address outside these limits, the processor will generate an "exception," which in the case of OS/2 will cause a "TRAP D" error to be displayed. This error will terminate the program, but nondestructively, since no other memory regions can be damaged by the error.

ALLOCATING MEMORY FROM C

There are a number of memory allocation routines provided by the C runtime library, that you can use to acquire memory blocks for your data. These should be used in preference to those provided by OS/2 when possible, since they make your program more portable to future operating system versions. All of these functions return a pointer of type **void**, which you must then cast to be a pointer of the correct type.

malloc(int size) returns a near or far pointer, depending of memory model.

_fmalloc(int size) returns a far pointer regardless of model.

_nmalloc(int size); returns a near pointer regardless of model.

halloc(long size, int vsize); returns a huge pointer to an array of **size** elements, each **vsize** bytes long.

Now there is no guarantee that huge data arrays larger than 64K will have their segments contiguous in physical memory, and, in fact, the OS/2 functions that these C functions call actually obtain selectors to 64K segments and a selector increment between segments. However, all this selector arithmetic is handled automatically by the C compiler, and there is no need for the data to be physically contiguous unless you are doing data acquisition using some hardware feature of an acquisition card. We will deal with this in the chapters on writing device drivers for OS/2.

OS/2 MEMORY ALLOCATION FUNCTIONS

All of the OS/2 system functions start with the prefix "Dos." This is meant to indicate that they are operating system functions and that they will also work in the DOS compatibility box, but they are not, strictly, DOS functions. The C-library routines listed above call those OS/2 functions to allocate memory. The lower-level functions for allocating memory directly are discussed below. For most applications, you will probably never need to use these functions directly, but it is useful to see what the C library is doing under the covers in case a memory protection fault occurs that you can't explain.

In OS/2 terminology, when you allocate memory, OS/2 returns a *selector value* that is the value of a location in the descriptor table. To convert a descripter to an address you must make it the upper 16 bits of a 32-bit pointer. The macro MAKEP is provided to do this:

```
float *x;
x = MAKEP(sel, 0);    /* x is now a pointer     */
                      /* to the address selected */
```

The memory allocation functions are

```
DosAllocSeg(size, &sel, fl); /*returns selector to memory*/

DosReallocSeg(size, sel);    /*change the size of segment*/

DosFreeSeg(sel);             /*free the allocated segment*/
```

where

size   is the number of bytes to allocate. This can vary from 1 to 65535 bytes and a value of zero means 65536 bytes.

sel   is the 16-bit selector value obtained when memory is allocated.

fl   can have the values

0x0001   the segment is shareable through DosGiveSeg

0x0002   the segment is shareable through DosGetSeg

0x0004   the segment may be discarded in low-memory situations

0x0008   the segment may be decreased in size, even if shared.

Huge memory is allocated using

```
DosAllocHuge(numsegs, size, &sel, /*returns selector to */
             maxsegs, flags); /* a huge region       */

DosReallocHuge(numsegs, size, sel);
```

where

numsegs   is the number of 65536-byte segments requested.

size   is the size of the last non-64K segment.

maxsegs   is the maximum number of segments you may reallocate to include.

The selected **sel** that is returned is a huge segment selector, but since the segments allocated may not be continuous in memory, it is necessary to find out the number that must be added to the selector to get the next segment selector. This is done with

```
DosGetHugeShift(&shift);
```

where **shift** is the number of places you must shift a bit left to get the value
to add to one selector to access the next selector. This is all handled automatically from C, however, for arrays that you declare **huge**.

Suballocation

OS/2 1.2 allows you to access about 1400 different selectors, and thus you
can only make about 1400 calls to DosAlloc. Since many times you only
need a small amount of memory for a short time, OS/2 provides a method to
allocate a large segment of memory and then suballocate it into small pieces
as needed. This is in fact what the **malloc** call does automatically.

```
/*initialize a segment for suballocation */
DosSubSet(sel, 1, size);

/*get offset for size bytes*/
DosSubAlloc(sel, &offset, size);

/*free sub-allocated memory*/
DosSubFree(sel, offset, size);
```

4 | Writing a Simple Multi-thread Program

In this chapter we will write a simple multithread program that prints a message once every second. In one thread, a timer will run and print messages, and in the other thread, we will monitor the keyboard.

The program first starts a timer thread. This timer thread will send "ticks" to a routine that will print a message each time the tick occurs. Meanwhile, another thread will monitor the keyboard and put any characters that are typed into a structure. This structure is then monitored by the same routine that is printing the tick messages and will exit if the letter "q" is struck. To keep our examples simple, we will not use the Presentation Manager in this first example.

SEMAPHORES

In OS/2 a *semaphore* is a memory location that can be accessed by more than one thread or process. Semaphores have only two values, called "set" and "cleared" or one and zero. There are two types of semaphores in OS/2: *RAM semaphores* and *system semaphores*. RAM semaphores provide faster access to their contents, because they are actual memory addresses. System semaphores are created and opened like files and can be used by processes that do not share memory. In this example, we will use system semaphores because these communicate with the system timer functions. Semaphores are explained in more detail in Chapter 20.

To create a system semaphore, we use the call

```
DosCreateSem(exclusive, &hSem, szName);
```

where

exclusive   is 1 if only this process can access the semaphore and 0 if it can be shared.

& hSem   is a pointer to where the handle to the semaphore will be returned.

szName   is the name of the semaphore. This is a zero-terminated ASCII string like a filename that must contain the path name "\SEM\."

Then to set the semaphore we will use the call

```
DosSemSet(hSem);
```

The timer function will clear the semaphore every time we set it and we will simply wait, trying to change the semaphore from cleared to set. We can only set the semaphore when the timer has cleared it, and thus the call

```
DosSemRequest(hSem, timeout);
```

will block the execution of that thread until the the semaphore is cleared and it can reset it. The function will exit after **timeout** milliseconds or will block the thread indefinitely if **timeout** is set to -1.

CREATING A NEW THREAD

To create a new thread we simply use the **_beginthread** call, passing it the address of the C function that is to be executed and the address of a stack of at least 2000 bytes:

```
stack = malloc(2000);                    /*allocate stack memory*/
_beginthread(Procedure, stack, stksize, arg); /*start it */
```

where

Procedure   is the address of the procedure to be executed by the new thread.

stack   is the pointer to an array of at least 2000 bytes that is used by the new thread.

stksize   is the size of the stack in bytes.

arg   is an argument that is passed to the new thread. Usually this is a pointer to a structure of several data values, or a pointer to a value that the thread is to change.

You can also create a thread with the OS/2 call **DosCreateThread**, but if you do, you cannot make calls to a number of C-library functions, such as **printf** or **sprintf**. The C function **_beginthread** correctly initializes the C library and then makes its own call to the **DosCreateThread** function.

HUNGARIAN NOTATION

The above examples illustrate the concept of "Hungarian" notation in naming OS/2 variables. The notation was named after Microsoft programmer Charles Simonyi, who developed it. This notation scheme prefixes variable names with one or two lower-case characters describing the variable type and purpose. Some of the more common variable prefixes include:

h   A handle to an OS/2 object: timer, semaphore, window, etc.

sz   A zero-terminated ASCII string: the usual C string type.

lp   A long pointer to a variable.

THE MAIN TIMER ROUTINE

The main routine in our TIMER program will simply create and set the semaphore, start the timer, create a thread and loop looking for the character "q" and print the message "tick" each time the semaphore clears and can be reset.

```
void main()
begin
        unsigned char *stk, c;
        HTIMER TimeHandle;
        HSEM hSem ;
```

```
/*create a system semaphore*/
DosCreateSem(1, &hSem, "\\SEM\\TIMER.TIM");

/*set the semaphore high */
DosSemSet(hSem);

/*start the timer with 1 second ticks */
DosTimerStart(1000L, hSem, &TimeHandle);
printf("Started timer at 1000 msec intervals.\n");

/*Create a keyboard monitoring thread */
stk = malloc(2000);                    /*get stack space  */
_beginthread(KeyTest, stk, 2000, &c); /*pass address of c*/
printf("Created second thread \n");

do
 begin
 DosSemRequest(hSem, -1L);   /*block thread until set sem*/
 printf("tick\n");           /*message at each semaphore */
 end
while(c != 'q');             /*other thread will change this*/

printf("Exiting \n");
DosExit(1, 0);               /*end all threads           */
end
```

WAITING FOR THE SEMAPHORE

The inner **do-while** loop simply issues calls to the **DosSemRequest** and waits for the semaphore to clear. In the outer loop, it checks the current value of the character **c** whose address was passed to the keyboard thread and exits when it becomes "q."

THE KEYBOARD THREAD

Finally, the thread that examines the keyboard simply loops "forever" calling the function **getch**, which has the form

```
*c= getch();                    /*get char from keyboard */
```

where ***c** refers to the contents of the address **c**. The entire routine is simply

```
void KeyTest(char *c)
/* This thread waits for characters to be struck and      */
/* stores them in the character variable whose address    */
/* is passed in the call                                  */
begin
do
   *c= getch();                 /* get char from keyboard    */
while (*c != 'q');              /* and check for 'q'         */
end                             /* exit if it is 'q'         */
```

EXITING WITH DOSEXIT

The **DosExit** function is used to terminate a program having a number of threads. The call has the form

```
DosExit(action, rcode);
```

where

action   is 1 if you want to terminal all threads and 0 if you only want to terminate the current thread.

rcode   is the return code you wish to pass from the program to the system.

This call allows us to make sure that all threads terminate when the program is finished.

COMPILING WITH IBM C/2

The IBM C/2 compiler requires that you define every function that you will call with a *function prototype* or definition of the type of each argument and the function's return type. All of the OS/2 functions are defined through the use of the include file **os2.h.** This file is actually a small header file containing a number of conditional includes that depend on whether various symbols are defined or not. These symbols are used as follows:

```
#define INCL_BASE      /* DOS and Kbd functions */
#define INCL_PM        /* Win PM calls          */
#define INCL_GPI       /* Graphics calls        */
#define INCL_DEV       /* device calls          */

#include <os2.h>       /* OS/2 calls defined    */
```

In this simple example, we are using only the BASE calls. In addition, every function in our program must have a function prototype definition at the top of the module. Here, we need to define the routine **KeyTest**. We also need the C-definitions file

cdefs.h

and the files

stdio.h

where **printf** is defined,

conio.h

and

process.h

where **_beginthread** is defined, and

stddef.h

and

malloc.h

where **getc** and **malloc** are defined. The correct include files to use for each library call are listed in the C Language Reference manual provided with your compiler.

```
/* Process with 2 threads executing */

#define INCL_BASE
#include <os2.h>
#include <cdefs.h>
#include <stdio.h>
#include <malloc.h>
```

```
#include <conio.h>
#include <process.h>
#include <stddef.h>

/*function prototypes (required)*/
void KeyTest(char *c);
/***********************************************************/
```

PASCAL-STYLE FUNCTION CALLS

The usual C programming style allows you to write functions that have vari-able numbers of arguments, because the number of arguments passed to the function is known only to the calling program. On a machine level, the argu-ments are pushed onto the stack before the function is called and removed from the stack by the calling program when the function returns. Calling functions in this way can lead to larger code modules, since every single call to a function must provide its own stack cleanup after the return from the function.

The Pascal-style function call is one in which the *called* routine removes the arguments from the stack before returning. Since the stack is cleaned up only in one place, the generated code in more complex programs can be as much as 10-20% smaller. For this reason, as well as for more internal reasons, all OS/2 functions are called in Pascal style, as well as all functions that you write that are to be called from OS/2, such as thread procedures and window procedures.

COMPILING THE TIMER PROGRAM

The command for compiling this program is

```
cl /c /AL /W2 /G2sc /Os /Zpe timer.c
```

where

/c   means compile but do not link.

/AL   means compile using the large memory model.

/**W2**   means generate error messages at warning level #2.

/**G2**   means generate code for the 80286.

/**Gs**   means remove stack probes.

/**Gc**   means generate Pascal-style function calls.

/**Os**   means optimize for size.

/**Zp**   means pack structure members.

/**Ze**   means enable language extensions (such as the **pascal** keyword).

The Multithread Include Files

A library is provided with the C compilers called LLIBCMT.LIB, which contains the *multithreaded* library functions. These functions store no values internally and can be called from several threads at once, since they are totally reentrant. All of these functions have Pascal-style calls and require different function prototypes in the header files. These header files are stored in the

```
include\mt
```

subdirectory and you can make them the default for your use by setting the environment variable INCLUDE as follows:

```
set INCLUDE=c:\include\mt;c:\include;
```

LINKING THE TIMER PROGRAM

When you run the IBM Linker/2 you will find that it requests a name for a .DEF file as well as the names of .OBJ and .LIB files. This .DEF file contains the stack size as well as other information that we will use under the Presentation Manager in later chapters. If you simply type

```
link timer
```

the linker will ask you for the following:

```
Run File [TIMER.EXE]:
List File [NUL.MAP]:
Libraries [.LIB]:
Definitions File [NUL.DEF]:
```

You can press the Enter key for each of the above questions except the last two. You must enter the names of the libraries OS2.LIB and LLIBCMT.LIB and the name of the .DEF file, usually TIMER.DEF. This file contains the following minimum information:

```
NAME    TIMER
DESCRIPTION 'Timer Sample Program'
STUB 'OS2STUB.EXE'

CODE MOVEABLE
DATA MOVEABLE MULTIPLE

HEAPSIZE 1024
STACKSIZE 4096
```

The NAME statement should correspond with the name of the executable program file. The DESCRIPTION statement inserts text into the program module, and can be used to embed copyright statements and other similar information. The STUB statement appends DOS-executable code to the program, and the file OS2STUB.EXE contains the statement "This program will not run in DOS mode." The CODE and DATA statements define the attributes of code and data segments of the program and are simply set to their default values for this program. Finally, the HEAPSIZE and STACKSIZE statements allow you to reserve a predetermined amount of space for the program's heap and stack. Arrays and automatic variables are generally taken from the stack space and global and static variables from the heap.

USING AN AUTOMATIC RESPONSE FILE

You can use an automatic response file to answer the linker questions by simply making a file called TIMER.L containing

```
timer.obj /A:16 /NOD
timer.exe
timer.map
llibcmt.lib+
os2.lib
timer.def
```

leaving a blank line for the default libraries. Then you can simply type

```
link @timer.l
```

to link your file.

USING THE MAKE UTILITY

The MAKE/2 program provides a simple method of compiling and linking programs containing multiple modules, where the MAKE program checks to see if the current file has a later time and date than any of the files it depends on. The syntax for declaring these dependencies is

```
file: depfile1 depfile2 depfil3
    commands to execute
```

In addition, if MAKE/2 discovers that one of the dependent files is itself dependent on other files whose dependencies are declared later in the make file, it will compile those first. The complete MAKE file TIMER.MAK for this simple TIMER example is

```
## TIMER MAKE file
timer.exe: timer.obj
    link @timer.l /A:16 /NOD;

timer.obj: timer.c
    cl /c /AL /W2 /G2sc /Os /Zpe timer.c
```

To us MAKE, you simply type

```
MAKE TIMER.MAK
```

and the program will scan all of the target files. If timer.exe is older than timer.obj, it will examine timer.obj's dependencies and if timer.obj is older than timer.c, it will compile timer.c using the command given. Then it will link timer.obj according to the timer.l file and make timer.exe.

While using MAKE for this simple example seems trivial, it can be a very valuable program development tool when a program has several modules and you change only one of them. Then MAKE will recompile only those modules that have changed.

The example shown here is specifically for the version of MAKE provided with IBM's C/2 1.1 compiler. Other versions of MAKE, including those from Microsoft, may analyze the dependencies between files differently and expect the final target file last rather than first. Check the documentation for your version of MAKE if these examples do not work correctly.

RUNNING THE TIMER PROGRAM

To run the program under OS/2, simply type TIMER at the prompt. The program will print out

```
C>TIMER
Started timer at 1000 msec intervals.
Created second thread.
tick
tick
tick
tick
tick
```

until you press "q." Then it will print

```
Exiting
C>
```

and exit back to OS/2.

5 Using the Presentation Manager

The Presentation Manager (PM) is one of several possible screens that can run under OS/2. It provides a consistent visual interface for programs along with device-independent graphics. In addition, it features pull-down menus, mouse interaction, and the ability to run tasks or programs in multiple windows.

There are some fundamental programming differences when you operate in a windowing environment. In particular, the size and position of the window owned by your program are managed by the system. You as a user can grab and resize or reshape a window, or convert it from a window to a small icon pattern at the bottom of the screen. However, whenever a window is moved or sized, the system redraws its borders and menu bars, but *you* as the programmer must repaint the contents of that window.

This is a fairly important distinction from other types of graphics programs, where you can be more or less certain that the screen is the way it was when you drew it. Here, any window may attempt to be resized, which will affect other windows' position and contents. When such resizing occurs, your window receives a *PAINT message*, along with coordinates that tell you which part of the window needs redrawing if only part of the window needs to be repainted. The upshot of this is that windows must be prepared to loop, checking for messages that must be acted on at all times.

Each window has associated with it a *window procedure*, which is in fact a subroutine that is called by OS/2 when an event occurs that might affect that window. When the window procedure is called, the four arguments that are passed to it are called a *window message*.

WINDOW MESSAGES

In the Presentation Manager, a *message* consists of four values that are sent to the windows procedure:

hWnd   the handle for that window (16 bits)

message   a message number (16 bits)

mp1   a 32-bit parameter value

mp2   a second 32-bit parameter value

As before, a handle is just a number by which an object in the PM is identified. The types of messages that may be received by a window include:

- Window creation

- Window resizing

- Window repainting

- Mouse movement

- Mouse buttons

- Keyboard character

- User-defined messages

- Messages from other windows

WINDOW DATA TYPES AND CONSTANTS

The PM include files define a large number of data types and constant values that are used throughout PM programming. As is customary in C, all constants and defined types are represented entirely in uppercase, while variables are represented in lowercase or a mixture of cases.

OS/2 Data Types

LONG   a 32-bit signed integer, same as type "long"

ULONG   a 32-bit unsigned integer

SHORT   a 16-bit signed integer, same as type "int" or "short"

USHORT   a 16-bit unsigned integer, same as type "unsigned int"

CHAR   same as type "char"

UCHAR   an unsigned char

MPARAM   a 32-bit message parameter value

MRESULT   a 32-bit message reply value

FAR   same as "far" keyword

PASCAL   same as "pascal" keyword

BOOL   a short value that can be either TRUE or FALSE

BYTE   an unsigned char type

VOID   the "void" data type

PVOID   a pointer to a value having the void data type

OS/2 Structures

Some of the more common structures used in OS/2 include:

RECTL   The dimensions of a rectangle in four integer values: xLeft, xRight, yBottom, and yTop.

POINTL   The x,y coordinates of a point in two long values: pointl.x and pointl.y.

HANDLE   a handle to a PM object

HWND   a handle to a window

HPS   a handle to a Presentation Space

HMQ   a handle to a Message Queue

HSEM   a handle to a Semaphore

PM Messages

A large number of values representing bit fields, colors, and messages have been defined as constants. The most important of these are the following WM_ messages:

WM_CREATE   A window is being created, but not yet shown.

WM_PAINT   The window needs to be repainted.

WM_CLOSE   The window is about to be closed.

WM_QUIT   The window is being closed.

WM_SIZE   The window is being resized. Mp1 contains the old x and y sizes, and mp2 contains the new x and y sizes.

WM_CHAR   A keyboard character has been struck. The upper word of mp2 contains the character code and the lower part the scan code.

WM_COMMAND   A menu command has been selected. Mp1 contains the command value.

WM_MOUSEMOVE   The mouse has been moved. The upper part of mp1 contains the x-position and the lower part the y-position.

WM_BUTTON1DOWN   The left mouse button has been depressed. The upper part of mp1 contains the x-position and the lower part the y-position. Analogous messages for button-up and for button 2 also exist.

STRUCTURE OF A PM PROGRAM

Presentation Manager programs are constructed so that the central loop is a *window procedure*, or function that is called by OS/2, passing to it the four arguments that constitute a message. For a window procedure to run, you must tell OS/2 its address and some general information about the window. This is done by *registering the window class*. In addition, you must create a *message queue*, an internal structure where messages accumulate before they are received by various windows. Thus, the overall structure of a PM program is:

1. Initialize the PM facility (WinInitialize).

2. Create a message queue (WinCreateMsgQueue).

3. Register the window class by name (WinRegisterClass).

4. Create the window and display it (WinCreateStdWindow).

5. Loop getting messages, until WM_QUIT is posted (WinDispatchMsg).

6. Destroy the window and the message queue (WinDestroy...).

7. Terminate the program (WinTerminate).

All of the messages that are dispatched end up being received as arguments by your program's window procedure. Within the window procedure, you simply interpret the messages using a **switch** and take action as necessary.

A SIMPLE HELLO PROGRAM

To illustrate how to write a simple program to display a message on the screen, let's design a program to display "Hi there" on the screen in blue letters on a black background. The coordinates of the window start with (0,0) in the lower left corner, and we will display our message at (50,50). In this first program we will only process the WM_PAINT message and leave all other messages to be processed by the default message-handling routine.

Initializing the PM and the Message Queue

The first thing we must do in a PM program is to initialize the Presentation Manager services and set up a message queue. This is done in the first part of our program as follows:

```
#define INCL_PM
#include <os2.h>
#include <cdefs.h>
#include <string.h>
#include "helloj1.h"

/* required function prototypes */
MRESULT FAR PASCAL HelloWndProc( HWND, USHORT,
                                         MPARAM, MPARAM );
void cdecl main(void);
/******************************************************/
void cdecl main ()                        /*C main routine*/

begin
        QMSG qmsg;              /*defining a message queue */
        HAB    hAB;             /*handle to anchor block    */
        HMQ    hmqHello;        /*handle to message queue   */
        HWND   hWnd;            /*client area window handle*/
        HWND   hFrame;          /*frame window handle       */
        ULONG flCreate;         /*window create flag bits   */

hAB = WinInitialize (NULL);  /*init and get anchor handle*/
hmqHello = WinCreateMsgQueue(hAB, 0); /*create msg queue */
```

The **WinInitialize** function returns a value called a handle to an *anchor block*, which is used in the following **WinCreateMsgQueue** call. This handle is also used in some timer and closing calls.

Register the Window Class

Then we register the window class as a *class name*. These class names are zero-terminated ASCII strings containing any desired name. Usually you relate the class name to the program or window's function.

```
/*register the Window class*/
WinRegisterClass (hAB,                /*handle to anchor block */
    (PCH)"Hello",                     /*name of window class   */
    (PFNWP)HelloWndProc,       /*address of window procedure */
    CS_SIZEREDRAW |CS_SYNCPAINT, /*use these flags           */
    0 ) ;                             /*number of "extra" bytes*/
```

In this call, we pass the anchor block handle **hAB** and the class name "Hello," and the address of the window procedure **HelloWndProc**. Then we set two style bits, CS_SIZEREDRAW and CS_SYNCPAINT, which say that the window should receive a paint message whenever the window is resized, and should be repainted synchronously. A *synchronous-paint* window will be redrawn *whenever* a paint message occurs, while an *asynchronous* window will be redrawn after there are no other messages in the queue, so that several paint regions may be combined into a single operation. The final argument is the number of extra bytes that should be reserved as part of the window structure. These bytes can be used to pass arguments to a window, obviating the need for global variables. For the moment, however, we will simply set this value to zero.

Create the Window and Display It

To create the window, we simply call WinCreateStdWindow, passing it a number of style bits and the class name of the window. We also include the title to be put across the title bar of the window. This function actually creates two windows, a *frame window* and an interior window called the *client window*, which is a child of the frame window.

The frame window consists of the active segments surrounding the client area, including the title bar, menu bar, system box, maximize and minimize boxes, and the frame border used for sizing the window.

The call to the create function has the form

```
WinCreateStdWindow(hParent, style, &ctrlbits, szClassname,
            szTitle, clientstyle, resource, id, &hClient);
```

where

hParent   The handle of the parent to this window. The window is constrained to move about only within the boundaries of its parent. Here we will say that the window is the child of HWND_DESKTOP, a window filling the entire screen.

style   Generally main windows are set to the style WS_VISIBLE. Child windows are set to style bits such as FS_BORDER, and made visible in a separate command controlling their size and position. There are also a number of other FS_ control bits that have identical functions to the FCF_ control bits described below, which are present only for evolutionary reasons.

& ctrlbits   This is a pointer to a 32-bit word containing bits describing the type of border, title bar, menu, min-max arrow boxes, and system menu box, as well as whether the program has an icon to display.

szClassname   This is the string containing the name of the window class. It is this name that determines the address of the window procedure that is to receive the messages.

szTitle   This is the title to be placed in the window title bar. If the style bits include FCF_TASKLIST, the program's filename is placed in the title bar and this text appended to it.

clientstyle   The style bits for the client window inside the frame window are usually just WS_VISIBLE.

resource   If this value is NULL then any menu information is to be found in the program file. Otherwise this is a handle to a module that contains these definitions.

id   This must be a non-zero frame window identifier. If you create a main or child window that has an icon or menu associated with it, it is this value that must be used in defining that menu and icon in the resource file. Then, when the window is created, these objects are automatically loaded.

& hClient   The handle to the client window is returned in this argument.

The example below illustrates how to set the FCF_ bits and open a standard window.

```
flCreate = FCF_MINMAX | FCF_SIZEBORDER | FCF_SYSMENU |
           FCF_TITLEBAR | FCF_SHELLPOSITION | FCF_ICON;

/*create the window */
hFrame = WinCreateStdWindow(
         HWND_DESKTOP,    /*as child of the desktop window*/
         WS_VISIBLE | FS_ICON ,
         &flCreate,        /*control data bits           */
         (PSZ)szClassName,  /*this name refers to class*/
         (PSZ)szMessage,    /*title across top bar      */
         WS_VISIBLE,        /*"main" window visible      */
         NULL,              /*menu is in resource file */
         HELLOICON,         /*icon identifier           */
         &hWnd);            /*client area handle        */
```

The long word **flCreate** contains a number of option bits to select the style of the window to be displayed. The bits we have chosen above are a reasonable default set. The complete set of options bits includes:

FCF_TITLEBAR   The window has a title bar.

FCF_SYSMENU   The window has the left corner system menu box.

FCF_MENU   The window has menus.

FCF_SIZEBORDER   The sizing border is to be shown so the window's size and shape can be manipulated.

FCF_MINBUTTON   The window should display the down-arrow minimize button.

FCF_MAXBUTTON   The window should display the up-arrow maximize button.

FCF_MINMAX   The window should have both minimize and maximize buttons.

FCF_VERTSCROLL   The window should have a vertical scrollbar.

FCF_HORZSCROLL   The window should have a horizontal scrollbar.

FCF_DLGBORDER   The window should have the dialog box style border.

FCF_BORDER   The window should have a single line border.

FCF_SHELLPOSITION   The window should be positionable on the PM shell display. This bit is **required.**

FCF_TASKLIST   The name of the main window program should be added to the task box list.

FCF_NOBYTEALIGN   Do not align windows on byte boundaries of the display.

FCF_NOMOVEWITHOWNER

                             Do not move the child window with its owner.

FCF_ICON   The window has an icon.

FCF_ACCELTABLE   There is an accelerator table of keystrokes to be loaded.

FCF_SYSMODAL   The window is modal: no other window can be active while it is active.

FCF_SCREENALIGN   Align child windows on byte boundaries.

FCF_MOUSEALIGN   Align the mouse cursor on byte boundaries.

PM is very particular that you only define the bits that describe features you actually have in this program. For example, do not specify FCF_MENU if you have no menus or FCF_ICON if you do not specify the name of an icon file in your resource file. In fact, such programs will compile and link properly but will "mysteriously" refuse to run.

As we noted, the class name we selected when we registered the window class is used as the third argument and is the only way that OS/2 can tell which window procedure is to receive the messages for that window. The text in **szMessage** is "Hello World" and becomes the name in the title bar across the top of the window.

This call returns the handle to the window frame in **hFrame** and the handle to the window in **hWnd**.

Loop Getting Messages until Quit Is Posted

The two calls below get messages and dispatch them. If **WinGetMsg** returns NULL, this is equivalent to the WM_QUIT message (which has a NULL value) and the while loop terminates.

```
/*get messages from the input queue and dispatch them */
while ( WinGetMsg( hAB, (PQMSG)&qmsg, (HWND)NULL, 0,0) )
    begin
    WinDispatchMsg(hAB, (PQMSG)&qmsg);
    end
```

Terminate the Program

The three statements below destroy the frame window and the message queue and terminate the program. When the frame window is ordered closed, it automatically sends close messages to its child window: the client window, so all windows are destroyed by this command.

```
/* once the program is over,            */
/* destroy the window and message queue */
WinDestroyWindow(hFrame);
WinDestroyMsgQueue(hmqHello);
WinTerminate (hAB);                    /* the TERMINATOR!!! */
end
```

THE WINDOW PROCEDURE

Obviously, the real work of the program is not done in the main function, but in the **HelloWndProc** window procedure. This function receives all the messages sent to the window, and either acts on them or passes them on to the function **WinDefWindowProc,** which performs the default action for

that message.

In the window procedure shown in Figure 5-1 we check the value of **message** in a switch statement and then either execute the paint routine or pass the message on to the default window procedure. Obviously, in a more versatile program, we might interpret quite a number of messages in this switch statement.

The bulk of this routine's activity is in the WM_PAINT case. Here we see the **WinBeginPaint** and **WinEndPaint** calls bracketing code that determines the rectangle size and where to write the string on the screen.

PRESENTATION SPACES

When **WinBeginPaint** is called, it returns a handle to a Presentation Space. A *Presentation Space* is an internal table of drawing attributes such as color, background, line type, font, and so forth that can be associated with any device on which you can draw graphics. The Presentation Manager defines three levels of Presentation Spaces:

1. A cached micro PS

2. A micro PS

3. A normal PS

The *cached micro PS* is used most commonly for simple drawing operations. This PS table exists within the Presentation Manager and is created each time you need it, with default attributes assigned. It is the fastest one to create and use for simple drawing operations, but it does not remember attributes from one use to the next.

```
/*************************************************************/
/* The window procedure receives messages and acts on them
   or passes them on for default processing. Minimally, it
   must respond to WM_PAINT, and may respond to WM_CREATE
   and WM_CLOSE                                             */
/*************************************************************/
MRESULT FAR PASCAL HelloWndProc(HWND hWnd, USHORT msg,
                                MPARAM mp1, MPARAM mp2)


begin
    HPS     hPS;            /*handle to presentation space  */
    RECTL   rc;             /*rectangle definition structure*/

switch (msg)               /*interpret messages            */
begin
 case WM_PAINT:
   hPS = WinBeginPaint(hWnd, (HPS)NULL, (PWRECT)NULL);

   /*get current window dimensions*/
   WinQueryWindowRect(hWnd, &rc);

   WinFillRect(hPS, &rc, CLR_BLACK); /*fill it with black*/
   rc.xLeft = 50;                    /*write at (50,50)   */
   rc.yBottom = 50;
   rc.yTop = 100;
   rc.xRight = 150;
   WinDrawText(hPS, strlen("Hi there!"), "Hi there!",
                     &rc, CLR_BLUE, CLR_BLACK, DT_LEFT);
   WinEndPaint(hPS);                 /*end painting routine*/
   break;

 default:
   return( WinDefWindowProc( hWnd, msg, mp1, mp2));
   break;
end /*switch*/

return((MPARAM)OL);
end
```

Figure   5-1. The Helloj1 Window Procedure

The *micro PS* must be created each time you need it, and can remember any set of attributes such as color, line type, etc., that you might need to keep constant from one paint invocation to another.

The *normal PS* allows you to keep a record of your graphics calls in a *graphics segment* associated with the PS memory and then play back these commands quickly when repainting is required. You can also edit and modify these graphics segments easily. In addition, the normal PS is the only PS that can be associated with more than one device. You can "detach" the normal PS from one device and reattach it to another device and have the stored graphics segment information played back on this new device.

THE PAINT ROUTINE

WinBeginPaint returns the handle to a *micro* presentation space, **hPS**. Then the function **WinQueryWindowRect** returns the size and position of the window in the RECTL structure **rc**. This will always be a structure in which the xLeft and yBottom values are zero, and the xRight and yTop values contain the window dimensions. In this case, however, we do not need to ever look at these values, but simply pass them on to the **WinFillRect** function, which clears the screen to black. All of the major colors are defined as constants having the prefix CLR_. In this case the background is filled with CLR_BLACK.

Ending the Paint Routine

The **WinEndPaint** function simply releases the cached micro presentation space, completing the paint routine. This also completes the window procedure, since the routine exits after completing this function. The **WinBeginPaint - WinEndPaint** calls often are used to bracket a paint routine, since they allocate and deallocate a presentation space. The complete call is

```
WinBeginPaint(hWnd, hPS, &rect);
```

where

hWnd   is the handle to the current window.

hPS   can be NULL if you want a PS allocated, or can be the handle
                to a current PS if one already exists.

& rect   returns the rectangle boundary of the region of the window that
                must be updated.

The **WinEndPaint** call tells PM that the screen region requiring update is
now valid, and either releases the allocated micro PS or restores the existing
PS to its state prior to the **WinBeginPaint** call.

THE DISPLAYED WINDOW

Once the program is compiled and linked, running it will give the display
shown in Figure 5-2. The parts of the window are as follows

The *system box* is the box containing the hollow dash in the upper left
corner. If you click on this box, you will get a small menu containing the
options shown in Figure 5-3. Clicking on any of these options causes that
window to be maximized to full screen, minimized to an icon, or moved to a
new location determined by moving the mouse and clicking at the new
location. Clicking on Close causes the window to be closed. You can also
close down any PM program without waiting for a menu by double clicking
the mouse on the system box.

The *title bar* contains the current program title or other information. If
you position the mouse pointer inside the title bar and press and hold the left
mouse button, you can move the window to a new position determined by the
position of the movable outline when you raise your finger from mouse
button 1. This is called *dragging* the mouse and indicates that you are dragging the figure as well.

The *minimize box* contains the down-arrow. If you click on it the window
shrinks to an icon in the lower left corner of the screen.

The *maximize box* contains the up-arrow. If you click on it the window
will expand to full screen, and the minimize box will change to an up-arrow
plus a down-arrow. If you click on this box, the window will shrink back to
its previous size. You can also maximize the window by double clicking on
the title bar, and reduce it to partial screen size by double clicking on the
title bar when the window is maximized.

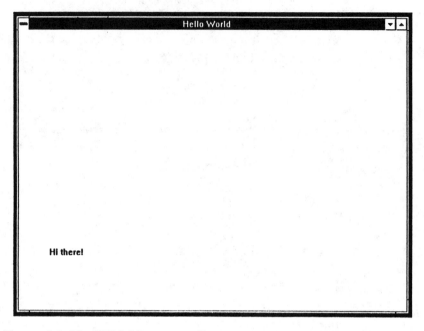

Figure   5-2. The HELLOJ1 program display

The **command bar** is the bar just below the title bar. It generally contains a list of top-level commands. When you click on the menu item, a drop-down list of commands appears. Since we haven't put any command detection in our first PM program, none of the commands that might appear in this menu will do anything.

The **frame** can be dragged to change the window's size and shape by placing the mouse pointer on the frame. Here it will change to a double-headed arrow. Holding down the left mouse button and moving the mouse allows you to move that side of the window frame to a new position, making the window larger or smaller. Dragging the mouse after selecting a corner of the frame allows you to move two sides at once.

FILES USED IN COMPILING A PM PROGRAM

The following files figure in preparing a PM program.

.C	The source code files
.MAK	The MAKE file
.H	The include file(s)

Restore	Alt+F5
Move	Alt+F7
Size	Alt+F8
Maximize	Alt+F9
Minimize	Alt+F10
Close	Alt+F5
Task Manager	Ctrl+Esc

Figure 5-3. The System Box Menu

.L	The Link file list
.DEF	The definitions file
.RC	The Resource file
.ICO	The icon image file
.DLG	The Dialog Box file(s)
.OBJ	The compiled object file before linking
.EXE	The executable program
.RES	The resource file compiled by RC or the dialog box editor
.DLL	A dynamic link library module to be linked at run time
.LIB	A library module to be linked to your program at link time

In this first program, we will not have any dialog boxes, so we can delay discussing the .DLG file, but we will need to have one of each of the other files.

The Icon File

The ICONEDIT program can be used to prepare a 32 x 32-pixel icon pattern to represent the program when its window is minimized to an icon. For this first example, we will make an icon file that simply has "Hi!" in the middle of the icon area as show in Figure 5-4.

The Include File

In this file we will define the one constant that we will use in this program:

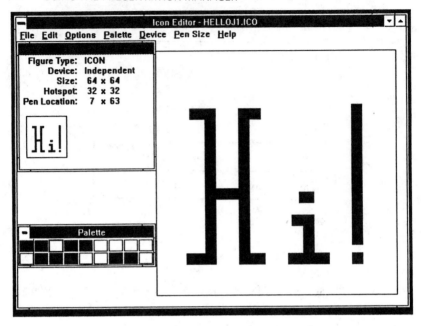

Figure 5-4. The ICONEDIT program display. The large square can be operated on pixel by pixel using the mouse, and the small icon area shows the final icon at normal viewing size.

```
#define HELLOWIND          1
```

We use this constant to refer to the frame window id in both the program and the resource files to define the window that the icon will be associated with.

The Definition File

This file is exactly like the one we prepared for the TIMER program, *except* for the **EXPORTS** statement.

```
NAME     HELLOJ1    WINDOWAPI
DESCRIPTION 'PM Hello Program'
STUB 'OS2STUB.EXE'

CODE MOVEABLE
DATA MOVEABLE MULTIPLE
```

```
HEAPSIZE 1024
STACKSIZE 4096
EXPORTS
    HelloWndProc @1
```

The EXPORTS statement is required for all PM programs compiled with /AL or /AS, and must contain a list of all window procedures that are to be called from OS/2. In this first program, we have only the one window procedure *HelloWndProc*. Each of these procedure names must be followed by a commercial sign (@) and an integer. These integers must each have different values: they usually start at 1 and each additional window procedure name simply has the next largest integer for its id number.

However, while we illlustrate the EXPORTS statement here for completeness, if you compile with the */Alfu* switches, this statement is unnecessary as the external references are provided automatically by the compiler.

The Resource File

The resource file contains definitions for icons, menus, accelerator keys that act as menu items, and string tables, such as Help files might use. In this example, our resource file contains only the name of the icon file:

```
/*********** Resource file for HELLOJ1****************/
#include "helloj1.h"

POINTER HELLOWIND  helloj1.ico
```

The Make File

To create a PM program, you must compile and link as usual, and then you must run **RC**, the resource compiler. The overall make file, then, must indicate these dependencies, and as before, the final module is listed first followed by the dependent modules.

```
#### Make file for HELLOJ1###################
helloj1.exe: helloj1.obj helloj1.rc helloj1.h
    link @helloj1.l;
    rc helloj1.rc

helloj1.obj: helloj1.c
    cl /c /Alfu /W2 /G2sc /Os /Zpe helloj1.c
```

The Link File

The link file lists the actual modules and libraries to be linked. These are as follows:

```
helloj1.obj /A:16 /NOD
helloj1.exe
helloj1.map
os2.lib+
llibcmt.lib
helloj1.def
```

Note that we will habitually compile our programs using the large memory model /Alfu and link them using the multithread library LLIBCMT.LIB. The /NOD switch tells the linker not to look in the default C libraries for the library functions, but instead to look only in the specified libraries. The /A:16 switch tells the linker to align segments on 16-byte boundaries, which again is required for OS/2.

We will assume that the environment variable INCLUDE is set to point to the multithread include files:

```
set INCLUDE=c:\INCLUDE\MT;c:\INCLUDE;
```

THE COMPLETE HELLOJ1 PROGRAM CODE

In the complete program we show below, we illustrate the complete window procedure in Figure 5-1 and the main program that creates the window in for the main program shown below. Since the main program remains the same throughout all further examples, we will seldom show it again completely, but will concentrate on the window and graphics functions.

```
/******   Basic Presentation Manager Prototype Program ***/
/* Displays a blue "Hello World" on a black background    */
/**********************************************************/
#define INCL_PM
#include <os2.h>
#include <cdefs.h>
#include <string.h>
#include "helloj1.h"

MRESULT FAR PASCAL HelloWndProc( HWND, USHORT,
                                 MPARAM, MPARAM );
/**********************************************************/
/********** M a i n    F u n c t i o n*********************/
/* The main() function in a PM program registers the class
   of all windows and creates the main window. Then it gets
   and dispatches messages to that window until a WM_QUIT
   message is received, and closes down.              */
/**********************************************************/
void cdecl main ()                 /*C main routine*/


begin
  QMSG qmsg;                /*defining a message queue */
  HAB    hAB;              /*handle to anchor block   */
  HMQ    hmqHello;         /*handle to message queue  */
  HWND   hWnd;             /*client area window handle*/
  HWND   hFrame;           /*frame window handle      */
  ULONG flCreate;          /*window create flag bits  */

  hAB = WinInitialize (NULL); /*init and get anchor handle*/
  hmqHello =
    WinCreateMsgQueue(hAB, 0); /*creat msg queue*/

/*register the Window class*/
WinRegisterClass (hAB,          /*handle to anchor block  */
    (PCH)"Hello",               /*name of window class    */
    (PFNWP)HelloWndProc,  /*address of window procedure*/
    CS_SIZEREDRAW |CS_SYNCPAINT, /*use these flags        */
    0 ) ;                       /*number of "extra bytes  */

flCreate = FCF_MINMAX | FCF_SIZEBORDER | FCF_SYSMENU
         | FCF_TITLEBAR | FCF_SHELLPOSITION | FCF_ICON ;
```

```
/*create the window */
hFrame =
    WinCreateStdWindow(
            HWND_DESKTOP, /*as child of the desktop window*/
            WS_VISIBLE ,
            &flCreate,         /*control data bits         */
            (PSZ)"Hello",    /*this name refers to class*/
            (PSZ)"Hello World", /*title across top bar*/
            WS_VISIBLE,      /*"main"window visible      */
            NULL,              /*menu is in resource file*/
            HELLOWIND,         /*id of ICON in RC file   */
            &hWnd);            /*client area handle      */

/*get messages from the input queue and dispatch them */
while ( WinGetMsg( hAB, (PQMSG)&qmsg, (HWND)NULL, 0,0) )
    begin
    WinDispatchMsg(hAB, (PQMSG)&qmsg);
    end

/* once the program is over,               */
/* destroy the window and message queue */
WinDestroyWindow(hFrame);
WinDestroyMsgQueue(hmqHello);
WinTerminate (hAB);                  /* the TERMINATOR!!! */
end
```

CONCLUSIONS

Our first PM program certainly seems more complicated than the simple two- or three-line "Hello World" program that students of C are first shown. However, by having set up all of these functions we are now in a position to add any number of complex features with a minimum of effort. Further, we should certainly note that while the original C example printed its message and then exited, this example maintains a window and an icon at all times, and keeps the window display up to date, no matter how many other programs are running or might overlap it. The next step in our investigation is adding menu commands to the program, which follows in the next chapter.

6 Adding Menu Commands to Your Program

We have just seen that putting a movable, adjustable window on the screen is not terribly difficult and that drawing text is quite simple. However, a real program should be able to accept commands from the user and carry out useful work. To demonstrate a truly useful concept, we will design our first menu-driven program to change the "Hi there" text depending on the command selected.

THE MENU FOR HELLOJ2

In our first example, we will design a program that has a two-item menu that drops down from the "Commands" menu and displays the commands

Commands
Foogie
Moogie

We will write a program that will display the message "Foogie" if that command is selected from the menu, and "Moogie" if the other command is selected from the menu. We will further add code to exit from the program if the function key F3 is depressed.

In Presentation Manager programs, the text of menus and the commands they send can be stored in the resource or .RC file. The messages are just text enclosed in quotes and the commands are simply small integers. These integers are usually defined as constants and put in the include file:

```
#define HELLOWIND      1
#define HELLOCMD     101
#define HELLOFOO     102
#define HELLOMOO     103
```

Then the resource file can deal with these commands symbolically using the MENU directive. For this program, the resource file will contain:

```
#include "helloj2.h"
POINTER HELLOWIND  helloj2.ico


MENU HELLOWIND PRELOAD
BEGIN
    SUBMENU "Commands",    HELLOCMD
       BEGIN
       MENUITEM "Foogie", HELLOFOO
       MENUITEM "Moogie", HELLOMOO
       END
END
```

The meaning of this is very simple: the text following the SUBMENU directive will appear on the menu bar, and the text of the MENUITEMs will appear when you click the mouse on the menu bar text. Once the menu has appeared, you can click on any of the menu items and the message having that number will be sent to the program as a WM_COMMAND message.

Note that the constant HELLOWIND is the frame window identifier, and it must be associated with both the icon and the menu to be loaded with this window. Similarly, if you create a number of windows and subwindows, each having menus (or icons), the frame window identifiers for each of them must be unique and the same as those used when each **WinCreateStdWindow** call is made.

You can nest the SUBMENU commands to any depth, so that a menu item may bring up more menus as desired.

```
MENU HELLOMENU PRELOAD
BEGIN
    SUBMENU "Commands", HELLOCMD
        BEGIN
        MENUITEM "command1", COMMAND1
        SUBMENU "multicommand", COMMANDMULT
            BEGIN
            MENUITEM "command2", COMMAND2
            MENUITEM "command3", COMMAND3
            END
        END
END
```

Each submenu and menu item must have a constant associated with it although each constant need not be unique.

Separators You can use the special menu item MIS_SEPARATOR to draw a line between groups of menu items in a pull-down menu.

```
    SUBMENU "multicommand", COMMANDMULT
        BEGIN
        MENUITEM "command2", COMMAND2
        MENUITEM "",NULL,MIS_SEPARATOR
        MENUITEM "command3", COMMAND3
        END
    END
```

INTERPRETING MENU COMMANDS

When a user selects a command from a menu, the message WM_COMMAND is sent to that window with the lower 16 bits of the first parameter (mp1) containing the command constant listed alongside the menu. Inside the window procedure, we write a second switch statement to interpret the commands when WM_COMMAND is received.

```
case WM_COMMAND:                           /*interpret commands*/
    switch(LOUSHORT(mp1))
        begin
        case HELLOFOO:                  /*change text to Foogie*/
            strcpy(mstring,"Foogie");
```

```
        break;

   case HELLOMOO:                    /*change text to Moogie*/
        strcpy(mstring,"Moogie");
        break;

   default:                         /*else do nothing     */
        return(WinDefWindowProc(hWnd, message, mp1, mp2));
   end
WinInvalidateRect(hWnd, NULL, FALSE); /*force repaint  */
break;
```

In this program, we use the macro LOUSHORT to obtain the value of the lower ;il.LOUSHORT macro word of mp1. This macro is defined in

```
os2def.h
```

and is automatically included when we define INCL_PM.

This code simply copies the string "Foogie" into the string **mstring** if the message HELLOFOO is received and copies the string "Moogie" into the string if HELLOMOO is received. Then it calls the function **WinInvalidateRect**, which in turn forces the window to be repainted. The arguments to this call are

```
WinInvalidateRect(hWnd, &rect, scope);
```

where

hWnd   is the handle to the window to be repainted.

&rect   is the pointer to the RECTL structure containing the region to be invalidated or NULL if the whole window is invalid.

scope   is TRUE if children of hWnd are to be included or FALSE if they are to be included only if the parent does not have the WS_CLIPCHILDREN style.

INITIALIZING THE WINDOW

In this example, we have substituted **mstring** for the message "Hi there" of the previous example. We copy the correct string into **mstring** depending on the message. It is critical, therefore, that this variable be *static* since it must retain this value from one call to the window procedure to the next. In addition, we must *initialize* this string with some value when we first start up the window. You can do this by intercepting the WM_CREATE message and initializing the string:

```
static char mstring[80];

switch (message)                        /*interpret messages*/
begin
    case WM_CREATE:
        strcpy(mstring, "Hi there"); /*initialize message*/
        break;
```

The WM_CREATE message is sent to the window procedure before the WinCreate... call returns, which is before the window is made visible. Therefore, you cannot draw anything at create time, but you can initialize constants needed for later drawing.

INTERCEPTING FUNCTION KEYS

Whenever any keyboard key is depressed, a WM_CHAR message is sent to the window having the input focus. When this happens, the upper word of mp2 contains the scan code and the lower word the ASCII character code. Function keys, of course, do not have character codes, but their scan codes have been defined as VK_Fn code, where VK stands for "virtual key." Here we use the macro SHORT2FROMMP to get at the upper word of the message:

```
case WM_CHAR:
    if (SHORT2FROMMP( mp2) == VK_F3)  /* F3 causes WM_QUIT*/
        begin
        WinPostMsg(hWnd, WM_QUIT, OL, OL); /*terminate    */
        end
    break;
```

Note that we do not actually exit from the routine here, since this would leave the window active. Instead, we post the WM_QUIT message to the window, so that the default window processing will close the window. The final running window is shown in Figure 6-1.

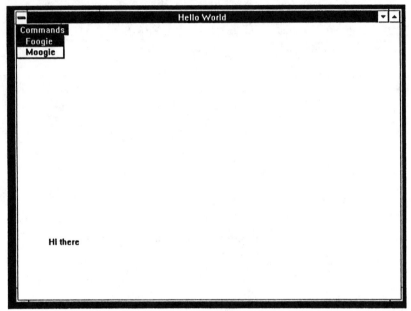

Figure 6-1. The HELLOJ2 program display

The complete program text is shown below. The main program that sets up the window differs from the main program at the end of Chapter 5 only in that the style **FCF_MENU** is included in the **flCreate** flag.

```
#define INCL_PM
#include <os2.h>
#include <cdefs.h>
#include <string.h>
#include "helloj2.h"

MRESULT FAR PASCAL HelloWndProc( HWND, USHORT, MPARAM,
                                 MPARAM);
/**************************************************************/
/*************** M a i n   F u n c t i o n ***************/
/* The main() function in a PM program registers the class
   of all windows and creates the main window. Then it gets
   and dispatches messages to that window until a WM_QUIT
```

```
    message is received, and closes down.                    */
/**********************************************************/
void cdecl main ()                    /*C main routine*/


begin
  QMSG qmsg;                /*defining a message queue  */
  HAB     hAB;             /*handle to anchor block     */
  HMQ     hmqHello;        /*handle to message queue    */
  HWND    hWnd;            /*client area window handle  */
  HWND    hFrame;          /*frame window handle        */
  ULONG flCreate;          /*window create flag bits    */


hAB = WinInitialize (NULL);/*init and get anchor handle*/
hmqHello = WinCreateMsgQueue(hAB, 0); /*creat msg queue*/


/*register the Window class*/
WinRegisterClass (hAB,        /*handle to anchor block*/
     "Hello2",                /*name of window class   */
     HelloWndProc,         /*address of window procedure*/
     CS_SIZEREDRAW |CS_SYNCPAINT, /*use these flags    */
     0 ) ;                    /*number of "extra bytes*/


flCreate =
     FCF_TITLEBAR | FCF_MINMAX |FCF_SYSMENU | FCF_MENU |
     FCF_SIZEBORDER | FCF_BORDER |
     FCF_SHELLPOSITION | FCF_ICON;


/*create the window */
hFrame =
WinCreateStdWindow(
          HWND_DESKTOP, /*as child of the desktop window*/
          WS_VISIBLE | FS_ICON,
            &flCreate,           /*control data bits      */
              "Hello2",        /*this name refers to class*/
              "Hello World", /*title across top bar      */
              WS_VISIBLE,     /*"main"window visible     */
              NULL,           /*menu is in resource file */
              HELLOWIND,      /*frame window id-you pick */
              &hWnd);         /*client area handle       */
```

```
/*get messages from the input queue and dispatch them    */
while ( WinGetMsg( hAB, &qmsg, (HWND)NULL, 0, 0) )
    begin
    WinDispatchMsg(hAB, &qmsg);
    end

/*once the program is over,
    destroy the window and message queue */
WinDestroyWindow(hFrame);
WinDestroyMsgQueue(hmqHello);
WinTerminate (hAB);                     /* the TERMINATOR!!! */
end
/********************************************************/
/* The window procedure receives messages and acts on them
   or passes them on for default processing. Minimally, it
   must respond to WM_PAINT, and may respond to WM_CREATE
   and WM_CLOSE                                         */
/********************************************************/
MRESULT FAR PASCAL HelloWndProc(HWND hWnd, USHORT msg,
                                MPARAM mp1, MPARAM mp2)


begin
    HPS     hPS;            /*handle to presentation space   */
    RECTL   rc;            /* rectangle definition structure*/
    static char mstring[80];

switch (msg)                          /*interpret messages*/
begin
 case WM_CREATE:
    strcpy(mstring, "Hi there");   /*initialize message    */
    break;

 case WM_COMMAND:                     /*interpret commands    */
    switch(LOUSHORT(mp1))
        begin
        case HELLOFOO:               /*change text to Foogie*/
            strcpy(mstring,"Foogie");
            break;

        case HELLOMOO:               /*change text to Moogie*/
            strcpy(mstring,"Moogie");
```

```
      break;

    default:                        /*else do nothing      */
        return(WinDefWindowProc(hWnd, msg, mp1, mp2));
    end
  WinInvalidateRect(hWnd, NULL, FALSE); /*force repaint */
  break;

case WM_PAINT:
   hPS = WinBeginPaint(hWnd, (HPS)NULL, (PWRECT)NULL);

   /*get current window dimensions*/
   WinQueryWindowRect(hWnd, &rc);

   WinFillRect(hPS, &rc,CLR_BLACK); /*fill it with black*/
   rc.xLeft = 50;                        /*write at  (50,50)*/
   rc.yBottom = 50;
   rc.yTop = 100;
   rc.xRight = 150;
   WinDrawText(hPS, strlen(mstring), mstring, &rc,
              CLR_BLUE, CLR_BLACK, DT_LEFT);
   WinEndPaint(hPS);                     /*end painting routine*/
   break;

case WM_CHAR:
   if (SHORT2FROMMP( mp2) == VK_F3) /* F3 causes WM_QUIT */
      begin
      WinPostMsg(hWnd, WM_QUIT, OL, OL); /*termimate      */
      end
      break;

default:                            /*pass on other messages*/
      return( WinDefWindowProc( hWnd, msg, mp1, mp2));
      break;
end /*switch*/

return(OL);
end
```

CHANGING MENU ITEMS

Disabling and Enabling Items

In programs where you must have data present before you can perform operations on it, you might find it useful to *disable* any menu items that cannot be used without data. This is done by sending the particular menu item an MM_SETITEMATTR message to set new item attributes.

Now, a menu item is generally known by its value, but you can only send messages to windows. Therefore you must get the window handle of that menu item using the function **WinWindowFromID**. Further, since the window containing the menus is not the client window but the *frame* window, you need to get the handle to the frame window to start. This is done with the **WinQueryWindow** function:

```
hFrame =
 WinQueryWindow(hWnd,
           QW_PARENT, FALSE);    /*get the frame handle*/
```

Then, you get the handle to the menu window by making the call

```
hMenu =
  WinWindowFromID(hFrame, FID_MENU); /*get handle to menu*/
```

Changing the Menu Item Attributes

The MM_SETITEMATTR message allows you to set any of the following menu attributes:

MIA_CHECKED	The menu item is checked.
MIA_DISABLED	The menu item is grayed and not selectable
MIA_FRAMED	The menu item is framed.
MIA_NODISMISS	If this item is true, the pull-down menu containing this item will not be hidden before sending the message to the window that this item has been selected.

The two message parameters sent with this message have the following format:

```
WinSendMessage(hMenu, MM_SETITEMATTR, (itemval, submenus),
```

where

itemval   is the menu item to change.

submenus   is TRUE if submenus are to be searched and FALSE if not.

mask   is the mask describing which bits are to be changed.

attrib   is the attributes to be changed.

Note that to grey an item or disable it, you *set* the MIA_DISABLED bit, and to enable the item you *clear* it. Thus, to disable an item you might write

```
hFrame =
  WinQueryWindow(hWnd,
            QW_PARENT, FALSE);      /*get the frame handle*/
hMenu =
  WinWindowFromID(hFrame, FID_MENU); /*get handle to menu  */
  WinSendMsg(hMenu, MM_SETITEMATTR, /*disable menu        */
            MPFROM2SHORT(HELLOFOO, TRUE),
            MPFROM2SHORT(MIA_DISABLED, MIA_DISABLED));
```

and to enable the item,

```
  WinSendMsg(hMenu, MM_SETITEMATTR,   /*enable menu        */
            MPFROM2SHORT(HELLOFOO, TRUE),
            MPFROM2SHORT(MIA_DISABLED, NULL));
```

Similarly, to check the menu item, you could write

```
  WinSendMsg(hMenu, MM_SETITEMATTR,   /*check menu         */
            MPFROM2SHORT(HELLOFOO, TRUE),
            MPFROM2SHORT(MIA_CHECKED, MIA_CHECKED));
```

ADDING MENU ITEMS DYNAMICALLY

To add menu items to an existing menu bar, you must add a main menu item with an associated submenu and then add submenu items. To insert a main menu item on the title bar, you send the *frame* the **MM_INSERTITEM** message, where **mp1** points to a MENUITEM structure and **mp2** contains a pointer to the text to be displayed. The MENUITEM structure has the form

```
typedef struct _MENUITEM
  begin
  SHORT iPosition;     /*position in the menu, or MIT_END*/
  USHORT afStyle;      /*style, usually MIS_TEXT        */
  USHORT afAttribute;  /*usually NULL                   */
  USHORT id;           /*id value sent when item is selected*/
  HWND hwndSubMenu;    /*handle of submenu              */
  ULONG hItem;         /*usually NULL                   */
  end MENUITEM;
```

Now, insert a main menu that has submenus, we must have the handle to the submenu in advance. We obtain it by using the **WinCreateMenu** call, which returns the handle to a menu that we place in this structure. Thus, to create a main menu called "User" we write

```
    MENUITEM mu;   /*menu item structure            */

hFrame =
    WinQueryWindow(hWnd, QW_PARENT, FALSE); /*get frame*/
hMenu =
    WinWindowFromID(hFrame, FID_MENU); /*get menu handle*/
  mu.iPosition = MIT_END;              /*add at end     */
  mu.afStyle = MIS_TEXT | MIS_SUBMENU;   /*set style    */
  mu.afAttribute =  NULL;
  mu.id = 110;                         /*command value  */
  mu.hwndSubMenu =
      WinCreateMenu(hFrame, NULL);     /*create submenu */
  mu.hItem = NULL;
  WinSendMsg(hMenu, MM_INSERTITEM, (MPARAM)&mu,
                              (MPARAM)"User");
```

Now, to insert items in the submenu under the main menu item "User," we simply get the structure back, and insert into *its* submenu

```
WinSendMsg(hMenu, MM_QUERYITEM,
          MPFROM2SHORT(110,TRUE), (MPARAM)&mu);
hSubMenu = mu.hwndSubMenu;              /*get submenu handle*/
mu.hwndSubMenu = NULL;                  /*no more submenus  */
mu.id = 111;                           /*set new command   */
mu.iPosition = MIT_END;                /*insert at end     */
mu.afStyle = MIS_TEXT;                 /*text style        */
mu.afAttribute =  NULL;
mu.hItem = NULL;
WinSendMsg(hSubMenu, MM_INSERTITEM,
          (MPARAM)&mu,
          (MPARAM)"Math");             /*insert "Math"     */
WinSendMsg(hFrame, WM_UPDATEFRAME,
                   NULL, NULL); /*redraw frame           */
```

7 | The Keyboard in OS/2 PM

USING THE KEYBOARD WITH PM PROGRAMS

For people who are afraid of mice, it is possible to issue most commands directly from the keyboard. If you look at the main menu of most complete programs, you will discover that each item in the menu bar has one character underlined. For example, the ICONEDIT program has the following command line:

*F*ile *E*dit *O*ptions *C*olor *O*pen *S*ize E*x*it

You can access any of these commands by pressing *and releasing* the Alt key. The "File" item will be highlighted. Then, you can select any of the menus by simply pressing the highlighted character: F, E, O, C, P or X. The case of the character you press does not matter. When you do this, that menu will appear, again, with some character underlined. If you press "F" the File menu will appear:

```
New
Open
Save        Alt+F3
Save As...
```

You can select an item from that menu by either moving the highlight bar down to the item with the cursor arrow keys, or by pressing the underlined character. For example, to save the current file, just press "S." Thus, you can, in every case, select a menu item and execute it in three key strokes: here, "Alt," "F," and "S."

SELECTING UNDERSCORED CHARACTERS

The Resource compiler allows you to indicate the character that is to be underscored in your menu items and recognized by the keyboard command processor by simply preceding the character with the "~" character.

```
MENU HELLOMENU PRELOAD
BEGIN
    SUBMENU "~Commands", HELLOCMD
        BEGIN
        MENUITEM "~Foogie", HELLOFOO
        MENUITEM "~Moogie", HELLOMOO
        END
END
```

MENU ACCELERATORS

PM also provides you the ability to use single keystrokes to select commonly used functions. For example, we have already seen how we can intercept the F3 function key as a WM_CHAR message to exit from a program. We can also define particular keystrokes, usually Alt and Ctrl combinations, as ones that will send the same command messages to the program as do the menu items themselves. This is done through a *menu accelerator* table. The following accelerator table is made part of the Hello program by including it in the resource file:

```
ACCELTABLE HELLOWIND PRELOAD
BEGIN
    "f", HELLOFOO, CHAR, ALT
    "m", HELLOMOO, CHAR, ALT
END
```

This table simply says that the keystroke Alt/f will send the message HELLOFOO to the current window, and that the keystroke Alt/m will send the message HELLOMOO to the current window. These will then be processed in exactly the same way as if the commands had been selected from the menu.

Virtual Keys

You can also specify function keys, alone or combined with ALT, SHIFT, or CONTROL, for a number of additional accelerators. Instead of being of type CHAR, these are specified as of type VIRTUAL. Since the codes for these virtual key symbols are not known to the resource compiler, you must include the <os2.h> file in the resource file.

```
#include <os2.h>
#include "helloj.h"

ACCELTABLE HELLOLABL PRELOAD
BEGIN
   "f",   HELLOFOO, CHAR,          ALT
   "m",   HELLOMOO, CHAR,          ALT
   "f",   HELLOFOO, CHAR,          CONTROL
   VK_F1, HELLOFOO, VIRTUALKEY
   VK_F1, HELLOFOO, VIRTUALKEY, SHIFT
END
```

Loading the Accelerator Table

If you do not specify PRELOAD, the final step in using the accelerator table is loading the table when you open your main window. You must specify the style bit FCF_ACCELTABLE when you create the window:

```
flCreate =
     FCF_TITLEBAR | FCF_MINMAX |FCF_SYSMENU | FCF_MENU |
     FCF_ACCELTABLE | FCF_SIZEBORDER | FCF_BORDER |
     FCF_SHELLPOSITION | FCF_ICON;
```

or you must load the table when you are ready to use it:

```
WinLoadAccelTable(hAB, NULL,
              HELLOACCEL);    /*load the accelerators*/
```

where NULL indicates that the table is in your resource file, and HELLOWIND is the id number of the frame window, defined in the helloj3.h file:

```
#define HELLOWIND    1
#define HELLOCMD     101
#define HELLOFOO     102
#define HELLOMOO     103
```

THE WM_CHAR MESSAGE

We have already seen that the lower word of **mp2** contains the "virtual key code" needed to recognize function keys. These virtual key codes have been defined by OS/2 to eliminate the conflicts inherent in different versions of PC keyboards. In the original PC, the *scan codes* for each key were simply their numerical position on the keyboard, with the 10 function keys taking positions along the left side of the keyboard. Since then at least three other versions of the PC keyboard have appeared from IBM alone, with additional versions from other manufacturers, some with numeric keypads, some with cursor keys, and some with neither. To insulate the user from these differences the keyboard driver returns a series of "virtual" key codes whose numerical value has nothing to do with any series of scan codes, but is consistent for all keyboards. This is simply an example of the attempts of the PM designers to make the system completely device independent.

In fact, the two message parameters contain a wealth of information that makes the identification of keys and their associated shift keys simple and unambiguous. Parameter one contains the following information:

flags	repeat	scancode

and parameter **mp2** contains

ascii char	virtual code

The **flags** have the following values

KC_CHAR	If set, this key has a valid character value in **mp2**.
KC_SCANCODE	If set, this key has a valid scancode value in **mp1**.
KC_VIRTUALKEY	Indicates that the virtual key code is valid.
KC_KEYUP	If set, this is a key-up transition. Otherwise the key was pressed down.
KC_PREVDOWN	The key was previously down. Otherwise it was previously up.
KC_DEADKEY	This is a "dead" key. Your program must display any desired character for this key without advancing the cursor.
KC_COMPOSITE	The character code is formed by combining this key with the previous dead key.
KC_INVALIDCOMP	The character code is not a valid composite with the previous dead key.
KC_LONEKEY	Indicates if this key is pressed or released without any other key being pressed or released at the same time.
KC_SHIFT	A shift key is also down.
KC_ALT	An ALT key is also down.
KC_CTRL	A control key is also down.

The other values in these message parameters are

repeat The number of times the key has been repeated.

scancode The raw scan code for this key. You should always use the virtual key code instead.

char The ASCII code for the character. This is zero for all control and function keys, as well as for the cursor keys.

virtual   The virtual key code. This value is 0 if **flags** does not have KC_VIRTUALKEY set.

The Virtual Keys

The following virtual keys have been defined by PM.

VK_BREAK	VK_ESC	VK_INSERT
VK_BACKSPACE	VK_SPACE	VK_DELETE
VK_TAB	VK_PAGEUP	VK_SCRLLOCK
VK_BACKTAB	VK_PAGEDOWN	VK_NUMLOCK
VK_NEWLINE	VK_END	VK_ENTER
VK_SHIFT	VK_HOME	VK_SYSRQ
VK_CTRL	VK_LEFT	VK_F1
VK_ALT	VK_UP	VK_F2
VK_ALTGRAF	VK_RIGHT	:
VK_PAUSE	VK_DOWN	VK_F24
VK_CAPSLOCK	VK_PRINTSCRN	

8 Using Dialog Boxes with the Presentation Manager

The recommended way of entering and changing information in a program is using a *dialog box.* This is a pop-up box that allows the user to enter values, select options, and type in text. The shape and layout of these boxes can be edited graphically using the DLGBOX editor.

TYPES OF DIALOG ITEMS

There are several types of items that you can put in a dialog box for the user to select. Each of these is actually a little child window whose characteristics and messages have been preprogrammed to behave in standard ways.

Push buttons   A box with a word or two inside that can be selected with the mouse. Usually, these are used for selections such as "OK" or "Cancel."

Radio button   One of a series of round buttons, labelled at the side. Only one of these buttons can be depressed at a time. PM defines radio buttons as those where selecting one button causes PM to unselect any other button of the group. Normal radio buttons require that your program do the selecting and unselecting.

Check boxes   A series of square boxes that can be "checked" or "unchecked" to indicate selection of one or more options. They differ from radio buttons in that more than one can be checked at a time.

Text box   A box containing static text that cannot be edited.

Edit box   A box containing text that can be edited.

List box   A box containing a list of selections, such as filenames. Any item in the list can be selected. List boxes come with vertical scroll bars built in so the user can use the mouse to scroll through a large list.

multiline edit boxes A box containing several lines of text that can be edited.

Scroll bars   Horizontal and vertical scroll bars can be used to scroll horizontally through wide text or vertically through many lines of text. Selecting the scroll bar position causes messages to be sent to the dialog box to redraw the contents.

DESIGN OF THE CHGCOLOR PROGRAM

We are going to write a program to display an empty window with red background and the single item "Command" in its menu bar. When the menu is pulled down, the command "Dialog" appears. When "Dialog" is selected, a dialog box will pop up with three radio buttons, labelled "Red," "Green," and "Blue." Two push buttons, labelled "OK" and "Cancel," appear at the bottom as illustrated in Figure 8-1.

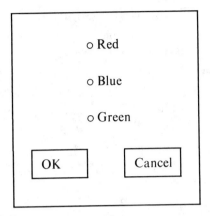

Figure   8-1. The design of the dialog box

The button representing the current screen color will be highlighted. When a button is selected and the "OK" push button is selected, the dialog box disappears, and the screen changes to that color. If "Cancel" is depressed, the dialog disappears and no color change occurs.

CREATING A DIALOG BOX

The first thing to do in creating a dialog box is to design its layout. You do this by running the DLGBOX program and arranging the various elements on the screen in a logical order for your purposes. When you start DLGBOX, you are presented with the menu

File   Include   Edit   Control   Options   Exit

Always start by selecting Edit, and "New Dialog" from the Edit menu. You will immediately be asked for the Dialog Box identifier. This can be a number (the default is 256) or it can be a symbolic variable. Enter the symbolic name COLORDIALOG for the box, and DLGBOX will assign it the first unused value starting at 256. A square box will appear on the screen that you can move around by pointing the mouse inside the box, holding the left button down, and moving the mouse to drag the box to a new position. You can also change the box's shape by dragging any side or corner to a new position.

Then, to put controls inside the box, select them from the "Control" menu. Let us select "Radio Button" from this list. A small box will appear that you can move within your dialog box. When you have moved it to the right position, press the left mouse button and a dialog will appear, asking you for the Button Control Style. The choices will appear as shown in Figure 8-2 Select "Auto Radio Button" and give the button text a message such as "Red" and an identifier such as BUTN_RED. An *auto* radio button or check box will darken when the user clicks on it and any other radio button will "pop out" and become light again. You should always use the auto feature of these dialog elements.

Push buttons allow you to check the *default* feature for one of them so that the default "OK" or "Cancel" is the one that is automatically selected if you just press Enter when the dialog box is active. In this case, select the default box for OK. Continue doing this until you have arranged a box as shown in Figure 8-3, where the elements of the box have the following symbolic identifiers:

COLORDIALOG   The dialog box as a whole.

BUTN_RED   The button labelled "Red."

BUTN_BLUE   The button labelled "Blue."

BUTN_GREEN   The button labelled "Green."

ID_OK   The OK push button. ID_OK should always be given the numeric value of 1.

ID_CANCEL   The Cancel push button. ID_CANCEL should always be given the numeric value of 2.

Then select "Save" from the file menu to save the dialog box. You will be asked for the name of the box and the name of the include file in which you wish to store the symbolic values you just generated. We will save the dialog box as COLOR.DLG and the include file as CDIALOG.H.

After you have selected options and positioned a dialog item on the screen, you can still change its style or even its button type by selecting that dialog element with the mouse, and then selecting "Styles" from the "Edit" menu. The same menu will pop up for you to select options.

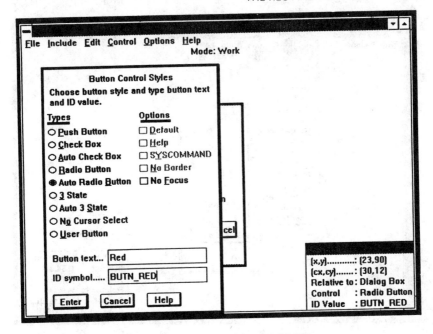

Figure 8-2. Selection of button attributes in the DLGBOX program

THE RES AND DLG FILES

The DLGBOX editor creates two files having the root name you select when you save the file: COLOR.DLG and COLOR.RES. The RES file is the resource-compiled version of the DLG file and may be combined directly with the EXE file using the RC compiler. The DLG file contains the same information in an ASCII format and can be copied into a general resource file for that program. If you look at the .DLG file, you will find that it contains the coordinates and characteristics of the elements of the dialog box:

```
DLGINCLUDE 1 "CDIALOG.H"

DLGTEMPLATE COLORDIALOG LOADONCALL MOVEABLE DISCARDABLE
BEGIN
  DIALOG "", COLORDIALOG, 94, 85, 79, 125, FS_NOBYTEALIGN |
            FS_DLGBORDER | WS_VISIBLE | WS_CLIPSIBLINGS |
            WS_SAVEBITS
  BEGIN
    CONTROL "Blue", BUTN_BLUE, 23, 67, 40, 14, WC_BUTTON,
            BS_AUTORADIOBUTTON | WS_GROUP | WS_TABSTOP |
```

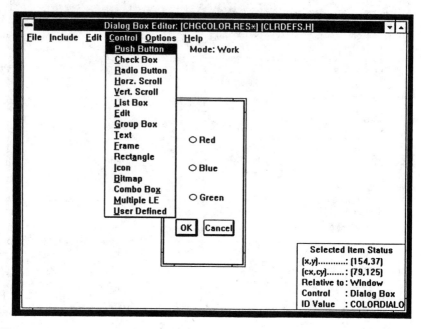

Figure 8-3. The CHGCOLOR dialog box design. Note the default box around the OK button.

```
        WS_VISIBLE
CONTROL "Green", BUTN_GREEN, 24, 45, 42, 12, WC_BUTTON,
        BS_AUTORADIOBUTTON | WS_TABSTOP | WS_VISIBLE
CONTROL "Red", BUTN_RED, 23, 90, 30, 12, WC_BUTTON,
        BS_AUTORADIOBUTTON | WS_TABSTOP | WS_VISIBLE
CONTROL "OK", ID_OK, 10, 20, 24, 14, WC_BUTTON,
        BS_PUSHBUTTON | WS_GROUP | WS_TABSTOP |
        WS_VISIBLE
CONTROL "Cancel", ID_CANCEL, 39, 20, 34, 14, WC_BUTTON,
        BS_PUSHBUTTON | WS_TABSTOP | WS_VISIBLE
END
END
```

There are two ways of getting this information into your program: by *putting* it in your resource file and by *including* it in your resource file. To include it in your resource file, simply add the statement

```
rcinclude color.dlg
```

to your resource file. It turns out, however, that if you have several dialog boxes in your program that all refer to the same include file for the definitions of their symbolic values, it is preferable to simply copy the text from the .DLG file into your resource file using your favorite text editor. If you include several .DLG files that start with the same DLGINCLUDE statement, the resource compiler will produce an .EXE file that cannot be loaded because of these apparent duplicate definitions. You can, however, put a number of dialogs in a single DLG and RES file, and selct any one of them for later editing as your program develops.

DIALOG BOX DESIGN

A dialog box allows you to select any of a number of options, including entering text and values. The user should be able to make a number of changes to his work and still be able to inspect the values in the box before closing the box and making the values permanent. Therefore, it is customary that all such boxes have a pair of push buttons marked "OK" and "Cancel." If "OK" is pushed then the currently selected values become permanent, and if "Cancel" is selected, the previous values remain in force. To be consistent with standard usage of dialog boxes, the messages DID_OK and DID_CANCEL have been defined as having the values 1 and 2, respectively, in pmwin.h.

STARTING A DIALOG BOX

A dialog box procedure is really just a special kind of window procedure. It must be declared by name in an EXPORTS list in the .DEF file (unless you compile with /Alfu), but does not need to have its class registered, since all dialog box procedures are of the same window class. You call a dialog box with the call

```
WinDlgBox(HWND_DESKTOP, hWnd, Dlgproc, resid, dlgid,
          &params);
```

where

HWND_DESKTOP   is the parent window handle of the dialog window. Making the desktop the parent is recommended so the box can appear anywhere on the screen.

hWnd   is the handle of the owner window. This is usually the calling window.

Dlgproc   is the dialog box's window procedure address.

resid   is the resource file handle containing the template for the dialog box.   If this is linked into the program's EXE file, as is usually the case, this handle must be NULL.

dlgid   The id value of the dialog box. This is the symbolic name you chose when you first created the dialog box using DLGBOX.

& params   This can be a pointer to a data word or structure that you want to pass to the dialog box as an argument.

Dialog boxes called in this fashion are said to be *modal* and prevent you from accessing any other window until this dialog is closed. You can also use the **WinLoadDlg** call along with **WinShowWindow** to create a *modeless* dialog box that will allow processing in other windows simultaneously.

THE DIALOG WINDOW PROCEDURE

The dialog box window procedure is much like any other window procedure: messages are received and interpreted. However, since the dialog box is really a special class of window and all of the dialog features are actually little child windows, the messages that are received are somewhat ;il.child windows different.

The first message the dialog box receives is a WM_INITDLG message, and it is intended to be used to set up the initial status of the box when it appears. Dialog boxes should always represent the current status of variables in the program rather than some arbitrary set of default values. Thus, at initialization time, you might set the text of certain messages and check particular boxes and "push" a particular radio button.

WRITING THE CHGCOLOR PROGRAM USING A DIALOG BOX

We will now write an example that will have one menu item "Dialog." We have already designed the dialog box for this example and now need only process the messages in the dialog window procedure.

Calling the Dialog Box Procedure

We will call the dialog box procedure with a pointer to the current color passed as the argument:

```
WinDlgBox(HWND_DESKTOP,    /* parent window            */
          hWnd,            /* owner window             */
          ColorDialogProc, /* window procedure         */
          NULL,            /* template in resource file */
          COLORDIALOG,     /* dialog id                */
          &buttoncolor);   /* address of current color */
```

and upon return from the dialog box, we will force a screen repaint in the new color by invalidating the entire screen:

```
WinInvalidateRect(hWnd, NULL, FALSE); /* force repaint */
```

The WM_INITDLG Message

When we first enter the dialog box, we want the radio button to be pushed that indicates the current background color of the screen. The parameter **mp2** contains the pointer or value that we passed to the dialog on startup. In this case, it will contain the color whose button we wish to highlight.

Here we check the current color of the screen and send the proper radio button the message BM_SETCHECK, which not only causes this button to be checked, but also unchecks any other radio buttons.

```
        static int localcolor,              /*  copy of color  */
                 *buttoncolor;              /*  pointer to color*/
case WM_INITDLG:
  buttoncolor = (int *)mp2;  /*save address of color      */
  localcolor = *buttoncolor; /*copy into local variable   */

  switch(localcolor)         /*check button for current color*/
     begin
     case CLR_RED:           /* if red, save ID of red button*/
        button = BUTN_RED;
        break;
     case CLR_BLUE:          /*if blue save id of blue button*/
        button = BUTN_BLUE;
        break;
     case CLR_GREEN:         /*if green, save green button id*/
        button = BUTN_GREEN;
        break;
     end
     /* set the button whose ID was saved to "checked"    */
     WinSendDlgItemMsg(hWnd, button, BM_SETCHECK,
               MPFROMSHORT( TRUE), MPFROMSHORT(0));
     return((MRESULT)TRUE);
  break;
```

The parameter **mp2** contains a pointer to the value of the current color. We copy this to a local color variable that we change each time a button is pushed. However, we don't change the actual color unless the OK is selected, so we save the address of the color in another variable. Note that these must both be *static* variables so that their values will remain between messages passed to the dialog box. Note particularly that we *must* return TRUE from the WM_INITDLG message to tell PM that we have processed this message, so that it doesn't carry out default processing and push some other button. When the program first calls the dialog box, it should press the Red button, so the dialog looks like that in Figure 8-4.

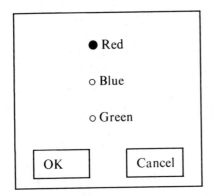

Figure   8-4. The initial setting of the dialog box

Finding Out if a New Button Has Been Pressed

If the user points at a radio button (or check box) and clicks the left mouse button, the message WM_CONTROL is sent from the radio button child window to the dialog window procedure. The lower word of the first parameter **mp1** is set to the value BN_CLICKED and the upper word to the id of the button that was clicked. We can recognize this by processing the WM_CONTROL messages:

```
case WM_CONTROL:                        /*control buttons clicked*/
   if (SHORT2FROMMP(mp1)==BN_CLICKED)  /*if it was clicked*/
   switch (SHORT1FROMMP(mp1))
     begin
     case BUTN_RED:
        localcolor = CLR_RED;    /*set local color to red  */
        break;
     case BUTN_GREEN:
        localcolor = CLR_GREEN; /*set local color to green*/
        break;
     case BUTN_BLUE:
        localcolor = CLR_BLUE;   /*set local color to blue */
        break;
     end
   break;
```

Recognizing the OK and Cancel Buttons

When the user clicks on an ordinary push button, the message WM_COMMAND is sent to the dialog window with the lower word of mp1 equal to the id of the push button that sent the message. Here we need only recognize ID_OK and ID_CANCEL and either do or do not change the GlobalColor.

```
case WM_COMMAND:                        /*OK or Cancel clicked    */
   switch(SHORT1FROMMP(mp1))
      begin
      case ID_OK:
         *buttoncolor = localcolor; /* send out new color */
         WinDismissDlg(hWnd, TRUE); /* if OK exit          */
         return((MRESULT)TRUE);
         break;
      case ID_CANCEL:                      /* if cancel...        */
         WinDismissDlg(hWnd, FALSE);/* leave color alone   */
         return((MRESULT)TRUE);
         break;
      end
```

THE MAIN WINDOW PROCEDURE

The command processor in the main window procedure simply has to look for the WM_COMMAND message, and if the command is CDIALOG, then start the dialog box:

```
case WM_COMMAND:
   switch(LOUSHORT(mp1))
      begin
      case CDIALOG:
         WinDlgBox(HWND_DESKTOP,          /* start dialog box*/
                   hWnd,                   /*Window id        */
                   ColorDialogProc,        /*dialog proc      */
                   NULL,
                   COLORDIALOG,            /*id of dialog     */
                   NULL);
         WinInvalidateRect(hWnd, NULL, FALSE);/*force repaint*/
```

```
    break;

  default:
      return(WinDefWindowProc(hWnd, message, mp1, mp2));
  end
break;
```

Then, when the dialog box closes, the paint routine always invalidates the screen, forcing a repaint to the new background color. The paint routine itself is just like ones we have seen before:

```
/*get size and repaint background*/
case WM_PAINT:
      hPS = WinBeginPaint(hWnd, (HPS)NULL, (PWRECT)NULL);
      WinQueryWindowRect(hWnd, &rc);
      WinFillRect(hPS, &rc, buttoncolor);
      WinEndPaint(hPS);
      break;
```

THE COMPLETE CHGCOLOR PROGRAM

In the code that follows, we illustrate the main window procedure and the dialog box procedure. The main program is identical to that shown in -- Fig 'MAIN' unknown --, except that the **FCF■MENU** frame window creation flag bit is set.

```
/*****Color changing program-- illustrating dialog boxes**/
#define INCL_PM
#include <os2.h>
#include <cdefs.h>
#include "clrdefs.h"

MRESULT FAR PASCAL ColorWndProc( HWND, USHORT, MPARAM,
                                                MPARAM );
MRESULT EXPENTRY ColorDialogProc( HWND, USHORT, MPARAM,
                                                MPARAM );
/***************************************************************/
/************** M a i n    F u n c t i o n**************/
/***  has been illustrated before                    **/
```

```
/****************************************************************/
MRESULT EXPENTRY ColorDialogProc(HWND hWnd, USHORT msg,
                                      MPARAM mp1, MPARAM mp2)

begin
        static int localcolor, *buttoncolor;
        int button;
        MRESULT rmsg;

switch(msg)
begin
case WM_INITDLG:
  buttoncolor = (int *)mp2;
  localcolor = *buttoncolor; /*copy into local variable  */

  switch(localcolor)      /*check button for current color*/
    begin
    case CLR_RED:         /* if red, save ID of red button*/
      button = BUTN_RED;
      break;
    case CLR_BLUE:        /*if blue save id of blue button*/
      button = BUTN_BLUE;
      break;
    case CLR_GREEN:     /*if green, save green button id */
      button = BUTN_GREEN;
      break;
    end

    /* set the button whose ID was saved to "checked"  */
    WinSendDlgItemMsg(hWnd, button, BM_SETCHECK,
            MPFROMSHORT( TRUE), MPFROMSHORT(0));
  return((MRESULT)TRUE);
  break;

case WM_CONTROL:                      /*control buttons clicked*/
  if ( SHORT2FROMMP(mp1) == BN_CLICKED) /*if clicked...  */
    switch (SHORT1FROMMP(mp1))
      begin
      case BUTN_RED:
        localcolor = CLR_RED;   /*set local color to red */
        break;
```

```
        case BUTN_GREEN:
          localcolor = CLR_GREEN;/*set local color to green*/
          break;
        case BUTN_BLUE:
          localcolor = CLR_BLUE;  /*set local color to blue*/
          break;
        end
    break;

  case WM_COMMAND:                     /*OK or Cancel clicked*/
    switch(SHORT1FROMMP(mp1))
        begin
        case ID_OK:
          *buttoncolor = localcolor; /* send out new color */
          WinDismissDlg(hWnd, TRUE); /* if OK exit          */
          return((MRESULT)TRUE);
          break;
        case ID_CANCEL:                      /* if cancel... */
          WinDismissDlg(hWnd, FALSE);        /* leave alone  */
          return((MRESULT)TRUE);
          break;
        end

  default:
        return(WinDefDlgProc(hWnd, msg, mp1, mp2));
  end
  return((MRESULT)FALSE);
  end
/*************************************************************/
MRESULT FAR PASCAL ColorWndProc(HWND hWnd, USHORT msg,
                                    MPARAM mp1, MPARAM mp2)
begin
        HPS     hPS;            /*handle to presentation space*/
        RECTL   rc;
        static buttoncolor;

switch (msg)
begin
    case WM_CREATE:
        buttoncolor = CLR_RED; /* initialize color to red*/
        break;
```

```
    case WM_COMMAND:
        switch(LOUSHORT(mp1))
                begin
                case CDIALOG:
                 WinDlgBox(HWND_DESKTOP, /*start dialog box*/
                            hWnd,
                            ColorDialogProc,
                            NULL,
                            COLORDIALOG,
                            &buttoncolor);

                    /* force repaint                            */
                    WinInvalidateRect(hWnd, NULL, FALSE);
                    break;

                default:
                    return(WinDefWindowProc(hWnd, msg, mp1, mp2));
                end
        break;

    case WM_PAINT:      /*get size and repaint background*/
            hPS =
                WinBeginPaint(hWnd, (HPS)NULL, (PWRECT)NULL);
            WinQueryWindowRect(hWnd, &rc);
            WinFillRect(hPS, &rc, buttoncolor);
            WinEndPaint(hPS);
            break;

default:
    return( WinDefWindowProc( hWnd, msg, mp1, mp2));
    break;
end /*switch*/

return((MRESULT)0L);
end
```

The CHGCOLOR Resource File

```
#include <os2.h>
#include "clrdefs.h"

POINTER COLORWIND   chgcolor.ico

MENU COLORWIND PRELOAD
BEGIN
   SUBMENU "Commands", COLORCMD
      BEGIN
      MENUITEM "Dialog", CDIALOG
      END
END


rcinclude chgcolor.dlg
```

The CHGCOLOR Definitions File

The following shows the contents of the file clrdefs.h.

```
NAME    CHGCOLOR  WINDOWAPI

DESCRIPTION 'Color Demo Program'

STUB 'OS2STUB.EXE'

CODE MOVEABLE
DATA MOVEABLE MULTIPLE

HEAPSIZE 1024
STACKSIZE 4096

EXPORTS
    ColorWndProc @1
    ColorDialogProc @2
```

TEXT BOXES AND STRING TABLES

A text box is a field of static text that can be displayed but not edited in a dialog box. Usually such fields are used as labels beside the entry fields and list boxes, but they are not limited to one line and can contain quite a large amount of text. Such text boxes are usually loaded from *string tables*.

String Tables

String tables are another feature of the resource file. They allow you to keep all text that might be application or national language dependent in a file external to the program. A string table consists of the STRINGTABLE declaration followed by any number of strings, each with symbolic or numerical labels:

```
STRINGTABLE
BEGIN
CLOSEDOOR, "Close the door!"
WIPEFEET, "Wipe your feet!"
END
```

Then instead of putting the text directly in a message box, for example, you *load* the string from the string table and display it:

```
char mstring[BUFMAX];
/*get the string*/
WinLoadString(hAB, NULL, CLOSEDOOR, BUFMAX, mstring);
/*display it*/
WinMessageBox(HWND_DESKTOP, hWnd, mstring, "", MB_OK);
```

This effectively isolates the actual text from your program, and in another version of the program you could link the same EXE file with a resource file containing

```
STRINGTABLE
BEGIN
CLOSEDOOR, "Fermez la porte!"
WIPEFEET, "Essuyez-vous les pieds!"
END
```

In both cases, the constants CLOSEDOOR and WIPEFEET are small integers defined in an include file.

Loading Strings into a Text Box

You can also use a series of strings to load a long text message, such as a help text using a sequence of **WinLoadString** commands and concatenating them into a long string, which will automatically be word-wrapped to be displayed on several lines.

```
STRINGTABLE
BEGIN
T1,   "The programming of text from string tables into text boxes"
T1+1, "is not difficult. The strings are read into the text box"
T1+2, "using the WinLoadString function, and are word-wrapped into"
T1+3, "the text box, if the appropriate option is checked in the"
T1+4, "box when it is created with the dialog editor. Then you can"
T1+5, "scroll through the text box, no matter how long it is, by"
T1+6, "receiving messages from the scroll bar and moving through"
T1+7, "the text a line at a time."
END
```

Then, you can load the code using a loop:

```
char text[1500],        /*for all of help text    */
     buf[80];           /*one line if text        */
int id, i;

id = T1;                /*start with first id     */
                        /*of this string table    */
strcpy(text,"");        /*start with null string  */
for (i=0; i< TEXTMAX; i++)
     begin
     WinLoadString(hAB, NULL, id++, BUFMAX, buf);
     strcat(text, buf);      /*add string to text string*/
     strcat(text," ");       /*add a space between strings*/
     end

/*load into the text box*/
WinSetDlgItemText(hWnd, TEXTBOX, text);
```

SCROLL BARS

Scroll bars appear automatically on list boxes such as we will be using to select filenames, and can also be made part of any standard window if you want to scroll a large image through a smaller viewing area.

You can also include a scroll bar directly in a dialog box alongside a text box and use it to scroll through a large amount of text. If you include a vertical scroll bar, clicking the mouse on it will generate a WM_VSCROLL message, and a horizontal scroll bar will cause a WM_HSCROLL message.

When the scroll messages are received in a dialog box, the upper part of **mp2** contains one of the following messages:

SB_LINEUP	The mouse has clicked on the upper arrow.
SB_LINEDOWN	The mouse has clicked on the lower arrow.
SB_PAGEUP	The mouse has clicked on the area above the slider, or the PgUp key has been pressed.
SB_PAGEDOWN	The mouse has clicked on the area below the slider, or the PgDn key has been pressed.
SB_SLIDERPOSITION	Sent to indicate the final position of the slider. The lower part of **mp2** contains a normalized value between 0 and 100 representing the percent of full scale (bottom = 100, top =0).
SB_SLIDERTRACK	Sent every time the slider position changes.
SB_ENDSCROLL	Sent when the user has finished scrolling.

Each of these messages occurs when the slider has been moved by the user. The slider is not actually redrawn in this position, however, unless your program accepts this new position. Then it must send the slider a message indicating the new position:

```
hScroll =
    WinWindowFromID(hWnd, VSCROLL); /*get the scroll bar id*/
WinSendMsg(hScroll, SBM_SETPOS, (MPARAM)posn, NULL);
```

The SLIDEBOX Program

The SLIDEBOX program illustrates how to bring up a dialog box consisting of a vertical scroll bar, a text box and an OK push button as shown in Figure 8-5. The main program and the main window procedure of the SLIDEBOX program are identical to those shown earlier except for the command to start the dialog box:

```
case WM_COMMAND:                      /*interpret commands   */
    switch(LOUSHORT(mp1))
        begin
        case SHOWDLG :                /*change text to Foogie*/
          WinDlgBox(HWND_DESKTOP, hWnd, BoxDlg, NULL, LDLG,
                    NULL);
          break;

        default:                      /*else do nothing      */
          return(WinDefWindowProc(hWnd, msg, mp1, mp2));
        end
```

The dialog procedure is shown below:

```
void LoadWin(HAB hAB, HWND hWnd, int scroll, int max)
begin
        int i;
        char text[BUFMAX], buf[BUFMAX];
strcpy(text, "");
while (scroll < max)
    begin
    WinLoadString(hAB, NULL, scroll++, BUFMAX, buf);
    strcat(text," ");
    strcat(text, buf);
    end
WinSetDlgItemText(hWnd, TEXTBOX, text);
end
/**********************************************************/
MRESULT EXPENTRY BoxDlg(HWND hWnd, USHORT msg,
                                    MPARAM mp1, MPARAM mp2)
begin
        int i, itemid, posn;
        static scroll, max;
```

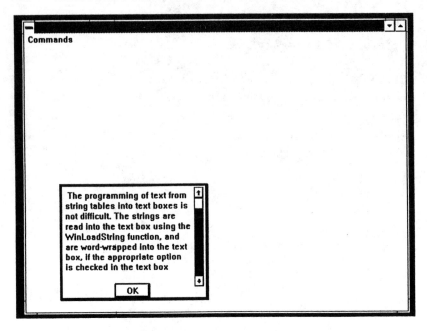

Figure 8-5. The SLIDEBOX program display

```
        static HWND hScroll;
        BOOL draw;

switch (msg)
 begin
 case WM_INITDLG:
  hScroll =
    WinWindowFromID(hWnd, VSCROLL);  /*get scroll bar id */
    scroll = T1;                      /*initialize text box*/
    max = T1 + TEXTMAX;               /*maximum line to load*/
    LoadWin(hAB, hWnd, scroll, max);/*load text into box*/

    /*be sure dialog is active*/
    WinPostMsg(hWnd, WM_BUTTON1DOWN, OL, OL);
    return (TRUE);
    break;

 case WM_VSCROLL:
    draw = TRUE;           /*indicates box should be redrawn*/
    switch(SHORT2FROMMP(mp2))
       begin
```

```
case SB_LINEDOWN: /*go down one line              */
   if (++scroll > max ) then scroll = max - 1;
   break;

case SB_LINEUP:                    /*go up  one line     */
   if (--scroll < T1) then scroll = T1;
   break;

case SB_PAGEDOWN:                  /*page down            */
   scroll += 5;
   break;

case SB_PAGEUP:                    /*page up              */
   scroll -= 5;
   if (scroll < T1) then scroll = T1;
   break;

case SB_SLIDERPOSITION:            /* move to new        */
                                   /* slider position    */
   scroll =
       ((LOUSHORT(mp2) * (long)TEXTMAX)/100L) + T1;
   break;

default:
     draw = FALSE;        /*do not redraw on other msgs*/
end
if (draw) then
     /*redraw text box                */
     LoadWin(hAB, hWnd, scroll, max);
/*set slider positon*/
posn = (scroll - T1)* 100 / TEXTMAX;
WinSendMsg(hScroll, SBM_SETPOS, (MPARAM)posn, NULL);
break;

case WM_COMMAND:
   switch(SHORT1FROMMP(mp1))
     begin
     case DID_OK:
       WinDismissDlg(hWnd, TRUE);
       return(TRUE);
       break;
```

```
        end
      break;

  default:
      return(WinDefDlgProc(hWnd, msg, mp1, mp2));
  end
  return((MRESULT)FALSE);
  end
```

THE MULTILINE EDIT BOX

One of the most useful functions in OS/2 1.2 is the addition of the multiline edit (MLE) box. This is actually a fairly full-featured text edito that can be used to operate on text buffers up to 65535 bytes long. To use an MLE box, simply create a dialog box with the dialog box editor that has a MLE edit box and, at the minimum, an OK and Cancel button.

Then, in processing your dialog, you need to load text into the MLE box at WM_INITDLG time and read it back out when OK is pressed. You do this by establishing a buffer and sending messages to the MLE box to import or export text.

Text is sent to the MLE box as a single buffer of up to 65536 bytes in length, with newline characters separating lines. There are actually three text formats allowed, one from programs written for Microsoft Windows, and two others. The most common are MLEFIE_CFTEXT and MLFIE_NOTRANS. The NOTRANS format guarantees that the text will be re-exported in exactly the same form it was imported, while the MIFIE_CFTEXT format translates CR, CR-LF and LF-CR as line break characters on import. To import text to the MLE box you do the following:

```
/*------------------------------------------------------*/
/* Initialize the MLE edit box and load it              */
/*------------------------------------------------------*/
        ULONG i, posn, result, bytes, rc;

case WM_INITDLG:
  buf =  malloc(MAXBUFLEN);          /*allocate text buffer*/
  strcpy(buf,
  "Initial text on display");        /*put text in it      */
```

```
WinSendDlgItemMsg(hWnd, MLEBOX,
    MLM_SETIMPORTEXPORT,        /*set address of buffr*/
    (MPARAM)buf,
    (MPARAM)MAXBUFLEN);         /*maximum size        */
WinSendDlgItemMsg(hWnd, MLEBOX,
    MLM_FORMAT,                 /*set the format      */
    (MPARAM)MLFIE_CFTEXT,
    NULL);
result = strlen(buf);          /*get the text size   */
posn = 0;                      /*position to start   */
WinSendDlgItemMsg(hWnd,
    MLEBOX,                     /*import the text     */
    MLM_IMPORT,
    (MPARAM)&posn,             /*starting here       */
    (MPARAM)result);           /*this size           */
return ((MRESULT)TRUE);        /*and exit            */
break;
```

Getting the edited text back from the MLE box just amounts to exporting the text back to the buffer and storing it: the format and buffer address do not have be set again. The first parameter to the **MLM_EXPORT** message is the position in the buffer where the text is to be inserted. After the export is completed, this parameter contains the number of bytes exported.

```
/*----------------------------------------------------------*/
/* Export the text back from the MLE box and store it       */
/*----------------------------------------------------------*/
case WM_COMMAND:                    /*OK or Cancel clicked   */
  switch(SHORT1FROMMP(mp1))
    begin
    case DID_OK:
      posn = 0;                     /*insert position        */
      bytes = MAXBUFLEN;
      WinSendDlgItemMsg(hWnd,
        MLEBOX,
        MLM_EXPORT,                 /*export the text        */
        (MPARAM)&posn,             /*becomes # exported     */
        &bytes);                   /*number length changes  */
      /*store the text in a file                             */
      f = fopen("words.txt","w"); /*open the file          */
      for (i=0; i <= posn; i++)
```

```
        fputc(buf[i], f);        /*put chars in file     */
     fclose(f);                  /*then close the file   */
  case DID_CANCEL:               /*start here if cancel  */
     free(buf);
     WinDismissDlg(hWnd, TRUE);
     return((MRESULT)TRUE);
     break;
```

The trickiest things about the MLE box are the use of the two parameters to the messages. Both are *pointers* to longs and both get changed during the calls. Be sure that you use longs for these variables and be sure that you reset the value of the position before calling EXPORT. The text will not necessarily end with a null byte after you have edited, so you must be careful to use the position count value. Finally, you should note that the buffer may be longer when you export it than it was when you started and allow space for it.

USING HELP HOOKS TO DISPLAY HELP MESSAGES

A *hook* is a routine that intercepts messages before they are sent to specific windows. You can set a hook to intercept specific classes of messages and send them to special window procedures. To do this, you use the command **WinSetHook**, which has the calling sequence

```
WinSetHook(hAB, hmq, hooktype, hookproc, modid);
```

hooktype   one of the following hook types:

        HK_HELP any occurrence of WM_HELP, MIS_HELP, BS_HELP, or MB_HELP.

        HK_INPUT called when messages are removed from the message queue before being returned by **WinGetMsg** or **WinPeekMsg**.

        HK_JOURNALPLAYBACK whenever a message is to be played back.

        HK_JOURNALRECORD after input it translates into WM_CHAR or WM_BUTTON1_DBLCLCK for recording messages into a journal.

	HK_SENDMSG called whenever **WinSendMSg** is called.
hookproc	The address of a procedure to be called by the hook.
modid	The id of a resource if loaded, or NULL if being installed in the system message queue.

When a message is intercepted by one of these hooks, the hook procedure is called with the following parameters:

```
helphook(hAB, mode, topic, subtopic, &rect);
```

where

mode	is **HFM_MENU, HFM_MD, HFM_WINDOW,** or **HFM_APPLICATION,** indicating the mode in which help has been requested.
topic	In menu mode this is the menu id: in message box mode this isthe message id; and in standard mode this is a window id.
subtopic	In menu mode, this is a command id; in message box mode this is a control id; and in standard mode this is the id of the window with the focus or -1 if none.
& rect	The address of a RECTL structure containing the screen area from which the help was requested.

As you can see, if you carefully give each window and message box a known id, you can tell the context from which help was detected and decide which help message to display. You can request help at any time by pressing F1, which has the default WM_HELP accelerator associated with it, by selecting Help from the menu or by selecting a HELP push button in a message or dialog box.

1. If you request help by pressing F1 while a top-line menu item is selected, the topic will be the id of this menu item and the subtopic will be -1.

2. If you request help from a drop-down menu item, the topic will be the top-line menu item and the subtopic the id of the selected item.

3. If you request help from the main window, the subtopic will be the main window id.

4. If you select a help button from a message box, the topic will be the window id specified in the **WinMessageBox** call.

5. If you select a help button from a dialog box, the subtopic will be the dialog id used to reference the dialog template in the resource file.

From the id passed to the hook, you can select the correct text strings from the string table and load and display them.

9 Using the Help System in OS/2 PM

OS/2 1.2 has a sophisticated help system that allows you to write and format help screens using a simple scripting language and include index entries and links to additional screens so that each help screen can take on the features of a *hypertext* system.

The help screens can be written using any text editor and formatted by including *markup* commands that are identical to those used in IBM's Bookmaster text processing system. Thus, you can write a manual for your program using Bookmaster and include the same text in the same form in the help screens.

MARKING UP HELP SCREEN TEXT

A markup language is a series of symbols that tell some text formatting program how to space, format, and index the text that makes up a help screen (or manual). In OS/2 the program that compiles the help files is called IPFC for the Interactive Presentation Facility Compiler. Nearly all of the commands in a help file begin with a colon and end with a period. Many occur in pairs such as

:ol.   begin an ordered list
:eol.   end the ordered list

where the second of the two is the same command as the first but preceded with the letter "e."

The tags that we use to mark up the text divide into groups as follows:

- headers
- linking commands
- lists and definitions
- formatting commands
- index entries

Formatting Commands

Formatting commands are used to affect the layout of text on the page, as well as the structure of the document:

:userdoc. -:euserdoc.   Must start and end any IPF source file.

:p.   Starts a new paragraph.

:hp1. - :ehp1.   Sets the text between the markers in *italics*.

:hp2.-:ehp2.   Sets the text between the markers in **bold-face.**

Headers

Headers are used to label groups of paragraphs and start individual help panels. They range from #1 to #6 heads and are specified as follows:

:h1.   chapter head— used to start a panel

:h2.   principal subhead— starts panels

:h3.   secondary subhead— also starts panels

:h4.-:h6.   minor subheads— do not start panels

The IPFC program requires that you start with :h1. heads and use them in sequence down to the lowest level you plan to use, without leaving any intermediate heads out.

Lists

There are four types of lists allowed by IPFC:

> simple lists
>
> ordered lists
>
> unordered lists marked with *bullets*
>
> definition lists

The above list of names of lists is a *simple list*, where each element starts on a new line. An *ordered list* is simply a numbered series of items, and an *unordered list* is a list of items preceded by bullets:

- unordered list

- each item is marked

- using a bullet

The markup symbols for these lists are

:sl.	begin simple list
:esl.	end simple list
:ol.	begin ordered list
:eol.	end ordered list
:ul.	begin unordered list
:eul.	end unordered list
:li.	begin a new list item of any of these types

Thus, the markup code for an unordered list like that shown above would be

```
:ul.
:li.unordered list
:li.each item is marked
:li.using a bullet
:eul.
```

Each of the preceeding lists can also be modified with the **compact** modifier to print with less space between lines.

Definition Lists

A *definition list* is one in which a boldfaced column of items appears at the left, with an indented series of definitions adjacent to them. A definition list for the list types appears just above. There are four markup symbols used in specifying definition lists:

:dl tsize=*nn*.   start a definition list with a left column width of *nn*.

:dt.   Start a definition tag to appear in the left-hand column.

:dd.   Start a definition to appear in the right-hand column.

:edl.   end a definition list.

As with the other lists, these can be compressed by including the **compact** modifier as part of the **dl** marker. A typical definition list might look like the following:

lists   used to enumerate data
hp tags   used to highlight phrases
headers   used to start sections of a document

The above definition list is typed in as

```
:dl tsize=10 compact.
:dt.lists
:dd.used to enumerate data
:dt.hp tags
:dd.used to highlight phrases
:dt.headers
:dd.used to start sections of a document
:edl.
```

LINKING PANELS TOGETHER

The most powerful part of the help system in OS/2 is the ability to click the mouse on a highlighted word and have a new panel appear describing that feature in more detail. To highlight a word or phrase that you wish to have linked to another panel, you use the **:link.** marker around the phrase

```
:link reftype=hd res=2000.
reading files
:elink.
```

This says to link the phrase "reading files" to a header of a panel whose id is 2000. Then, that panel should begin with a header that contains that id number:

```
:h2 res=2000.Reading in Files
```

You should realize that the symbolic values that you define for these panels could be related to window identifiers within your OS/2 program. However, while it is common to refer to each window by a symbolic identifier, IPFC requires that these integer values be referred to only as numbers. It is up to you to make this association either with comments or with values in the Help table, which becomes part of your resource file.

One method of using the symbolic constants defined in an include file to represent these integers is to use the C preprocessor, which will read in the include files and substitute the values for the named constants. This produces an output file with an ".i" extension which you can then process with IPFC. To use the preprocessor simply type

```
cl /c /P ipfile.ipf
```

This will produce the output file names "ipfile.i." You will need to edit this file to remove about 50 lines of blank lines which are inserted by the C preprocessor. Certain other C symbols are also converted, most typically ".e" is converted to ".E0," and must be restored before running IPFC. Other third party vendors will probably also produce tools which will take care of this step.

Constants Used by HELPJ

We will use the following constants in the HELPJ program below. We define them here so you can see the relationship between the named constants and the integer values we will use to define help panels in the IPF file.

```
#define PROGWIND          1

#define MAIN_HELPTABLE    2000
#define SUBHELP           2010
#define EXTENDED_HELP     2020
#define HELP_FOR_HELP     2030
#define KEYS_HELP         2040

#define FILEMENU          100
#define OPEN              110
#define EXIT              120

#define DISPLAY           200
#define LINETYPE          210
#define SETCOLOR          220

#define EDIT              300
#define MOVESIZE          310
```

This file defines the window id, the help table ids and the menu values.

THE HELP RESOURCE FILE

When you create a help file, you must include information on the help messages to be processed in your program's resource file. These include a main line help menu on the menu bar, a main help table, and a help subtable.

```
/***  Resource file for the HELPJ program*****************/
#include "helpj.h"
#include <os2.h>
POINTER PROGWIND  helpj.ico

MENU PROGWIND PRELOAD
BEGIN
  FiSUBMENU "    FILEMENU
      BEGIN
        MENUITEM "&eqvOpen...",  OPEN
        MENUITEM "Exit",         EXIT
      END
    SUBMENU "&eqvDisplay",       DISPLAY
```

```
    BEGIN
    MENUITEM "LineType",  LINETYPE
    MENUITEM "Color",     SETCOLOR
    END
  SUBMENU "&eqvEdit",          EDIT
    BEGIN
    MENUITEM "Move/Size", MOVESIZE
    END
  SUBMENU "Help", WM_HELP
  begin
   MENUITEM    "&eqvHelp for help...", HELP_FOR_HELP
   MENUITEM    "&eqvExtended help...", SC_HELPEXTENDED,
               MIS_SYSCOMMAND
   MENUITEM    "&eqvKeys help...",     SC_HELPKEYS    ,
               MIS_SYSCOMMAND
   MENUITEM    "Help &eqvindex...",    SC_HELPINDEX   ,
               MIS_SYSCOMMAND
  end
END


HELPTABLE MAIN_HELPTABLE
BEGIN
    HELPITEM PROGWIND, SUBHELP, EXTENDED_HELP
END


HELPSUBTABLE SUBHELP
BEGIN
        HELPSUBITEM    EDIT,    EDIT
        HELPSUBITEM    FILEMENU, FILEMENU
        HELPSUBITEM    DISPLAY, DISPLAY
        HELPSUBITEM    LINETYPE, LINETYPE
END
```

For each panel that you want displayed, you must have an entry in the HELPSUBTABLE. This associates the window id's with the panel id's.

Interpreting the Help Messages

The main line Help menu by convention includes the commands "Help for Help," "Extended Help," and a "Help Index." You may also include the menu item "Keys Help" and copy that help text from the sample provided in the OS/2 1.2 Toolkit. The "Help for Help" menu item posts a WM_COMMAND message with **mp1** set to the message in the menu, which you then intercept in your main window procedure and post the message HM_DISPLAY_HELP.

```
case WM_COMMAND:
    switch (SHORT1FROMMP(mp1));      /*Get the command value*/
    begin
    case HELP_FOR_HELP:
        WinSendMsg( hHelpInst, HM_DISPLAY_HELP, OL, OL);
        break;
    end
    break;
```

The three remaining help menu selections post system commands that result in actions by OS/2 PM directly. Selecting "Extended Help" causes the system to post a WM_HELP message that is intercepted by the help instance processor, causing a display of the main help panel for your program.

The "Keys Help" selection posts the message HM_QUERY_KEYS_HELP, which you respond to by posting the number of the window panel where your keys help message begins. This is the text you copied from the toolkit HElP example. You can also easily omit this panel unless you have additional special keys you wish to explain, since it is available under the main PM "Help for Help" window. The messages to cause the keys help to appear are

```
case HM_QUERY_KEYS_HELP:
    return( (MRESULT) KEYS_HELP);
    break;
```

The "Help Index" menu item posts the message SC_HELPINDEX, which causes a display of all the items indexed in your help IPF file. You can click on these index items and go directly to that point in the help panels.

INDEXING ITEMS

The Help manager and the IPFC compiler also provide the ability to generate an alphabetical index of topics. These are automatically linked to their appearance in the text and clicking on the "Options" menu of the help window will allow you to select an index.

There are two levels of indexing provided: **:i1.** and **:i2..** To make a main line index entry, simply include the word preceded by the **:i1** tag:

```
:i1.File menu
```

To include subindex entries, you simply give the main entry a symbolic name that you then refer to in all subindex entries:

```
:i1 id=filemen.File menu
:i2 refid=filemen.opening files
```

THE COMPLETE HELP IPF FILE

Below we show a simple help file with some linked panels. Note that the main panel is given the res value 2020, which is equal to the EXTENDED_HELP value in the symbol definitions. This equality is required if you want a main help panel to appear when you press F1 or select the "Extended Help" menu item.

```
:userdoc.
:title.Help for Display/2
:body.
:h1 res=2020.Help for Main Screen
:p. To use this package, simply click on any pull-down
menu and select from the menu which appears. While a menu
is pulled down, you can press F1 for help on that topic.
:dl tsize=15.
:dt.:link reftype=hd res=100.File:elink.
:dd.read in ASCII data files.
:dt.:link reftype=hd res=200.Display:elink.
:dd.Change the data display
:dt.:link reftype=hd res=300.
Edit
:elink.
```

```
:dd.move, size, and erase data.
:edl.
:hl res=100.File Menu
:il.File menu
The File menu allows you to read in data files
:hl res=200.Display Menu
:il.Display menu
The display menu allows you to change the color and line
type.
:dl tsize=10.
:dt.:link reftype=hd res=210.
Linetype
:elink.
:dd.Allows you to change the line type
:dt.Color
:dd.Allows you to change the line color
:edl.
:h2 res=210.Line Type
:p.This command brings up a dialog box allowing
you to select the line type using a series of radio
buttons.
:hl res=300.Editing the Display
:p.The Edit Menu allows you to move lines around on
the screen.
:index.
:euserdoc.
```

Compiling a Help File

Once you have created your help text file using a text editor, you simply compile the file using the IPFC compiler. It is conventional to give the help source file the extension .IPF and the compiled file the extension .HLP. The following command produces the file HELPJ.HLP:

```
IPFC HELPJ.IPF
```

The help file must be accessible when you start the program that requires it. You can put it either in the same subdirectory as the program you are running or in a subdirectory specified by the environment variable HELP.

REGISTERING A HELP INSTANCE

A program will invoke these help features if a help initialization structure is filled with the correct values and a help instance is created and associated with the main window frame. To load the help initialization structure **hmi**, you fill it as follows:

```
HELPINIT hmi;                       /*declare help structure*/
HWND     hHelpInst;                 /*help instance window  */

hmi.cb = sizeof(HELPINIT);          /*size of help structure*/
hmi.ulReturnCode = NULL;
hmi.pszTutorialName =NULL;
hmi.phtHelpTable =                  /*value of help table   */
     (PVOID)(0xffff0000 BitOR MAIN_HELPTABLE);
hmi.hmodAccelActionBarModule = NULL;
hmi.idAccelTable = NULL;
hmi.idActionBar = NULL;
hmi.pszHelpWindowTitle="Example Help Window"; /*title bar*/
hmi.hmodHelpTableModule = NULL;
hmi.usShowPanelId = NULL;
hmi.pszHelpLibraryName="HELPJ.HLP"; /*name of help file   */
```

Then you must create the help instance and associate it with the current *frame* window:

```
/*create the help instance*/
hHelpInst = WinCreateHelpInstance(hAB, &hmi);

/*associate with a window*/
WinAssociateHelpInstance(hHelpInst, hFrame);
```

Once these functions are executed, then either pressing function key F1 or selecting Extended help will automatically bring up the main help window. The display of the help window using the text above is illustrated in Figure 9-1.

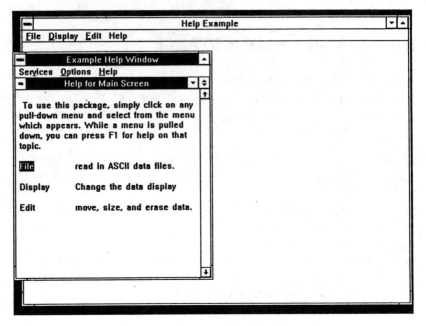

Figure 9-1. A Help example window

10 Using the Graphics Presentation Interface

OS/2 PM has an extensive set of calls for drawing graphical images on the screen, all having the prefix Gpi. These calls allow you to draw lines, curves, boxes, markers and fonts, fill areas, and move bitmaps on the screen. You have the ability to set the line type, color, and fill pattern and draw a number of different point markers in a few simple calls.

PRESENTATION SPACES

All Gpi calls have the handle to a presentation space as an argument. Recall that there are three types of presentation spaces

- cached micro
- micro, and
- normal

The cached micro presentation space is an existing internal table that is initialized and passed to you when you make a **WinBeginPaint** call. It has no memory from previous invocations and you must set the color, line type, marker type, and font each time you use it.

The micro presentation space is created with the **GpiCreatePS** call with the option GPIT_MICRO bit set. A micro presentation space is useful when you need to create and reuse a PS with a number of settings that differ from the defaults.

139

The normal presentation space is created with the **GpiCreatePS** call with the option GPIT_NORMAL bit set. A normal presentation space not only allows you to save various settings and colors, but also allows you to record all of your graphics drawing commands in a *graphics segment* that can be played back rapidly each time you want to repaint the screen. In addition, a normal segment can be used for drawing both on the screen and on other devices simply by associating a new *device context* with the presentation space and redrawing the segment on the new device.

GRAPHICS COMMANDS

Many of the Gpi drawing commands operate on a POINTL structure that gives the current x and y location where the operation is to take place. Note that you must pass the *address* of the point structure.

```
POINTL pt;           /* point structure          */

pt.x = 50;           /* set x-coordinate         */
pt.y = 100;          /* set y-coordinate         */

GpiMove(hPS, &pt);   /* move to that point       */
pt.x = 200;          /* set a new x-value        */
GpiLine(hPS, &pt);   /* draw a line to that point */
```

Graphics Coordinate Space

Usually, you make calls to graphics functions using units of *pixels* or *pels*. These two terms are used in different engineering disciplines but have identical meaning. The coordinate system of a PM screen has (0,0) in the lower left corner and a maximum (x,y) value in the upper right corner. You can always find out the current size of your window with the **WinQueryWindowRect** call, which returns the coordinates of the window in a RECTL structure.

It is also possible to tell PM that a window is to use a different coordinate system, such as 0.1 millimeters or 0.01 inches, by setting suitable option bits in the GpiCreatePS call, but these bits are only interpreted accurately when the graphics are drawn to a plotter or printer. The representation on a screen is not exact.

The GpiCreatePS Call

This call has the form

`GpiCreatePS(hAB, hDC, &size, options);`

where

hAB   is the handle to the anchor block.

hDC   is the handle of a device context with which the presentation space is to be associated. This value must be non-null if the GPIA_ASSOC bit is set in the options, or if a micropresentation space is specified.

size   is the address of a SIZEL structure, containing the long value of the x size in

`siz.cx`

and the y size in

`siz.cy.`

options   is a series of bits defining the units, format, and type of PS.

   units   describes the screen units

      PU_ARBITRARY any convenient units
      PU_PELS   units are pels or pixels
      PU_LOMETRIC units of 0.1 mm
      PU_HIMETRIC units of 0.01 mm
      PU_LOENGLISH units of 0.01 inch
      PU_HIENGLISH units of 0.001 inch
      PU_TWIPS units of 1/1440 inch

   format indicates whether the segments will be retained in long or short format. Can be set to GPIF_LONG or GPIF_SHORT or GPIF_DEFAULT, which is the same.

type   type of presentation space. Select GPIT_NORMAL or GPIT_MICRO.

association   can   be   set   to   GPIA_ASSOC   or GPIA_NOASSOC. If associate is set then hDC must be a valid handle to a device context, obtained with **DevOpenDC**.

DRAWING A SPECTRUM

A **spectrum** is a series of data points acquired at evenly spaced time intervals. They are best displayed by drawing a series of continuous lines between adjacent points. If there are a large number of data points, you may have to scale the data to fit into your window. In this case, the space between data points will be calculated as a fractional number of pixels so that the entire spectrum will fit into the window. As a simple algorithm, the Paint procedure consists of

1. Get the current window width.

2. Divide the width by the number of points. The result is the *x increment*.

3. Move the drawing point to the leftmost position.

4. Draw a line to each successive y-point, incrementing the x-pixel position by the amount calculated.

This can be represented as follows:

```
xinc = (long)(65536L*(float)rc.xRight /(float)XDIM);
err=GpiSetColor(hPS, CLR_WHITE);
xpos = 0L;                    /*set initial x posn           */
pt.x = 0;
pt.y = x[0];                  /*set initial y posn           */
err=GpiMove(hPS, &pt);        /*move to first point          */
xpos += xinc;                 /*increment 32-bit to next x*/
for (i = 1; i < XDIM; i++)
   begin
   pt.x = (int)(xpos >> 16); /*get next x pos from top 16*/
   pt.y = x[i];              /*get next y                   */
   GpiLine(hPS, &pt);        /*draw line                    */
```

```
    xpos += xinc;                    /*fractional increment      */
    end
WinQueryUpdateRect(hWnd, &rc);  /*repaint window           */
WinValidateRect(hWnd, &rc, TRUE);
```

The disadvantage of this technique is obvious for large numbers of data points: it is very slow and can take one or more seconds to draw the spectrum on the screen.

Packing the Spectrum into a Buffer

A more efficient technique for drawing spectra consists of making up a *buffer* consisting of an array of the maximum and minimum data points in the group of points that would fall on top of each other when plotted on a screen of limited resolution. For example, if the screen width were 640 pixels, then a 4096-point spectrum would consist of 4096/640 or 6.3 data points superimposed on each pixel. Rather than drawing a series of lines between 6 points, we determine the maximum and minimum of the group of points that would be plotted on top of each other and simply draw a vertical line between these maxima for each pixel column:

```
pts_per_bin = (float)XDIM/(float)rc.xRight;
j = 0;
leftpnt = 0.0;
/*fill the buffer with mins and maxes*/
rightpnt = pts_per_bin;              /*size of one bin      */
while(rightpnt < XDIM)
    begin
    min = 10000;                     /*find max and min     */
    max = -10000;                    /*in each group        */
    for (i = (int)leftpnt; i < (int)rightpnt; i++)
      begin
      if (max < x[i]) then
          max = x[i];                /*set new maximum      */
      if (min > x[i]) then
          min = x[i];                /*set new minimum      */
      end
    buffer[j++] = min;               /*put min and max      */
    buffer[j++] = max;               /*in buffer            */
    leftpnt += pts_per_bin;          /*go on to next group*/
```

```
    rightpnt += pts_per_bin;        /*of points              */
    end
bufmax = j-1;                       /*remember how big the buffer is
WinInvalidateRect(hWnd, NULL, TRUE);
```

Then, to draw the spectrum, you only need to draw vertical lines at each x-pixel position:

```
j = 0;
pt.x = 0;
while (j < bufmax)          /*draw lines from display buffer*/
    begin
    pt.y = buffer[j++];
    GpiMove(hPS, &pt);      /*move to bottom of each bin     */
    pt.y = buffer[j++];
    GpiLine(hPS, &pt);      /*and draw line to top of bin    */
    pt.x++;
    end
```

Now, the only problem with this algorithm lies in the case of a lively or noisy spectrum in which the maximum value in one pixel column is less than the minimum in the adjacent column. In this case the spectrum would appear to have discontinuities. This is easily solved by checking the previous column's maximum and minimum before drawing the new column:

```
if (min > oldmax) then
    min = oldmax;           /*lower new min          */
if (max < oldmin) then
    max = oldmin;           /*raise new max          */
oldmax = max;               /*save for next column*/
oldmin = min;
```

Line Types

The default line type is solid and one pixel wide. You can change the line type to several other types using the call

```
    GpiSetLineType(hPS, type);
```

where **type** can be one of the following:

```
LINETYPE_DEFAULT          LINETYPE_LONGDASH
LINETYPE_DOT              LINETYPE_DASHDOUBLEDOT
LINETYPE_SHORTDASH        LINETYPE_SOLID
LINETYPE_DASHDOT          LINETYPE_ALTERNATE
LINETYPE_DOUBLEDOT        LINETYPE_INVISIBLE
```

Point Markers

You can *mark* data points with markers provided as part of the character set. These markers include a cross, plus, diamond, square, six-pointed star, eight-pointed star, solid diamond, solid square, dot, small circle, and blank. You select the type of marker with the call

```
GpiSetMarker(hPS, type);
```

where **type** is one of the following constants:

```
MARKSYM_CROSS             MARKSYM_SOLIDDIAMOND
MARKSYM_PLUS              MARKSYM_SOLIDSQUARE
MARKSYM_DIAMOND           MARKSYM_DOT
MARKSYM_SQUARE            MARKSYM_SMALLCIRCLE
MARKSYM_SIXPOINTSTAR      MARKSYM_BLANK
MARKSYM_EIGHTPOINTSTAR
```

Then, to draw the markers you use the call

```
GpiMarker(hPS, &point);
```

where **point** is a POINTL structure, just as is used in the **GpiLine** call.

Polylines and Polymarkers

If you have a series of lines to draw, as in a spectrum, and all are represented as a series of *(x, y)* data pairs as pixel coordinates, you can create an array of POINTL structures defining these drawings and issue a single call:

```
GpiPolyLine(hPS, count, &points);
```

where

hPS   is the Presentation Space Handle

count   is a long value representing the number of points to draw.

& points   is the pointer to an array of POINTL structures representing successive *(x, y)* coordinates.

Similarly, you can mark all the points in such an array using the

```
GpiPolyMarker(hPS, count, &points);
```

call.

Using the Polyline in a Buffered Display

If you create an array of POINTL values for drawing in succession and use the **GpiPolyLine** call to draw all the lines at once, it can be as much as 50% faster than a series of individual **GpiMove** and **GpiLine** calls. If we create a packed buffer of data points as above where each vertical line represents the maximum excursion of all the data points that would be drawn at that horizontal pixel location, we can pass this array directly to the **GpiPolyLine** call.

Now, since these lines are drawn from successive points, rather than from bottom to top each time, we must arrange for our buffer to draw one line "up" and the following one "down," to minimize screen drawing time. This can be done easily with the following code:

```
WinQueryWindowRect(hWnd, &rc        /*get the window size   */
pts_per_bin = (float)XDIM/(float)rc.xRight;
j = 0;
leftpnt = 0.0;                      /*fill the buffer with  */
up = TRUE;                          /*mins and maxes        */
oldmin = 0;                         /*remember last         */
oldmax = 0;                         /*min and max           */
xp =0;
rightpnt = pts_per_bin;             /*size of one bin       */
while(rightpnt < XDIM)
    begin
    min = 10000;                    /*find max and min      */
    max = -10000;                   /*in each group         */
    for (i = (int)leftpnt; i < (int)rightpnt; i++)
        begin
        if (max < x[i]) then
```

```
        max = x[i];               /*find current max        */
      if (min > x[i]) then
          min = x[i];             /*and min                 */
        end
    if (min > oldmax) then        /*make sure this min      */
        min = oldmax;             /*is not > old max        */
    if (max < oldmin) then        /*make sure this max      */
        max = oldmin;             /*is not < old min        */
    oldmax = max;                 /*remember this min and   */
    oldmin = min;                 /*max for next column     */
    if (up) then
        begin
        buffer[j].x = xp;         /*draw up from min to max*/
        buffer[j++].y = min;      /*put min & max in buffer*/
        buffer[j].x = xp++;
        buffer[j++].y = max;
        up = FALSE;               /*next one is drawn down  */
        end
      else
        begin
        buffer[j].x = xp;         /*draw down from max to min*/
        buffer[j++].y = max;      /*put min and max in buffer*/
        buffer[j].x = xp++;
        buffer[j++].y = min;
        up = TRUE;                /*next one is drawn up     */
        end
      leftpnt += pts_per_bin;     /*go on to next           */
      rightpnt += pts_per_bin;    /*group of points         */
      end
  bufmax = j - 1;                 /*remember size of buffer */
```

Then the PAINT routine is just the simple call

```
case WM_PAINT:
  hPS = WinBeginPaint(hWnd, (HPS)NULL, (PWRECT)NULL);
  WinQueryWindowRect(hWnd, &rc);      /*get current window */
                                      /* dimensions        */
  WinFillRect(hPS, &rc, CLR_BLACK);   /*fill it with black */
  GpiSetColor(hPS, CLR_WHITE);        /*draw white lines    */
  j = 0;
  GpiPolyLine(hPS, bufmax, buffer);   /*draw entire         */
```

```
                                        /* poly line        */
WinEndPaint(hPS);                       /*end paint routine */
break;
```

DRAWING CLOSED FIGURES

There are three types of figures that you can draw as closed shapes using simple Gpi calls: boxes, arcs, and areas. The simplest of these is drawn by the **GpiBox** command, which simply draws a box whose lower left corner is at the current drawing point, and whose upper corner is at the point defined in the call

```
        GpiBox(hPS, control, &pt, hround, vround);
```

where

hPS   is the Presentation Space Handle.

control   defines whether the box is to be filled, using the constants   DRO_FILL,   DRO_OUTLINE,   or DRO_OUTLINEFILL. DRO_OUTLINEFILL.

&pt   contains the coordinates of the diagonally opposite box corner.

hround   is the horizontal length of the full axis of the ellipse used for rounding the corners.

vround   is the vertical length of the full axis of the ellipse used for rounding the corners.

If either rounding parameter is NULL, the corners are not rounded.

DRAWING AN ARC

An *arc* is an ellipse or a segment of an ellipse and can, of course, include the circle. The shape of the ellipse is defined by an ARCPARAM structure consisting of two points on the edge of the ellipse, which produce perpendicular lines when drawn to the center of the ellipse. The structure consists of two *(x, y)* coordinate pairs called *(p, s)* and *(r, q)*. The structure has the form

```
typedef struct _ARCPARAMS
    {
    LONG lP;
    LONG lQ;
    LONG lR;
    LONG lS;
    } ARCPARAMS;
```

The default settings for these parameters produce a circle whose center is the drawing point (p=1, r=0, s=0, q=1). Thus, if you do not change the arc parameters, the **GpiFullArc** call will draw a circle. This call has the form

```
GpiFullArc(hPS, control, multiplier);
```

where

control   is DRO_FILL, DRO_OUTLINE or DRO_OUTLINEFILL

multiplier   is a fixed point fraction that determines the size of the arc. The largest allowed multiplier is 256.

The fixed point fraction can be constructed using the MAKEFIXED macro, where the first argument is the fixed point part and the second argument the fractional part. A typical call to draw a 20-pixel ellipse would be

```
GpiFullArc(hPS, DRO_OUTLINE, MAKEFIXED(20,0));
```

It is also possible to draw partial arcs, using the call

```
GpiPartialArc(hPS, &center, multiplier, start, sweep);
```

where

& center   is a POINTL structure describing the coordinates of the arc center.

multiplier   is a fixed point fraction that determines the size of the arc. The largest allowed multiplier is 256.

start   is the starting angle as a fixed point fraction.

sweep   is the sweep angle as a fixed point fraction.

Pattern Filling

Boxes, full arcs, and areas are filled with the current pattern if DRO_FILL is set. If you do nothing, this is a solid fill pattern. However by using the call

```
GpiSetPattern(hPS, pattern);
```

you can set the current pattern to one of the following:

PATSYM_DEFAULT	PATSYM_DIAG4
PATSYM_VERT	PATSYM_NOSHADE
PATSYM_HORIZ	PATSYM_SOLID
PATSYM_DIAG1	PATSYM_HALFTONE
PATSYM_DIAG2	PATSYM_BLANK
PATSYM_DENSE1 - PATSYM_DENSE8	

COLORS

OS/2 PM defines 16 different colors that correspond to the same colors available on the original PC color graphics adapter in character mode. You can set the current color for text, lines, markers, and areas using the **GpiSetColor** call

```
GpiSetColor(hPS, color);
```

where **color** is one of the following:

CLR_WHITE	CLR_DARKGRAY
CLR_BLACK	CLR_DARKBLUE
CLR_BLUE	CLR_DARKRED
CLR_RED	CLR_DARKPINK
CLR_PINK	CLR_DARKGREEN
CLR_GREEN	CLR_DARKCYAN
CLR_CYAN	CLR_BROWN
CLR_YELLOW	CLR_PALEGRAY
CLR_NEUTRAL	

The following special values for color settings can also be used:

CLR_FALSE   all bit planes are zeroes.

CLR_TRUE   all bit planes are ones.

CLR_DEFAULT   The device-dependent color that contrasts with its natural background.

CLR_BACKGROUND   The device's natural background color.

You can also set each of the primitive types (line, character, marker and area) to have their own independent color values using the **GpiSetAttrs** call, where you can set a mask so that the basic color is only changed for one of these types at a time. This is usually more programming than it is worth and we will not use it here.

FILLING AREAS

An *area* is a section of the drawing that starts and stops with commands you insert in the drawing sequence. You can fill an area regardless of shape by starting it with the **GpiBeginArea** call, drawing some lines, and then closing the area with the **GpiEndArea** call. If the area is not a closed figure, the close area call draws a line back to the beginning of the area to close it. The calls for starting and ending an area are

```
GpiBeginArea(hPS, options);

GpiEndArea(hPS);
```

where

options   can be BA_NOBOUNDARY or BA_BOUNDARY to draw boundary lines or not, and BA_ALTERNATE or BA_WINDING to define whether to construct the interior by the number of boundary crossings or not.

The following calls draw a filled equilateral triangle:

```
GpiBeginArea(hPS, BA_ALTERNATE);  /* begin area for filled*/
                                  /* triangle          */
GpiMove(hPS, &pos);               /* set first vertex  */
pt.x = pos.x + BOXWID;            /* move across x      */
pt.y = pos.y;                     /* leave y the same   */
GpiLine(hPS, &pt);                /* draw line across base*/
pt.x = pt.x - BOXWID/2;           /* back up x halfway   */
                                  /* for apex           */
pt.y = pos.y + BOXWID;            /* altitude == width  */
GpiLine(hPS, &pt);                /* altitude           */
GpiLine(hPS,&pos);                /* draw last line      */
GpiEndArea(hPS);                  /* fill area of triangle*/
```

PATHS AND LINE WIDTHS

There are analogous calls to start a drawing region called a *path*. A path can be used just like an area, to define a part of the screen to close and fill, but it is more often used to define a series of lines and curves that have a width greater than a single pixel. The call **GpiSetLineWidth** described in the reference manual has no effect in OS/2 PM 1.2 and is included for future expansion. However, the call

```
GpiSetLineWidthGeom(hPS, width);
```

has an effect when describing the drawing of a line or lines inside a *path*. In the current implementation of OS/2 PM, there can be only one path at a time and the calls to refer to that path always reference path number 1L. Once the path has been opened, you can issue any of a number of drawing commands. At the end of the group of drawings, you close the path and issue the **GpiModifyPath** call to indicate that wide lines are to be drawn, followed by the **GpiFillPath** command to fill the lines to this width. The following code draws a thick line and a thick box.

```
GpiSetLineWidthGeom(hPS, 4L);        /*set 4 pixel wide line*/
GpiBeginPath(hPS, 1L);               /*begin the path        */
GpiMove(hPS, &pos);                  /*move to first point   */
GpiLine(hPS, &pt);                   /*draw a line to 2nd pt*/
GpiMove(hPS, &pos);                  /*move to start of box  */
GpiBox(hPS, DRO_OUTLINE, &pt,
               NULL, NULL);   /*draw the box           */
GpiEndPath(hPS);              /*end the path           */
/* set up for wide lines */
GpiModifyPath(hPS, 1L, MPATH_STROKE);
GpiFillPath(hPS, 1L, FPATH_WINDING);  /* fill the path      */
```

ERROR CHECKING OF GPI CALLS

Many Gpi calls do not return error codes but instead return other values of
use in advanced programming. If you have a programming problem you
want to debug, the **WinGetLastError** call is useful.

```
err =
  WinGetLastError(hAB);   /*see if there has been an error*/
if (err != 0) then
   begin
   sprintf(buf, "Error = %x",err);   /*print it to buffer*/
   WinMessageBox(HWND_DESKTOP,
   hWnd, buf, "Graphics error",
   1, MB_OK);                        /*and put in message box*/
   end
```

To use it, you need the handle to the anchor block. If you debug using
Codeview or print out the error value in hexadecimal in a message box you
can look up the error number in the **pmerr.h** file.

11 Child Windows

One of the great advantages of OS/2 Presentation Manager is its ability to spawn a number of tasks and have each one associated with a visual indicator in its own window. Windows created by other windows are known as *child windows*. We have already seen a number of examples of child windows in dialog boxes, where all of the symbols representing various types of boxes are actually child windows preprogrammed to behave in standard ways.

USES OF CHILD WINDOWS

Child windows can be used to represent events taking place in separate tasks or to show information in different ways. For example, in a data acquisition program you could show the data being acquired in a child window while maintaining the main window for processing of user commands. Another common use of child windows is to allow the user to view data in a number of ways at the same time. For example, you might want to see data in both graphical and tabular form in two windows, and see how changing the data in one window affects the display in the other.

CREATING CHILD WINDOWS

Creating child windows is just as easy as creating the main window. However, it is customary to create child windows as "invisible" and then use the **WinSetWindowPos** function to make them visible at a position chosen by the program, rather than letting PM decide on default positions. Each child window must have its own window procedure and each procedure's name must be declared in an EXPORTS statement in the .DEF file unless you compile with the /Alfu compile switches.

INSTANCES OF THE SAME WINDOW

Now we are going to draw two small windows on the screen that have identical properties, except that one will be drawing a blue line and one a red line. Further, they will be drawing these lines at different rates, since we are sending timer messages at different frequencies to the two windows. However, there is now reason to clutter up our program (and memory) with two virtually identical window procedures for drawing red lines and blue lines. Instead, we can register the class of one single window type and create two windows of that class.

The only problem we will then have is telling from within the window procedure which color we are supposed to draw and where the current line is located. We will store the current color and line position in a structure pointed to by the extra bytes associated with each window.

THE CHILDREN PROGRAM

To illustrate the uses of child windows in a multitasking environment, we will write a program to display two small child windows. Then we will start two timers ticking at different rates, and have the timers send their "ticks" to the two windows. Whenever a window receives a tick, it will draw a line one pixel further to the right, and when the window is full horizontally, it will begin drawing from the left two pixel rows higher. To illustrate the ability to open and close windows, we will use two menu commands: one to turn on the windows, and one to destroy them.

In this program, the "tasks" are the timers themselves. The child windows all run as part of the main program, receiving messages asynchronously from the timer tasks.

Creating the Main Window

Creating the main window is exactly like creating the windows we have used previously, except that it is important that the style bit CS_CLIPCHILDREN be set when the class is registered. This tells PM that children of this window are not to be painted over when the main window is repainted.

```
/*register the main Window class*/
WinRegisterClass (hAB,
          (PCH)szClassName,
          (PFNWP)TimerWndProc,
          CS_SIZEREDRAW ICS_SYNCPAINT | CS_CLIPCHILDREN,
          0 );
```

Likewise, you must register the class of the child windows:

```
WinRegisterClass (hAB, /*child window class        */
          "Children", /*class name              */
          Child1WndProc, /*window procedure      */
          NULL,
          6 );        /*space for pointer and color value*/
```

The Child Window Procedures

Since both child windows do the same thing, their window procedures are identical, except that we draw one line in red and one in blue for contrast. They must interpret the WM_TIMER message that is received each time the timer ticks, and draw the line one pixel further. In order to tell which window we are currently executing, we need a way to pass arguments to each child window indicating the current line position and color. We do this by using the "extra bytes" feature of windows. When we register the class of the child window, we reserve 4 bytes for a pointer to a POINTL structure containing the current line coordinates and 2 more bytes containing the color of the line. Then, when we start these windows, we will put values in these extra bytes.

Starting the Timers

The timers can be started in a windowing environment using the call

```
WinStartTimer(hAB, hWnd, tid, time);
```

where

hAB	is the handle to the main window's anchor block.
hWnd	is the handle of the window to which the timer ticks are to be sent.
tid	is the timer id number: an arbitrary small integer below the value TID_USERMAX.
time	is the time in milliseconds between timer ticks.

Note that this **WinStartTimer** function eliminates the need for semaphores and for the **DosTimer** function.

Passing the Arguments to the Window Procedures

When we start the child windows, we use the usual **WinCreateStdWindow** call, referring to both windows by the same class name "Children." Then, immediately after the call, we set values into the extra window words using the **WinSetWindowULong** and Ushort commands.

```
WinSetWindowULong(hWnd1, 0, &redpnt);  /*pass the pointer*/
WinSetWindowUShort(hWnd1, 4, CLR_RED); /*amd the color   */
```

It is important to recognize that the WM_CREATE message is executed before the program returns from the **WinCreate** call, and therefore the arguments *are not yet there*. Thus, we cannot access them during WM_CREATE but only later when the window is visible. In this case, since there are actually two instances of the same window in operation, we cannot store these values in local static variables, but must request them from the window words each time we need to draw another pixel.

Drawing the Pixels at Each Timer Tick

Note that in order to keep the example simple, these child windows do *not* have a paint procedure, and if you decide to move or size the child windows, the line will not be redrawn from the beginning:

```
MRESULT FAR PASCAL ChildWndProc(HWND hWnd, USHORT msg,
                                MPARAM mp1, MPARAM mp2)


begin
    POINTL *point;   /*pointer to point structure          */
    int color;       /*and color obtained from extra bytes*/

switch (msg)
begin

    case WM_ERASEBACKGROUND:     /*tell PM to erase screen*/
        return(TRUE);
        break;

    case WM_TIMER:               /*draw new point on each tick*/
        point =
            (POINTL *)WinQueryWindowULong(hWnd, QWL_USER);
        color =
            (int)WinQueryWindowUShort(hWnd, QWL_USER+4);
        incrline(hWnd, point, color);
        break;

    default:
        return( WinDefWindowProc( hWnd, msg, mp1, mp2));
        break;
end /*switch*/
return(0L);                       /*message not processed*/
end /*child*/
```

Each child window must also receive and interpret the WM_ERASEBACKGROUND message since it is not doing any painting, and must return TRUE, which tells PM that it must erase the window's background. This message is sent whenever the child window is resized by the user.

Drawing the Lines in the Windows

The **incrline** function is called by the timer routine and draws a line across the screen a pixel at a time. For it to begin drawing, it must obtain a micro presentation space using the WinGetPS function, and release it when done.

```
hPS =
   WinGetPS(hWnd);            /*get presentation space handle*/
GpiSetColor(hPS, color); /* set the current color        */
lpPoint->x++;              /* increment the line length    */
if (lpPoint->x > XMAX) then    /* if the line is at the */
   begin                       /* end of the window     */
     lpPoint->x = 0;           /* reset the x-value      */
     lpPoint->y += 2;          /* and move up two lines */
   end
GpiSetPel(hPS, (PPOINTL)lpPoint);     /* set that pixel */
WinReleasePS(hPS);              /* release PS           */
```

Closing Child Windows

Just as you destroy the main window when your program terminates, you can destroy child windows when you are through with them. You simply use the call

```
WinDestroyWindow(hWndchild1Frame);
```

where the window you actually destroy is the *frame*. The client window is a child of the frame and is destroyed automatically when its parent is destroyed.

THE FINAL PROGRAM

When the program is run and the "Start" command selected, the two child windows appear as shown in Figure 11-1.

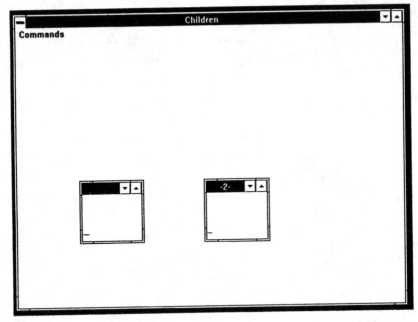

Figure 11-1. A display from the CHILDREN program

They disappear when "Stop" is selected. Note that since the timers run as separate tasks, you always have access to the menus.

```
/*********PM program with child windows and timer ********/
#define INCL_BASE
#define INCL_PM
#include <os2.h>
#include <cdefs.h>
#include <string.h>
#include "childefs.h"

        HAB     hAB;                    /*handle to anchor block*/


#define XMAX 100
#define SWP SWP_SIZE | SWP_MOVE | SWP_ACTIVATE | SWP_SHOW
MRESULT FAR PASCAL ChildWndProc(HWND hWnd, USHORT msg,
                                MPARAM mp1, MPARAM mp2);

MRESULT FAR PASCAL ParentWndProc(HWND hWnd, USHORT msg,
                                MPARAM mp1, MPARAM mp2);
```

```
POINTL bluepnt, redpnt;
/*****************************************************/
/************** M a i n    F u n c t i o n**************/
int  cdecl main ()                    /*C main routine      */

begin /* as before*/
end
/*****************************************************/
void incrline(HWND hWnd, PPOINTL lpPoint, USHORT color)

/* increments line to new position in either child window*/
begin
        HPS hPS;
        CHARBUNDLE cb;

  hPS = WinGetPS(hWnd);  /* get presentation space handle */
  GpiSetColor(hPS, color);
  lpPoint->x++;
  if (lpPoint->x > XMAX) then
     begin
     lpPoint->x = 0;
     lpPoint->y += 2;
     end
  GpiSetPel(hPS, (PPOINTL)lpPoint);
  WinReleasePS(hPS);
end
/*****************************************************/
MRESULT FAR PASCAL ChildWndProc(HWND hWnd, USHORT msg,
                                    MPARAM mp1, MPARAM mp2)

begin
        POINTL *point;     /*note that this is static*/
        int color;

switch (msg)
begin

  case WM_ERASEBACKGROUND:     /*tell PM to erase screen*/
     return(TRUE);
     break;
```

```
case WM_TIMER:               /*draw new point on each tick  */
    point = (POINTL *)WinQueryWindowULong(hWnd, QWL_USER);
    color = (int)WinQueryWindowUShort(hWnd, QWL_USER+4);
    incrline(hWnd, point, color);
    break;

default:
    return( WinDefWindowProc( hWnd, msg, mp1, mp2));
    break;
end /*switch*/
return(0L);                  /*message not processed*/
end /*child*/
/**********************************************************/
/*      Main window procedure for all messages          */
/**********************************************************/
MRESULT FAR PASCAL ParentWndProc(HWND hWnd, USHORT msg,
                                 MPARAM mp1, MPARAM mp2)


begin
    HPS     hPS;         /*handle to presentation space*/
    RECTL   rc;          /*rectangle for paint         */
    ULONG flCreate;
    HWND hWnd1, hWnd2;   /*child window handles        */
    static HWND
        hWnd1Frame, hWnd2Frame; /*child window frames*/


switch (msg)
begin

case WM_COMMAND:                 /*interpret menu commands   */
    switch(LOUSHORT(mp1))        /*in lower word of mp1      */
        begin
        /*open 2 new windows and set timers               */
        case STARTTIME:
            flCreate = FCF_TITLEBAR | FCF_SIZEBORDER |
                       FCF_MINMAX;

            bluepnt.x = 0;            /*initialize pointers */
            bluepnt.y = 10;          /*for drawing         */
            redpnt.x = 0;
            redpnt.y = 10;
```

```
        hWnd1Frame = WinCreateStdWindow( hWnd,
                    FS_BORDER,
                    &flCreate,          /*control data  */
                    "Children",         /*window class  */
                    "-1-",              /*window title  */
                    (ULONG)NULL,
                    (HMODULE)NULL,
                    2,
                    &hWnd1);     /*client area handle*/
        /*pass the pointer*/
        WinSetWindowULong(hWnd1, 0, &redpnt);
        /*and the line color*/
        WinSetWindowUShort(hWnd1, 4, CLR_RED);

        hWnd2Frame = WinCreateStdWindow(hWnd,
                    FS_BORDER,
                    &flCreate,          /*control data  */
                    "Children",         /*window class  */
                    "-2-",              /*window title  */
                    (ULONG)NULL,
                    (HMODULE)NULL,
                    3,
                    &hWnd2);     /*client area handle*/
        WinSetWindowULong(hWnd2, 0, &bluepnt); /*pointer*/
        WinSetWindowUShort(hWnd2, 4, CLR_BLUE);/*color  */

        WinSetWindowPos(hWnd1Frame, HWND_TOP,
                    100,100,100,100,SWP);
        WinSetWindowPos(hWnd2Frame, HWND_TOP,
                    300,100,100,100,SWP);

        WinStartTimer(hAB, hWnd1,
                    4, 200); /*start 2 timer threads    */
        WinStartTimer(hAB, hWnd2,
                    5, 300); /*sending ticks to windows*/
        break;

case STOPTIME:            /*destroy the 2 child windows*/
        WinDestroyWindow(hWnd1Frame);
        WinDestroyWindow(hWnd2Frame);
        break;
```

```
      default:
        return(WinDefWindowProc(hWnd, msg, mp1, mp2));
      end
  break;

case WM_ERASEBACKGROUND:
        return(TRUE);              /*message is processed*/
        break;

case WM_PAINT:
        hPS = WinBeginPaint(hWnd, (HPS)NULL, (PWRECT)NULL);
        /*get current window dimensions*/
        WinQueryWindowRect(hWnd, &rc);
        WinFillRect(hPS, &rc,
                      CLR_BLACK); /*fill it with black  */
        WinEndPaint(hPS);            /*end painting routine*/
        break;

default:
        return( WinDefWindowProc( hWnd, msg, mp1, mp2));
        break;
end /*switch*/

return(0L);
end
```

The CHILDREN Resource File

```
#include "childefs.h"
POINTER HELLOWIND  children.ico
MENU HELLOWIND PRELOAD
BEGIN
    SUBMENU "Commands", HELLOCMD
        BEGIN
        MENUITEM "Start", STARTTIME
        MENUITEM "Stop", STOPTIME
        END
END
```

12 | Using the Mouse in OS/2 Programs

In many OS/2 PM programs, the mouse is the main method of communicating with the program. You use the mouse to select menu items, interact with dialog boxes, and point at program objects. To use the mouse in your own programs, you need to intercept the messages that the mouse sends to the window it is moved over. These messages are

WM_MOUSEMOVE	The mouse has moved over the current window.
WM_BUTTON1DOWN	The left button has been pressed.
WM_BUTTON1DBLCLK	The left button has been pressed twice.
WM_BUTTON2DOWN	The right button has been pressed.
WM_BUTTON2DBLCLK	The right button has been pressed twice.
WM_BUTTON1UP	The left button has been raised.
WM_BUTTON2UP	The right button has been raised.

In each case, **mp1** contains the x and y coordinates of the mouse position.

A SIMPLE MOUSE ETCH-A-SKETCH

The window procedure fragment that follows draws a line to the current mouse position each time the WM_MOUSEMOVE message is received.

```
case WM_MOUSEMOVE:
  pt.x = SHORT1FROMMP(mp1);   /* x and y coords      */
  pt.y = SHORT2FROMMP(mp1);   /* are packed in mp1 */
  GpiLine(hPS, &pt);          /* draw line to        */
                              /* new mouse position */
  break;
```

Window Initialization

To implement this simple procedure, we have to make a few changes in the way we have done things in the past. First, we are not doing our drawing from inside a WM_PAINT message, and thus we cannot use **WinBeginPaint**. But, in order to have a handle to a PS to use for this simple drawing, we must create and *keep* a presentation space during the entire life of the window. This also gives us the chance to specify the color of the line only once, during initialization. We will also need to set the cursor position (pointer) to a known spot before we start. We make this part of our initialization as well, setting the pointer to (0,0) with the WinSetPointerPos call. Note that since we want to use the PS throughout the life of the window, it must be a *static* variable.

```
case WM_CREATE:
  hPS = WinGetPS(hWnd);          /*get cached PS        */
  WinSetPointerPos(HWND_DESKTOP,
                   0, 0);        /*set pointer          */
  GpiSetColor(hPS, CLR_WHITE);   /*and drawing color   */
  break;                         /*keep it so we can    */
                                 /*draw on mouse moves*/
```

The Paint Routine

We do still need to process WM_PAINT messages, however, but only so that the background will be completely cleared when we start. However, since we are not using **WinBeginPaint** and **WinEndPaint** to start and finish our painting, we need to tell PM that we have now repainted the window and that it should remove further paint messages from the queue. We do this with the **WinValidateRect** call, which removes the specified rectangular region from the window's list of regions needing updating.

```
case WM_PAINT:
  WinQueryWindowRect(hWnd, &rc);   /*get current window   */
                                   /*  dimensions         */
  WinFillRect(hPS, &rc,CLR_BLACK);/*fill it with black   */
  WinValidateRect(hWnd,
                  &rc, FALSE); /*remove paint messages*/
  break;
```

Removing the Presentation Space

Whenever you have obtained a cached presentation space, or a normal PS, you must release it when the window is closed. This is done with the WinReleasePS call when the window receives a **WM_DESTROY** message:

```
case WM_DESTROY:
  WinReleasePS(hPS);   /*release PS when window is closed*/
  break;
```

Releasing the PS is quite important, because OS/2 may begin behaving strangely if these PS's are allowed to remain in use. The complete mouse window procedure is given below:

```
MRESULT FAR PASCAL MouseWndProc(HWND hWnd, USHORT msg,
                        MPARAM mp1, MPARAM mp2)


begin
        static HPS hPS;     /*handle to presentation space  */
        RECTL  rc;          /*rectangle definition structure*/
        POINTL pt;          /* point definition structure   */

switch (msg)                /*interpret messages            */
begin

case WM_CREATE:
  hPS = WinGetPS(hWnd);                 /*get cached PS      */
  WinSetPointerPos(HWND_DESKTOP,
                    0, 0);  /*set pointer        */
  GpiSetColor(hPS, CLR_WHITE);          /*and drawing color  */
  break;                                /*keep it so we can  */
                                        /*draw on mouse moves*/
```

```
case WM_MOUSEMOVE:
  pt.x = SHORT1FROMMP(mp1);      /*x and y coords are   */
  pt.y = SHORT2FROMMP(mp1);      /*packed in mp1        */
  GpiLine(hPS, &pt);             /*draw line to new     */
  break;                         /* mouse position      */

case WM_PAINT:
  WinQueryWindowRect(hWnd, &rc);   /*get current window  */
                                   /*  dimensions        */
  WinFillRect(hPS, &rc,CLR_BLACK);/*fill it with black   */
  WinValidateRect(hWnd,
                  &rc, FALSE); /*remove paint messages*/
  break;

case WM_DESTROY:
  WinReleasePS(hPS);             /*release PS when window*/
  break;                         /* is closed           */

default:
  return( WinDefWindowProc( hWnd, message, mp1, mp2));
  break;
end /*switch*/

return(0L);
end
```

DRAWING LINES ON BUTTON PRESSES

In our second example, we will set the beginning of a line segment the first time the left mouse button is pressed, and actually draw the line when the button is pressed again. To do this we will have to set a flag that remembers whether this is the first or second time the mouse button has been pressed. Now, since each mouse message represents a separate call to the window procedure, we cannot keep this flag as an automatic variable, but must make it *static* so that its value will remain between calls to the window procedure.

Initialization

Our initialization is quite simple: we must get a cached PS as before, set the
default line color, and set the flag **origin** to FALSE to indicate that no line is
being drawn:

```
static BOOL origin;     /*flag to indicate   */
                        /*  start of new line*/


switch (message)        /*interpret messages*/
begin


case WM_CREATE:
  origin = FALSE;               /*button not pressed yet  */
  hPS = WinGetPS(hWnd);         /*get cached PS           */
  GpiSetColor(hPS, CLR_WHITE);  /*and drawing color       */
  break;                        /*keep it so we can draw  */
                                /* on mouse moves         */
```

Drawing the Line Segments

In this program, all of the action takes place when a WM_MOUSEMOVE
message is received. If **origin** is not set, a new line is begun and a single pixel
is turned on at the start of the line and it is set to TRUE. If **origin** is turned
on then it draws a line and sets it back to false again.

```
case WM_BUTTON1DOWN:
  pt.x = SHORT1FROMMP(mp1);  /* x and y coords are   */
  pt.y = SHORT2FROMMP(mp1);  /* packed in mp1        */
  if (origin) then
    begin
    GpiLine(hPS, &pt);       /*draw line to new mouse  */
                             /*   position             */

    origin = FALSE;          /*indicate line is done   */
    end
  else
    begin
    GpiSetPel(hPS, &pt);     /*show start of next line  */
    GpiMove(hPS, &pt);       /*set drawing point locn   */
    origin = TRUE;           /*indicate new line starting*/
```

```
        end
    break;
```

MOVING OBJECTS ON THE SCREEN WITH THE MOUSE

One of the most easily understood program features for a new user is the ability to move objects around on the screen using the mouse. If the object is very simple, such as the box in the program below, it is acceptable to erase and redraw the entire object each time the mouse message is received. In more complex cases, you might want to draw a rectangle around the object that moves with the mouse and only redraw the object when the final position is determined.

In this example program, a 100 x 100 white box is displayed on the screen and moved around as the mouse moves. This movement is accomplished by setting the drawing mode to exclusive OR mode or XOR mode. In this drawing mode, redrawing the same lines a second time erases them from the screen. When the left mouse button is pressed, the program draws a filled red box at the current box position. Since the program continues, you can draw any number of red boxes on the screen with it. Of course, if the boxes overlap, the overlapping part will be black again, because the drawing mode remains as XOR.

Initialization

As in our previous examples, we will obtain a micro presentation space when the window is first created. We also need to set a flag **drawn** to indicate that the *first* box we draw can be drawn without erasing a previous one.

```
    static POINTL pt, ptcorner;      /* point structures    */
    static BOOL drawn;               /*flag if one drawn yet*/

switch (msg)                         /*interpret messages   */
begin

case WM_CREATE:
    hPS = WinGetPS(hWnd);            /*get cached PS        */
```

```
GpiSetColor(hPS, CLR_WHITE);        /*and drawing color    */
GpiSetMix(hPS, FM_XOR);             /*set drawing mode      */
                                    /*to exclusive OR       */
WinSetPointerPos(hPS, 100,100);     /*set pointer = 100,100*/
drawn = FALSE;                      /*no rect drawn yet     */
break;                              /*keep it so we can     */
                                    /*draw on mouse moves   */
```

Moving the Box

Then, each time a **WM_MOUSEMOVE** message is received, we erase the
previous box and draw a new one at the new mouse position:

```
case WM_MOUSEMOVE:
  if (drawn) then
      begin
      GpiMove(hPS, &pt);           /*erase box in old position*/
      ptcorner.x = pt.x  + 100; /*set box size to 100x100 */
      ptcorner.y = pt.y  + 100;
      GpiBox(hPS, DRO_OUTLINE,
            &ptcorner, OL, OL); /*XOR out old box           */
      end
      pt.x = SHORT1FROMMP(mp1); /* x and y coords are       */
      pt.y = SHORT2FROMMP(mp1); /* packed in mp1            */
      GpiMove(hPS, &pt);
      ptcorner.x = pt.x  + 100; /*set box size to 100x100    */
      ptcorner.y = pt.y  + 100;
      GpiBox(hPS, DRO_OUTLINE,
            &ptcorner, OL, OL); /*draw in new box            */
      drawn = TRUE;             /*erase all future boxes     */
      break;
```

Note that the **GpiBox** call uses the style DRO_OUTLINE to indicate that
only the outline of a box is to be drawn. The box is drawn at the current
drawing point specified by the last **GpiMove** or **GpiLine**, and is drawn so that
the upper right corners are specified by the point structure in the argument
ptcorner. Once we have drawn our first box, we set the **drawn** flag to TRUE
so that all future boxes are drawn after erasing the previous once. Note that
the **pt** structure is static so that the previous position will always be remembered.

Drawing a Filled Box

When the left mouse button is depressed, this program draws a filled red box at the current drawing point. This is done in just the same way as the **GpiBox** calls above, except that the style argument is changed to DRO_FILL.

```
case WM_BUTTON1DOWN:
  GpiMove(hPS, &pt);          /* move to current point    */
  pt.x = SHORT1FROMMP(mp1);   /* x and y coords are       */
  pt.y = SHORT2FROMMP(mp1);   /* packed in mp1            */
  ptcorner.x = pt.x + 100;    /*set box size to 100 x 100 */
  ptcorner.y = pt.y + 100;
  GpiSetColor(hPS, CLR_RED); /* fill box in red           */
  GpiBox(hPS, DRO_FILL,
        &ptcorner, 0L, 0L);  /*draw in new box            */
  GpiSetColor(hPS, CLR_WHITE);   /*reset color to white   */
  break;
```

THE MOUSE POINTER: VISIBILITY AND ACCESSIBILITY

In our examples so far, we have done nothing to affect the mouse pointer on the screen. Thus, in all of these examples, if the mouse pointer moves outside the current window, messages will not be received and the drawing or box motion will stop. While this is often what you want, there are occasions in which you might not want to lose a mouse message or get a multistep series of clicks and moves out of synch because the user has inadvertently moved the mouse just beyond the window border.

You can, however, capture all mouse messages to the current window by issuing the call

```
    WinSetCapture(HWND_DESKTOP, hWnd);  /*capture mouse*/
```

where **hWnd** is the handle of the window that is to receive all the mouse messages. Remember that once you do this, you have disabled all mouse pointer functions in other adjacent windows until you release the mouse. Issuing the same call with **hWnd** set to null releases mouse capture.

The mouse pointer can be made visible or invisible using the **WinShowPointer** call

```
WinShowPointer(HWND_DESKTOP, FALSE);    /*hide pointer*/
WinShowPointer(HWND_DESKTOP, TRUE );    /*show pointer*/
```

You must be careful, however, to be sure the pointer is turned back on before exiting from your program, since PM has no way of knowing that it should be turned back on if a process has made it invisible.

ROUTING MOUSE MESSAGES TO SUBROUTINES

As your programs begin to grow in complexity, it will become necessary to interpret mouse messages in different ways depending on what function the user is carrying out. This could lead to a rather convoluted structure in which the action taken on mouse messages depends on which command was last selected.

It is more desirable, however, to write subroutines or C functions in which a particular routine receives all the mouse messages for a given function, and another routine all the messages for that function. This can be done in OS/2 PM programming by directing these messages to *child windows*. These child windows are not some small section of the main window, but are in fact, *identical with* that window. Thus, by creating a child window that has the same dimensions a the main window, you can send all of the messages you wish to intercept to that window.

Definition of the Mouse-Child Program

We will write a program with a single menu item in a pull-down menu. This selection, "Box," will cause the program to remove the cursor pointer and display a moving white hollow box much like the one above. When the mouse button is pressed, the box will be filled with red and the cursor will reappear. To draw further boxes, the menu item must be selected again.

In these examples, we will draw the moving box from within the child window and draw a filled red box from within the child window. Then we will close the child window, but leave the red box on the screen. Since we will not be doing any drawing in the WM_PAINT routine, we will have to prevent the screen from being erased when a paint message is received by the window. In this case, we will have to do this for both the child and the main window so that the main window does not erase the box just drawn by the child window.

User-Defined Messages

Since each window receives messages separately as calls from PM, we will have to tell the parent window not to repaint when the child window closes by sending it a message. The easiest way to do this is by defining a user message NO_PAINT, which we send to the main window. PM has defined the constant WM_USER as the first message number not used by the system, and we can begin defining our own messages at this value. The following definitions make up the mouse4.h file:

```
#define MOUSEWIND       1
#define MOUSECMD        101
#define MRECT           102
#define NO_PAINT        WM_USER + 1
```

We will also make up a simple menu in the resource file as follows:

```
#include "mouse4.h"
POINTER MOUSEWIND   mouse4.ico

MENU MOUSEWIND PRELOAD
BEGIN
    SUBMENU "Commands", MOUSECMD
        BEGIN
        MENUITEM "Box", MRECT
        END
END
```

This will cause a command bar to appear with the "Commands" header and the drop-down menu containing "Box."

Sending and Posting Messages to Windows

There are two calls for getting messages to a window:

```
WinPostMsg(hWnd, message, mp1, mp1);   /*post a message*/
WinSendMsg(hWnd, message, mp1, mp1);   /*send a message*/
```

A message that is *posted* is put into the message queue and will be received in order from the main message dispatch loop. A message that is *sent* goes immediately to that window and the call does not return until the message is received and processed. In fact, **WinSendMsg** is equivalent to calling the window procedure directly. In nearly all cases, the **WinPostMsg** method is preferable, unless you have severe message timing constraints.

Creating the Child Window

To create a child window having the same dimensions as the parent, we use the **WinQueryWindowRect** call to fill a RECTL structure with the current window dimensions. Then, we create a window having these dimensions using the **WinCreateWindow** call. This call creates a pure window, without border, frame, or title bar, and its existence as a separate logical window is not apparent to the user.

```
case MRECT:
    WinQueryWindowRect(hWnd, &rc); /*get window dimensions*/
    WinCreateWindow(hWnd,              /*child window same   */
        "BoxWnd",                      /*  as main           */
        NULL,                          /* no text            */
        WS_VISIBLE,                    /* make it visible     */
        (SHORT)rc.xLeft,               /*position of window   */
        (SHORT)rc.yBottom,             /* same as parent      */
        (SHORT)(rc.xRight - rc.xLeft),
        (SHORT)(rc.yTop - rc.yBottom),
        hWnd,                          /*parent window        */
        HWND_TOP,                      /*on top of parent     */
        1,                             /*frame ID             */
        NULL,                          /* unused             */
        NULL);                         /*reserved             */
```

Determining the Child Window's Parent

To send a message to the parent window, telling it not to erase the screen, we need for the child window to know the handle of its parent. This can be done with the **WinQueryWindow** call, which has the form

```
hParent =                     /*get handle to parent window*/
  WinQueryWindow(hWnd, QW_PARENT, FALSE);
WinSendMsg(hParent, NO_PAINT,
               OL, OL);  /*tell it not to repaint        */
```

The complete list of window handles this call will return is

QW_NEXT	The window below the current window.
QW_PREV	The window above the current window.
QW_TOP	The topmost child window.
QW_BOTTOM	The bottommost child window.
QW_OWNER	The owner of the window.
QW_PARENT	The parent of the window.
QW_NEXTTOP	The next window in the owner window hierarchy which is subject to *z* ordering.

To further clarify this, the *parent* window restricts the movement of a child window to its size, while the *owner* window is the one that receives messages from the child. In many cases these are the same relationship, but for dialog box controls they could be different.

Hiding the Pointer

It is not particularly elegant to have the mouse pointer showing when the box is being moved around on the screen, so the pointer is hidden when the child window is opened and shown again when the pointer is destroyed.

The Complete Mouse-Child Program

```
/******* MOUSE 4 -- Mouse-Child Window Program **********/
/* Moves a rectangle around on the screen, and fills it   */
/* with red when the left button is clicked.              */
/**********************************************************/
#define INCL_PM
#include <os2.h>
#include <cdefs.h>
#include "mouse4.h"
/**********************************************************/
MRESULT FAR PASCAL MouseWndProc( HWND, USHORT,
                                      MPARAM, MPARAM );

MRESULT FAR PASCAL RectWndProc( HWND, USHORT,
                                      MPARAM, MPARAM );

void draw_box(HPS hPS, PPOINTL pt, int mode, int color);
/**********************************************************/
/*************** M a i n   F u n c t i o n***************/
/**********************************************************/
void cdecl main ()                 /*C main routine*/

begin
  QMSG   qmsg;              /*defining a message queue */
  HAB    hAB;              /*handle to anchor block   */
  HMQ    hmqMouse;         /*handle to message queue  */
  HWND   hWnd;             /*client area window handle*/
  HWND   hFrame;           /*frame window handle      */
  ULONG  flCreate;         /*window create flag bits  */

hAB = WinInitialize (NULL);   /*init and get anchor handle*/
hmqMouse = WinCreateMsgQueue(hAB, 0); /*create msg queue */

/*register the Window class*/
WinRegisterClass (hAB,       /*handle to anchor block    */
      "Mouse",               /*name of window class      */
      MouseWndProc,          /*address of window procedure*/
      CS_SIZEREDRAW,         /*use these flags           */
      0 ) ;                  /*number of "extra bytes    */
WinRegisterClass (hAB,       /*handle to anchor block    */
      "BoxWnd",              /*name of window class      */
      RectWndProc,           /*address of window procedure*/
```

```
        CS_SIZEREDRAW,        /*use these flags            */
        0 ) ;                 /*number of "extra bytes     */

flCreate = FCF_MINMAX | FCF_SIZEBORDER | FCF_SYSMENU
   |FCF_TITLEBAR | FCF_SHELLPOSITION | FCF_ICON | FCF_MENU;

/*create the window */
hFrame =
    WinCreateStdWindow(
        HWND_DESKTOP, /*as child of the desktop window*/
        WS_VISIBLE ,
        &flCreate,            /*control data bits          */
        "Mouse",              /*this name refers to class*/
        "Mouse 4",            /*title across top bar       */
        WS_VISIBLE | WS_CLIPCHILDREN,
        NULL,                 /*menu is in resource file */
        MOUSEICON,            /*frame identifier           */
        &hWnd);               /*client area handle         */

/*get messages from the input queue and dispatch them      */
while ( WinGetMsg( hAB, &qmsg, (HWND)NULL, 0,0) )
   begin
   WinDispatchMsg(hAB, &qmsg);
   end

/* once the program is over,                */
/* destroy the window and message queue */
WinDestroyWindow(hFrame);
WinDestroyMsgQueue(hmqMouse);
WinTerminate (hAB);
end
/************************************************************/
/* The window procedure receives messages and acts on      */
/*them or passes them on for default processing.           */
/*The only important command it receives is MRECT under    */
/*WM_COMMAND which opens a child window to receive mouse    */
/*motion messages. It also receives the user-defined       */
/*command NO_PAINT which prevents repainting of the main    */
/*window when the child window closes                      */
/************************************************************/
MRESULT FAR PASCAL MouseWndProc(HWND hWnd, USHORT msg,
```

```
                                        MPARAM mp1, MPARAM mp2)

begin
        HPS hPS;            /*handle to presentation space   */
        RECTL  rc;         /* rectangle definition structure*/

switch (msg)              /*interpret messages             */
begin

case WM_PAINT:
  hPS = WinBeginPaint(hWnd, (HPS)NULL, NULL);
  WinQueryWindowRect(hWnd, &rc);        /*get     dimensions*/
  WinFillRect(hPS, &rc, CLR_BLACK);     /*fill with black   */
  WinValidateRect(hWnd, &rc,
                    TRUE);    /*remove paint messages*/
  WinEndPaint(hPS);                     /*end paint routine*/
  break;

case NO_PAINT:
  WinValidateRect(hWnd, &rc,
                    TRUE);    /*remove paint messages*/
        break;

case WM_COMMAND:
  switch(LOUSHORT(mp1))
    begin
    case MRECT:
      WinQueryWindowRect(hWnd, &rc); /*get dimensions    */
      WinCreateWindow(hWnd,    /*child window same as main*/
        "BoxWnd",
        NULL,                      /*no text            */
        WS_VISIBLE,                /*make it visible    */
        (SHORT)rc.xLeft,           /*posn of window     */
        (SHORT)rc.yBottom,         /*same as parent     */
        (SHORT)(rc.xRight - rc.xLeft),
        (SHORT)(rc.yTop - rc.yBottom),
        hWnd,                      /*parent window      */
        HWND_TOP,                  /*on top of parent   */
        1,                         /*frame ID           */
        NULL,                      /* unused            */
        NULL);                     /*reserved           */
```

```
            break;
        end             /*switch*/


default:
        return( WinDefWindowProc( hWnd, msg, mp1, mp2));
        break;
end /*switch*/

return((MPARAM)OL);
end
/**********************************************************/
/* draws a 100 x 100 box from pt in color using          */
/* the drawing mode specified                            */
/**********************************************************/
void draw_box(HPS hPS, PPOINTL pt, int mode, int color)
begin
    POINTL ptcorner;

GpiMove(hPS, pt);                   /*move to current point */
ptcorner.x = pt->x  + 100;          /*set box size 100 x 100*/
ptcorner.y = pt->y  + 100;
GpiSetColor(hPS, color);            /*fill box in red       */
GpiBox(hPS, mode, &ptcorner,
            OL, OL);                /*draw in new box       */
end
/**********************************************************/
MRESULT FAR PASCAL RectWndProc(HWND hWnd, USHORT msg,
                            MPARAM mp1, MPARAM mp2)
/*======================================================*/
/* This window is physically identical with the parent  */
/* window. It receives mouse motion messages and moves a */
/* box around on the screen. When the left mouse button  */
/* is pressed, a red box is drawn at the current box     */
/* location and the window closes, sending a NO_PAINT    */
/* message to its parent so that the screen will not be  */
/* erased in the main window.                            */
/*======================================================*/
begin
  static HPS hPS;        /*handle to presentation space   */
  RECTL  rc;             /* rectangle definition structure*/
```

```
      static POINTL pt, ptcorner;      /* point structures   */
      static BOOL drawn;        /*tells if one drawn yet     */
      HWND hParent;             /*handle to parent window    */

   switch (msg)                 /*interpret messages         */
   begin

   case WM_CREATE:
      hPS = WinGetPS(hWnd);                  /*get cached PS      */
      GpiSetColor(hPS, CLR_WHITE);           /*and drawing color*/
      GpiSetMix(hPS, FM_XOR);                /*drawing mode=XOR  */
      WinSetPointerPos(hPS, 100,100);        /*pointer = 100,100*/
      WinShowPointer(HWND_DESKTOP,FALSE);    /*hide pointer      */
      WinSetCapture(HWND_DESKTOP, hWnd);     /*capture all       */
                                             /*  mouse movements*/
      drawn = FALSE;                         /*no rect drawn yet*/
      break;

   case WM_BUTTON1DOWN:
      pt.x = SHORT1FROMMP(mp1);              /* x and y coords   */
      pt.y = SHORT2FROMMP(mp1);              /*are packed in mp1*/
      draw_box(hPS, &pt, DRO_FILL, CLR_RED);
      WinDestroyWindow(hWnd);                /*exit from window*/
      break;

   case WM_MOUSEMOVE:
      if (drawn) then
         begin
         draw_box(hPS, &pt, DRO_OUTLINE,
                           CLR_WHITE); /*XOR out old box   */
         end
      pt.x = SHORT1FROMMP(mp1);              /* x and y coords   */
      pt.y = SHORT2FROMMP(mp1);              /*are packed in mp1*/
      draw_box(hPS, &pt, DRO_OUTLINE,
                        CLR_WHITE); /*draw new box      */
      drawn = TRUE;                /*erase all future boxes*/
      break;

   case WM_DESTROY:
      WinShowPointer(HWND_DESKTOP,TRUE ); /*show pointer      */
      WinSetCapture(HWND_DESKTOP, NULL); /*release mouse      */
```

```
WinReleasePS(hPS);                          /*release PS         */
hParent =                      /*get handle to parent window*/
   WinQueryWindow(hWnd, QW_PARENT, FALSE);
WinSendMsg(hParent, NO_PAINT,
                      0L, 0L);  /*tell it not to repaint*/
break;

case WM_PAINT:
   WinValidateRect(hWnd, NULL,
                      TRUE);      /*remove paint messages*/
   break;

default:
   return( WinDefWindowProc( hWnd, msg, mp1, mp2));
   break;
end /*switch*/

return((MPARAM)0L);
end
```

The screen display of the overlapping boxes is shown in Figure 12-1.

SUBCLASSING WINDOW PROCEDURES

Another way of accomplishing the same thing as we did with the identical child window is to *subclass* a window procedure. Any time you have a window procedure that is almost the one you need, but needs to interpret a few messages differently, it is possible to create a new window procedure that is called *before* the standard window procedure to intercept these messages. Instead of processing the remaining messages with **WinDefWindowProc** you instead call the parent window procedure directly to process them.

The advantages of creating a superimposed identical window are that you can write a completely self-contained window procedure with local static and automatic variables, and its own Presentation Space. From the point of view of controlling the pointer visibility and position, this is somewhat simpler. Further, a subclassed window procedure never receives a WM_CREATE message and has no way to initialize variables before receiving other messages.

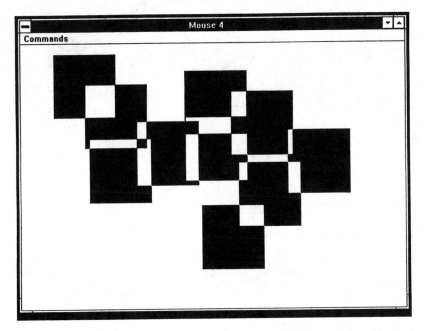

Figure 12-1. The boxes generated by the mouse-child box program.. Since the boxes are drawn in exclusive OR mode, they erase each other where they overlap.

The advantages of subclassing a window procedure are that the subclassing routine is somewhat simpler, since it only needs to process a few messages, but the disadvantage may occur if it is necessary to draw into the presentation space from the subclassed window. The subclassed procedure can only know the handle of the main window's PS if it is a global variable that it has access to, or if it is stored in the window words of that window.

In this final example, we will rewrite the main window procedure **MouseWndProc** and make the subclassed procedure a portion of the **RectWndProc** procedure. Our main window procedure now must have a cached presentation space that remains in existence throughout the window's life so that it can be available to the subclassed procedure as a global variable. We thus intercept the WM_CREATE message and create the PS, and set the drawing color and mix mode. When we receive the command MRECT, we set the pointer position, make the pointer invisible, set the global flag **drawn**, set the mouse capture, and subclass the window.

```
/*---------------------------------------------------------*/
/* main window procedure which subclasses when the         */
/* MRECT command is received                               */
/*---------------------------------------------------------*/
MRESULT FAR PASCAL MouseWndProc(HWND hWnd, USHORT msg,
                              MPARAM mp1, MPARAM mp2)
begin
    RECTL  rc;          /* rectangle definition structure   */

switch (msg)            /*interpret messages                */
begin

case WM_CREATE:
  hPS = WinGetPS(hWnd);              /*get cached PS         */
  GpiSetColor(hPS, CLR_WHITE);  /*and drawing color         */
  GpiSetMix(hPS, FM_XOR);            /*set drawing mode to XOR*/
  break;

case WM_PAINT:
  WinQueryWindowRect(hWnd, &rc); /*get current              */
                                 /* window dimensions        */
  WinFillRect(hPS, &rc, CLR_BLACK);  /*fill with black       */
  WinValidateRect(hWnd, &rc, TRUE);  /*remove paint msgs     */
  break;

case WM_COMMAND:
  switch(LOUSHORT(mp1))
    begin
    case MRECT:
      WinShowPointer(HWND_DESKTOP,
                          FALSE);     /*hide pointer         */
      WinSetPointerPos(hPS, 100,100);    /*set ptr=100,100   */
      WinSetCapture(HWND_DESKTOP, hWnd);/*capture all        */
                                    /*mouse movements        */
      drawn = FALSE;                   /*no rect drawn yet    */
      WinSubclassWindow(hWnd,
              RectWndProc);   /*and subclass the window      */
      break;
      end                            /*switch                */

default:
```

```
    return( WinDefWindowProc( hWnd, msg, mp1, mp2));
    break;
end /*switch*/

return((MPARAM)0L);
end
```

The subclassed window procedure, on the other hand, becomes simpler.
It only needs to receive the **WM_MOUSEMOVE** and the
WM_BUTTON1DOWN messages. When it receives the mouse move messages, it XORs out the old box position and draws a new one. When it
receives a button down message, it draws the final filled box, reshows the
pointer, unlocks the mouse capture, and reclasses the window so only the
main window receives messages. Note that the default message case now
only calls the main window procedure directly.

```
/*=========================================================*/
/* This window is a subclass of MouseWnd Proc. It          */
/* receives mouse motion messages and moves a box around   */
/* on the screen. When the left mouse button is pressed,   */
/* a red box is drawn at the current box location and      */
/* the subclass is removed, so that the main window        */
/* again receives all messages.                            */
/*=========================================================*/
MRESULT FAR PASCAL RectWndProc(HWND hWnd, USHORT msg,
                              MPARAM mp1, MPARAM mp2)

begin
    RECTL  rc;                      /* rectangle structure */
    static POINTL pt, ptcorner;     /* point structures    */


    switch (msg)                    /*interpret messages    */
    begin


    case WM_BUTTON1DOWN:
        pt.x = SHORT1FROMMP(mp1);              /* x and y coords */
        pt.y = SHORT2FROMMP(mp1);              /* are packed in mp1*/
        draw_box(hPS, &pt, DRO_FILL, CLR_RED);
        WinShowPointer(HWND_DESKTOP,TRUE );  /*show pointer      */
        WinSetCapture(HWND_DESKTOP, NULL);   /*release mouse     */
        WinSubclassWindow(hWnd, MouseWndProc); /*restore main    */
```

```
                                    /* window for all mesgs*/
      break;

case WM_MOUSEMOVE:
   if (drawn) then
      begin
      draw_box(hPS, &pt, DRO_OUTLINE,
                         CLR_WHITE); /*XOR out old box*/
      end
   pt.x = SHORT1FROMMP(mp1);    /*x and y coords are    */
                                /*    packed in mp1     */
   pt.y = SHORT2FROMMP(mp1);
   draw_box(hPS, &pt, DRO_OUTLINE,
                         CLR_WHITE); /*draw new box       */
   drawn = TRUE;                     /*erase all future boxes*/
   break;

default:
   MouseWndProc( hWnd, msg, mp1, mp2);   /*call main window*/
                                         /* for all others */
   break;
end /*switch*/

return((MPARAM)OL);
end
```

SCREEN VERSUS WINDOW COORDINATES

Since the mouse is always moving across the entire screen, even though the screen may contain a number of windows, the coordinates that the mouse messages return are always *screen coordinates,* having (0,0) at the lower left corner of the physical screen and the maxima at the upper right. By contrast, calls such as WinQueryWindowRect return values in *window coordinates,* where (0,0) is at the lower left corner of the current window.

This distinction is likely to be important if you want to set the mouse pointer to a particular position relative to the current window. The calls : hp2.WinSetPointerPos i1.WinSetPointerPos and **WinQueryPointerPos** refer to the pointer position in screen coordinates, but you may wish to set the pointer to some position relative to your current *window*. You can, however, make this conversion by using the **WinMapWindowPoints** call

```
WinMapWindowPoints(hFrom, hTo, &points, count);
```

where

hFrom   is the handle to the window from which the conversion is to be made. If the conversion is from screen coordinates, this should be HWND_DESKTOP.

hTo   is the handle to the window to which the conversion is to be made. If the conversion is to screen coordinates, this should be HWND_DESKTOP.

& points   is a pointer to an array of points defined as POINTL structures, or, in other words, long x and y values.

count   is the number of x,y point pairs to convert.

Thus, to set the pointer in the middle of a window, you would write

```
RECTL rc;        /*window rectangle*/
POINTL point;    /*one point structure*/

WinQueryWindowRect(hWnd, &rc);     /*get the window size */
point.x = rc.xRight / 2;          /*half of x width     */
point.y = rc.yTop /2;             /*half of y height    */
WinMapWindowPoints(hWnd, HWND_DESKTOP, &point, 1);
WinSetPointerPos(HWND_DESKTOP, point.x, point.y);
```

CHANGING THE POINTER SHAPE

Normally the mouse pointer is an arrow sloping diagonally upward, with its "hot spot" one pixel above and to the left of the point. It changes to a double-headed arrow when you move it across the boundary of a window with a sizable frame. There are a number of pointer icons you can obtain from the system and use as you wish, and the handle to these icons can be obtained by the **WinQuerySysPointer** call

```
HPOINTER hPtr;

hPtr =
    WinQuerySysPointer(HWND_DESKTOP, SPTR_HANDICON, TRUE);
```

where the icons you can obtain are

SPTR_ARROW   the arrow pointer

SPTR_TEXT   the text I-beam pointer

SPTR_WAIT   the hour glass

SPTR_SIZE   the size pointer

SPTR_MOVE   the move pointer

SPTR_SIZENWSE   the downward-sloping, double-headed arrow pointer

SPTR_SIZENESW   the upward-sloping, double-headed arrow pointer

SPTR_SIZEWE   the horizontal double-headed arrow pointer

SPTR_SIZENS   the vertical double-headed arrow pointer

SPTR_APPICON   the standard application icon pointer

SPTR_QUESICON   the question mark icon

SPTR_BANGICON   the exclamation mark

SPTR_NOTEICON   the note icon

Once you have obtained the handle to the desired icon, you must set that pointer and show it using the calls

```
WinSetPointer(HWND_DESKTOP, hPtr);       /*select pointer  */
WinShowPointer(HWND_DESKTOP, TRUE);      /*show the pointer*/
```

Because the system will change the pointer every time it leaves the current window, you must make these two calls *every time* you get a WM_MOUSEMOVE message, since the mouse may have just moved in from outside the window.

13 Building a Dynamic Link Library

OS/2 provides you with the unique ability to write library routines that can be loaded with your program at run time. This allows several programs to use the same routines and allows you to change the internal workings of such library routines without having to recompile and relink the programs that use them. In fact, you can view these dynamic link library modules (DLLs) as user-definable extensions to the operating system.

It is possible to write a series of functions in a module and compile them as usual and link them as ordinary parts of your program, and then later decide that these routines can be a DLL and, with virtually no changes, recompile and relink the same routines to be used in this new form.

The OS/2 program loader is signalled that a DLL is needed when the program is linked with a special small library file that indicates that all of the modules to be called are located in this DLL. Then OS/2 looks in the subdirectories specified in the LIBPATH statement in CONFIG.SYS to find these DLLs. The LIBPATH will always contain C:\OS2\DLL and may contain a number of other directories. In order to tell OS/2 to look in the current directory as well, you should include the ".;" statement in the search list. Once you have finished debugging your DLL, it is common to put it in a directory with other application-program level DLLs, such as C:\MYDLLS. Then you can be sure it will be accessed no matter which directory you are running from.

```
LIBPATH=.;C:\OS2\DLL;C:\MYDLLS;C:\OS2;
```

CREATING A SIMPLE DLL

There are a number of simple rules you must follow to create a DLL. The most important is that all of the function calls in a DLL will be far calls and all of the variables passed to the function will be referenced as far addresses. Since we have habitually linked with the large model library this will not present us any new challenges. In addition, you must compile your DLL C code using the /DDLL switch that defines **DLL** as a symbol. This forces some of the include files to provide different function prototypes.

In addition, you must compile the DLL functions so that DS is not equal to SS, which means that you use the switches /**Alfu**. Rather than linking with LLIBCE.LIB or LLIBCMT.LIB, the most common option is to link with LLIBCDLL.LIB, which provides all of the standard C- library functions in reentrant form. This will not work, however, if you will have more than one thread running in your DLL, although you can have several threads running in the calling program. For this case, you must create the CRTLIB libraries as discussed below.

Finally, the LLIBCDLL.LIB library uses the alternate floating point math library functions rather than the math coprocessor, and for these you must also use the CRTLIB functions.

THE PDLL LIBRARY

In this example, we jill write a small C function that applies the quadratic formula to three supplied coefficients and returns the two real roots, or an error flag if the result is complex. We see that the function and the surrounding code are no different than if we had created a module to link directly with a main program.

```
/* PDLL Library - with the quadratic formula evaluator    */
#include <cdefs.h>
#include <math.h>
#include <stdio.h>
#define INCL_BASE
#include <os2.h>
/*------------------------------------------------------------*/
BOOL FAR PASCAL quadform(double *x1, double *x2, double a,
```

```
                     double b, double c)
/* calculates the two roots of a 2nd order polynomial    */
begin
        double rad;
        BOOL valid;

/* calculate value under square root                      */
rad = b * b - 4.0 * a * c;

if (rad < 0) then
  valid = FALSE;    /*can't take square root of neg number*/
else
  begin
  valid = TRUE;    /* OK if >= 0                          */
  *x1 = (-b + sqrt(rad)) / (2.0 * a);    /*calculate root1*/
  *x2 = (-b - sqrt(rad)) / (2.0 * a);    /*calculate root2*/
  end
return(valid);              /*return flag for validity of answer*/
end
```

To compile this library module, we use the C command

```
cl /Zei /c /G2sc /W2 /Alfu /DDLL pdll.c
```

Then, to link the program to make a DLL, we use the following definitions file:

```
LIBRARY PDLL INITINSTANCE
PROTMODE
DESCRIPTION 'Quadratic DLL'
DATA MULTIPLE NONSHARED
HEAPSIZE 1024
EXPORTS
   QUADFORM @1
```

where we note the EXPORTS statement describes the name of the functions we are going to be able to access when the DLL is loaded. The INITINSTANCE statement describes the fact that each instance of the DLL requires some initialization code. This is required for all DLLs linked with LLIBCDLL.LIB.

Finally, we link the DLL using the following response file

```
pdll.obj /CO /A:16
pdll.dll /NOI
pdll.map
llibcdll.lib+os2.lib /NOD
pdll.def
```

WRITING A PROGRAM TO CALL THE DLL

Now we need to write a program to call the QUADFORM function in the
DLL. We will need to generate a function prototype for each function in the
DLL, which in this case is just the QUADFORM function. The

```
pdll.h
```

file contains the simple statement

```
BOOL FAR PASCAL quadform(double *x1, double *x2, double a,
                         double b, double c);
```

The program to call this function can be as simple as the following:

```
#include "pdll.h"
#include <stdio.h>
#include <cdefs.h>

/* simple example program to call the quadratic      */
/* calculator in a DLL                                */
void cdecl main()
begin
    double a, b, c, x1, x2;
    int valid;

a = 1.0;                            /*initialize coefficients */
b = 2.0;
c = 1.0;
valid =
    quadform(&x1, &x2, a, b, c);    /*call the DLL function*/
if (valid)                          /*print out the answer*/
    printf("x1 = %f, x2= %f\n", x1, x2);
else
```

```
    printf("complex roots: valid=%d\n", valid);
end
```

Compilation of this program proceeds as usual, with no indication that **quadform** won't be linked with the program directly:

```
cl /Zpei /c /G2sc /W2  /Alfu cquad.c
```

However, when you link the program, you include an **IMPORTS** statement in the .DEF file that gives the name of the DLL and the name of any referenced functions:

```
NAME    CQUAD
DESCRIPTION 'DLL Test Program'
STUB 'OS2STUB.EXE'
CODE MOVEABLE
DATA MOVEABLE MULTIPLE

HEAPSIZE 1024
STACKSIZE 4096

IMPORTS
   PDLL.QUADFORM
```

The link response file is no different than if no DLLs were referenced:

```
cquad.obj /CO /A:16 /NOD
cquad.exe /NOI
cquad.map
llibce.lib+os2.lib /NOD
cquad.def
```

Note that it is not necessary to link the main program with any special library.

LOADING A DLL AS NEEDED

One problem with linking all DLL calls using the IMPORTS statement is that the program will not run if even one of the referenced DLLs can not be found. This can lead to a portability problem, where some users may have all the DLLs in place and other may not.

Instead, you can load the DLLs as needed and issue error messages at run time if the DLLs can't be found. There are just two routines you need to use for this purpose:

```
err = DosLoadModule(objbuf, objlen,
                          modulename, &hMod); /*load a DLL*/

/*get address of function*/
err = DosGetProcAddr(hMod, procname, &procaddr);
```

where

err	is zero if there are no errors.
objbuf	contains the module name where the error occurred.
objlen	is the length of the **objbuf** buffer.
modulename	is the name of the DLL module (no path, no extension).
hMod	is the module handle returned by the first call and used by the second.
procname	is the name of the procedure within the DLL.
procaddr	is the far pointer to the procedure you want to call.

The following code illustrates exactly how to load and call a function in a DLL:

```
/* simple example program to load and call the quadratic */
/* calculator in a DLL                                    */
#define MAXLEN 80
#define INCL_BASE
#include <os2.h>
#include <stdio.h>
#include <cdefs.h>

void cdecl main()
begin
   double a, b, c, x1, x2;
   int valid, err;
   HMODULE hMod;
```

```
char objbuf[MAXLEN];
BOOL (far pascal *quadform)();      /*pointer to address*/

a = 1.0;                           /*initialize coefficients */
b = 2.0;
c = 1.0;
err = DosLoadModule(objbuf, MAXLEN, "PDLL", &hMod);
err = DosGetProcAddr(hMod, "QUADFORM", &quadform);
if (err == 0) then                 /*call the DLL function*/
    valid =(*quadform)(&x1, &x2, a, b, c);
if (valid)
    printf("x1 = %f, x2= %f\n", x1, x2); /*print  answer  */
else
    printf("complex roots: valid=%d\n", valid);
end
```

BUILDING THE C RUN-TIME DLL

If you wish to create a DLL that can work in a multithread environment and that will use the math coprocessor, you must build the special C run-time DLL CRTLIB.DLL. This will be loaded along with your DLL to provide reentrant versions of the C functions. Both IBM C/2 1.1 and Microsoft C 5.1 provide a batch CMD file that will link together a number of C run-time routines into a DLL. You must build this DLL and the accompanying C library

```
CRTLIB.DLL
CRTLIB.LIB
```

using the command file CDLLOBJS.CMD. You will then link your DLL with CRTDLL.OBJ followed by your own file to give your DLL the usual C startup code.

Linking a Program with CRTLIB.DLL

Linking amounts to specifying CRTDLL.OBJ as the first module, followed by your own module(s). You must specify the linker switches /NOI so that case is not ignored in the generated symbols and /NOD so that no default libraries are linked:

```
link @ filec.l
```

where the response file contains

```
crtdll.obj+filec.obj

filec.dll /NOI /CO
filec.map /M
crtlib.lib + os2.lib /NOD
filec.def
```

If the library routines use the Presentation Manager, you can then run the Resource Compiler to include any resources:

```
rc filec.rc filec.dll
```

The Definitions File

The .DEF file for a DLL must contain the LIBRARY statement, which defines the linked file as a DLL. Each function that you wish to call must be specified in the EXPORTS statement. Here you must be careful about the calling convention you use. If your functions are called using the Pascal calling convention, their names must be all uppercase. If your functions are called using the C calling convention, then they must match the case of the routines in the C module and must be *prefixed by an underscore (_)*.

```
LIBRARY FILEC
PROTMODE
DESCRIPTION "Any text"
DATA MULTIPLE NONSHARED
EXPORTS
     _GetFile
     FILEDIALOG
```

USING IMPLIB TO MAKE THE LIB FILE

Now that you have created your DLL, you must tell programs that they are to use it when they load. If you have quite a number of entry points it is easier to make an import library using IMPLIB than to specify all of them in the program's .DEF file. You do this by making a small LIB file that you link with each program that contains the information on the needed DLL. This LIB file is produced by the IMPLIB program

```
IMPLIB filec.lib filec.def
```

Then you simply link the resulting

```
filec.lib
```

with each program that will use the FILEC.DLL. All of the routines that were EXPORTed in the DLLs .DEF file will now be defined in the **filec.lib** file and will be linked automatically.

DEBUGGING A DLL

It is possible to use CodeView to debug a DLL if you compile it using the /Zi switch as we did here and link it using the /CO switch. Then, when you start up the program to be debugged, you *must* have the DLL in the *current* subdirectory. Then you start CodeView with the command

```
cvp -l filec prog
```

This tells CodeView that it will be debugging

```
prog.c
```

and

```
filec.dll.
```

14 | Printing Graphics and Text under OS/2

OS/2 is designed so that all requests to print are passed to the first part of a device driver that places them into a *spool file*. Then a spooler queue manager program (SPOOL.EXE) writes the file to disk and makes it a print job. When the printer or plotter is ready to print, the spooler queue processor program (PMPRINT.QPR) reads the file from the print queue and passes it to the second part of the device driver. The advantage of this process is that a number of requests to the same printer or printers can be queued by separate tasks and printed in sequence, but that all of them remain device independent.

The spooler queue manager is in fact the Print Manager program that starts automatically with OS/2 and displays a printer icon in the corner of the screen. You can click on the spooler icon and examine the contents of the queue for each device and remove or duplicate jobs in the queue. You actually select which devices are connected to which queues using the Spooler program. If you click on Setup in the Print Manager's menu, you will be able to select the printers currently installed and the queues to which they are attached.

PRINTERS, PORTS, AND QUEUES

Every printer on your system can have a Printer Name associated with it. Such printers can be local or can, in fact, be on a local area network. Each named printer must be associated with a printer hardware port, such as LPT1, LPT2, COM1, or COM2, etc. You must always associate each printer with a specific named queue. In addition, you must select a Device Driver program for each printer to be used. Often, it is convenient to simply use the Print Manager to select the current default printer and use the default name and queue.

When OS/2 PM is installed, the default printer is named PRINTER1, it is associated with the printer queue LPT1Q, it is connected to port LPT1, and the default device driver IBM4201 is selected. You can add device drivers and change printer connections using the Print Manager program, You can also create new queues with new names, but there can only be one *default* queue. Most standard PM programs work on the current default queue and if you wish to have your program work on several possible queues, you will have to install a menu with a list box to select the queue you wish to use. In the examples below we will operate on the default queue and assume that the user invokes the Control Panel program to change between queues.

THE OS2.INI PROFILE

Most of the parameters that are referred to as default parameters are included in the OS2.INI file in the c:\OS2 directory. This file contains the default screen colors, the default border width, the default printer names, the default queues, and the default fonts. You can examine the values in this file using the **WinQueryProfileString** function, which has the form

```
WinQueryProfileString(hAB, appname, keyname, default,
                      profile, maxstring);
```

where

hAB   is the handle to the anchor block

appname   is the name of the application program that requires initialization data.

keyname   is the name of the feature within the program for which we want information.

default   is the string that is returned in **profile** if the **keyname** can't be found.

profile   is the text string returned from the query.

maxstring   is the maximum length of the **profile** string.

PRINTING A SCREEN

Since PM printing or plotting is device independent, you should be able to take any screen of information and print or plot it. Printing or plotting the contents of a graphical screen can be quite simple if you are sure what device you are going to print on. In such a case, you simply initialize the contents of a DEVOPENSTRUC structure accordingly:

```
DEVOPENSTRUC dop
  = {(PSZ)"LPT1Q",        /*queue name                        */
     (PSZ)"IBM4201",       /*device driver name                */
     OL,                   /*driver data args                  */
     (PSZ)"PM_Q_STD",      /*data format                       */
     (PSZ)"comment",       /*optional comment                  */
     OL,                   /*queue processor name              */
     OL,                   /*optional queue processor parms*/
     OL,                   /*optional spooler parameters       */
     OL};                  /*optional network parameters       */
```

In the common case, however, you check the current status of the OS2.INI file and decompose the configuration string returned by the query profile string call. This first call looks for the "PM_SPOOOLER" text and returns the name of the default printer:

```
WinQueryProfileString(hAB, "PM_SPOOLER", "PRINTER", "",
                      szTemp, MAXLEN);


/*remove trailing semicolon*/
szTemp[strlen(szTemp)-1] = 0;
```

Then, we look for the string identified with the PM_SPOOLER_PRINTER text within the PM_SPOOLER application:

```
WinQueryProfileString(hAB, "PM_SPOOLER_PRINTER",szTemp, "",
                      szSplrPrntr, 256);
```

In the default case, this will return the string

> "LPT1;IBM4201;LPT1Q;;"

where

LPT1   is the name of the current port.

IBM4201 is the name of the current device driver.

LPT1Q   is the name of the current queue.

This can be somewhat more complex, however. If the current device driver is one of the plotters in the PLOTTERS.DRV file, then the entry point for that device is also specified. In addition, if there is more than one queue, all of the queue names are returned separated by commas, with the default queue first:

> "LPT1;PLOTTERS.IBM6180;LPT1Q,PLOT1Q;;"

In any case, we can clearly parse that string and put its substrings into the DEVOPENSTRUCT structure.

```
WinQueryProfileString(hAB, "PM_SPOOLER", "PRINTER", "",
                      szTemp, 80);
/*remove trailing semicolon                              */
szTemp[strlen(szTemp)-1] = 0;
WinQueryProfileString(hAB, "PM_SPOOLER_PRINTER",szTemp, "",
                      szSplrPrntr, 256);
strcpy(szPlot, szSplrPrntr);        /*get another copy */
pchScan = strchr(szSplrPrntr, ';'); /*look for ;       */
pchScan++;                          /*go just beyond it*/
pchScan = strchr(pchScan, ';');     /*look for 2nd ;   */
pchScan++;                          /*go beyond it     */
```

```
/*set next . , or ; to null                              */
*(pchScan + strcspn(pchScan, ".,;")) = 0;
dop.pszLogAddress =  pchScan;           /*logical queue name*/

pchScan = strchr(szSplrPrntr, ';');
pchScan++;
*(pchScan + strcspn(pchScan, ".,;")) = 0;
dop.pszDriverName = pchScan;            /*copy in driver name*/
dop.pszQueueProcName= NULL;             /*default queue proc */
dop.pszQueueProcParams=NULL;            /*no queue proc parms*/
dop.pszSpoolerParams=NULL;           /*default spooler parms*/
dop.pszNetworkParams=NULL;              /*def network parms  */
dop.pszDataType = "PM_Q_STD"; /*std queue data type*/
dop.pszComment = "comment";             /*any comment or NULL*/
```

The DRIVDATA Structure

The third argument in the DEVOPENSTRUC structure is the address of
another structure of variable length called the DRIVDATA structure. Since
the length and content of this structure vary with the device, its first entry is
the structure length in bytes, followed by the version number of the device
driver that it requires. The important field in this structure is the entry point
in a multiple device driver file such as PLOTTERS.DRV, which contains
drivers for a number of similar Hewlett-Packard and IBM plotters. If the
device driver has only one entry point, then this string must be NULL.

```
drivdata.cb = 44L;          /*length of this structure   */
drivdata.lVersion = 0L;     /*version of driver required */
dop.pdriv = &drivdata;      /*ptr to drive data structure*/

/* look for device name in device driver field*/
pchScan = strchr(szPlot, ';');
pchScan++;

i = strcspn(pchScan, "."); /*look for entry point name   */
if (i < strlen(pchScan)) then
    begin
    pchScan += i + 1;
    *(pchScan + strcspn(pchScan, ".,;")) = 0;
```

```
    /* get name of entry point                              */
    strcpy(drivdata.szDeviceName, pchScan);
    end
else
    strcpy(drivdata.szDeviceName, '''');    /*or null        */
```

THE PS, THE WINDOW, AND THE DEVICE CONTEXT

Thus far we have dealt with windows and with presentation spaces. When we consider devices besides the screen, we will also need to utilize *device contexts*. A *window* is a screen area that is maintained and refreshed by a particular routine, called a window procedure. A *presentation space* contains a table of values describing how the window is to be drawn, including font, character, line and marker colors, and line type. A *device context* is a device-specific table of values describing how a particular device is to be used for drawing. To confuse matters somewhat, a screen PS, such as those we have dealt with so far, contains some device-specific information, but this is not the case for printers and plotters, which require that you associate a device context with a presentation space before you begin drawing.

The Plotter Device Context

Now that we have loaded the DEVOPENSTRUCT, we can open a printer device context using the **DevOpenDC** call

```
DevOpenDC(hAB, type, token, count, &devopen, comp);
```

where

hAB   is the anchor block handle for this thread.

type   is the type of device context, which may be OD_QUEUED, OD_DIRECT, OD_INFO, OD_METAFILE, or OD_MEMORY

token   is a token to search for in OS2.INI. This is overridden by the DEVOPENSTRUC parameter. If the token is "*" no information is read from OS2.INI.

count   is the number of long entries in the DEVOPENSTRUC structure to read.

& devopen   is the address of a DEVOPENSTRUCT structure.

comp   is a handle to a device context compatible with the bit map to be used in this device context. Used only with the type OD_MEMORY.

To open the device context for a plotter, we simply call

```
hDC = DevOpenDC(hAB, OD_QUEUED, "*", 5L,
                (PDEVOPENDATA)&dop, NULL);
```

The Plotter Presentation Space

The plotter device context must finally be associated with a plotter presentation space, so that we can call the same drawing routines using this new **hPS.** We do this using the **GpiCreatePS** call, where we require a *normal* presentation space. We would also like this presentation space to draw full scale on whatever plotter we attach, regardless of its resolution and regardless of the size of the window on the screen. If we scale our drawing to the current window size, we can query that size and set these values into the SIZEL structure before creating the PS.

```
WinQueryWindowRect(hWnd, &rc); /*get current window size */
siz.cx = rc.xRight;             /*plot full size on device*/
siz.cy = rc.yTop;
hPSPrinter = GpiCreatePS(hAB, hDC, &siz,
                PU_ARBITRARY | GPIA_ASSOC | GPIT_NORMAL);
```

Note that the **hDC** is the one just created for the printer and that the **GPIA_ASSOC** bit must be set.

The DevEscape Printer Calls

When you are printing to a specific plotter or printer, you may have to tell it things you wouldn't need to tell a display, such as setting the printer mode to draft or letter quality, and ejecting the page at the end. The **DevEscape** function has the form

```
DevEscape(hDC, code, incount, &indata, outcount, &outdat
```

where

hDC   is the handle to the device context.

code   is the code to be sent to the device driver.

incount   is the number of bytes in the input data buffer.

indata   is the input data buffer.

outcount   is the number of bytes in the output data buffer.

outdata   is the output data buffer.

There are 11 escape codes defined in OS2 1.2, but the only ones we will use are

$$DEVESC\_GETSCALINGFACTOR$$
$$DEVESC\_STARTDOC$$
$$DEVESC\_ENDDOC$$
$$DEVESC\_NEWFRAME$$
$$DEVESC\_DRAFTMODE$$

THE COMPLETE PLOT ROUTINE

```
void plot(HAB hAB, HPS hPS, HWND hWnd)
begin
        CHAR szTemp[80], szSplrPrntr[256], szPlot[256];
        PCH pchScan;
        DRIVDATA drivdata;
        SIZEL siz;
        RECTL rc;
        HDC hDC;
        HPS hPSPrinter;
```

```
        long  ocount, odata;
        DEVOPENSTRUC dop;
        int err,i;

WinQueryProfileString(hAB, "PM_SPOOLER", "PRINTER", "",
                      szTemp, 80);
szTemp[strlen(szTemp)-1] = 0; /*remove trailing semicolon*/
WinQueryProfileString(hAB, "PM_SPOOLER_PRINTER", szTemp,
                      "", szSplrPrntr, 256);
strcpy(szPlot, szSplrPrntr);   /*get another copy        */
                               /*for device name parse   */
pchScan = strchr(szSplrPrntr, ';');   /*look for 1st ;    */
pchScan++;                            /*go just beyond it*/
pchScan = strchr(pchScan, ';');       /*look for 2nd ;    */
pchScan++;                            /*go beyond it      */

/*  set next . , or ; to null                            */
*(pchScan + strcspn(pchScan, ".,;")) = 0;
dop.pszLogAddress = pchScan;          /*logical queue name*/

pchScan = strchr(szSplrPrntr, ';');
pchScan++;
*(pchScan + strcspn(pchScan, ".,;")) = 0;
dop.pszDriverName = pchScan;     /*copy in driver name      */
dop.pszQueueProcName= NULL;      /*default queue processor */
dop.pszQueueProcParams=NULL;     /*no queue proc parms      */
dop.pszSpoolerParams=NULL;       /*default spooler parms    */
dop.pszNetworkParams=NULL;       /*default network parms    */
dop.pszDataType = "PM_Q_STD";    /*standard queue data type*/
dop.pszComment = "comment";      /*any comment can go here */

drivdata.cb = 44L;               /*length of this structure*/
drivdata.lVersion = 0L;          /*version of driver reqd  */
dop.pdriv = &drivdata;           /*ptr to driver data struct*/

/* look for device name in device driver field*/
pchScan = strchr(szPlot, ';');
pchScan++;

i = strcspn(pchScan, ".");       /*get entry point name    */
if (i < strlen(pchScan)) then
```

```
   begin
   pchScan += i + 1;
   *(pchScan + strcspn(pchScan, ".,;")) = 0;
   strcpy(drivdata.szDeviceName, pchScan);
   end
else
   strcpy(drivdata.szDeviceName, "");    /*or null          */

hDC = DevOpenDC(hAB, OD_QUEUED, "*", 5L,
                (PDEVOPENDATA)&dop, NULL);

WinQueryWindowRect(hWnd, &rc); /*get current window size */
siz.cx = rc.xRight;             /*plot full size on device*/
siz.cy = rc.yTop;
hPSPrinter = GpiCreatePS(hAB, (HDC)hDC, &siz,
                PU_ARBITRARY | GPIA_ASSOC | GPIT_NORMAL);

DevEscape(hDC, DEVESC_GETSCALINGFACTOR, 0, NULL,
                &ocount, &odata);
DevEscape(hDC, DEVESC_STARTDOC, 4L, "Plot",
                &ocount, NULL);

drawscreen(hPSPrinter);          /*draw on this device    */
DevEscape(hDC, DEVESC_NEWFRAME, OL, NULL,
                   0, NULL); /*page eject               */
DevEscape(hDC, DEVESC_ENDDOC, OL, NULL,
                0, NULL);     /*close the document     */
GpiAssociate(hPSPrinter, NULL); /*disassoc from display  */
DevCloseDC(hDC);               /*discard the DC         */
GpiDestroyPS(hPSPrinter);      /*and the PS             */
end
```

15 | Communicating Through Serial Ports

Many devices that you might wish to connect to your computer can be connected using the computer's *serial ports* or COMM ports. These ports provide a standard method of communicating with devices using the RS-232 standard for serial communication. Data are sent through RS-232 ports as 8-bit bytes, but the the bytes are decomposed into a bit stream and sent serially and reassembled into 8-bit quantities at the other end.

BAUD RATES

Since the data are sent a bit at a time, the data rate or *baud rate* is roughly equivalent to the number of bits per second. Each character or byte of data actually consists of 1 start bit, 8 data bits, and 1 or 2 stop bits, so the baud rate is about 11 times higher than the character transfer rate. Data rates vary from 110 baud for historical reasons up to 9600 or 19,200 baud. PS/2 computers alllow transfer at 19.2 kbaud but AT hardware only allows baud rates up to 9600 baud. Clearly, the higher the data rate the better, and most modern instruments allow transfer at 9600 baud.

PARITY

All ASCII characters can be represented unambiguously in 7 bits (0-6), and bit 7 of the serially transmitted character is sometimes used as a *parity bit.* There are four cases for the parity bit:

Null Bit 7 is always 0.

Odd Bit 7 is on if it makes the total number of bits on odd.

Even Bit 7 is on if it makes the total number of bits on even.

Mark Bit 7 is always on.

THE COM DEVICE DRIVER

A copy of the COM port device driver is loaded for each active COM port in your machine if you specify that this driver is to be loaded at OS/2 installation time or if you have the statement

```
DEVICE=COM01.SYS
```

or

```
DEVICE=COM02.SYS
```

The COM01 driver is loaded for AT-class machines and the COM02 driver for PS/2 machines. These drivers provide interrupt-driven service of data transmission through a series of simple calls to the **DosDevIOCtrl** function. It is also possible to select the handshaking technique used.

PIN ASSIGNMENTS OF RS-232 CONNECTORS

The primary COM port on PS/2s is a 25-pin male connector. Additional ports on plug-in cards and the ports on AT-class machines are 9-pin connectors. The pin assignments are shown in Table 15-1.

Table 15-1. Pin Assignments on Serial Connectors			
Signal	**25-pin**	**9-pin**	**Description**
	1		Protective Ground
TD	2	3	Transmit Data
RD	3	2	Receive Data
RTS	4	7	Request to Send
CTS	5	8	Clear to Send
DSR	6	6	Data Set Ready
GND	7	5	Signal Ground
DCD	8	1	Data Carrier Detect
DTR	20	4	Data Terminal Ready
RI	22	9	Ring Indicator

The primary purpose of serial communication was originally to connect a terminal to a modem, a modem to a phone line, and at the other end another modem to a computer. Serial ports are classified as DCE (Data Communications Equipment), such as modems, and DTE (Data Terminal Equipment), such as computers. DCE connectors have pins 2 and 3 and pins 5 and 20 reversed, so that a straight-through cable between DCE and DTE connectors has RD connected to TD and Clear to Send connected to Data Terminal Ready. More commonly, two computers or other devices with DCE connectors must be attached, and this requires a "crossed cable" or "null modem" cable which has pins connected as shown in Table 15-2.

Table 15-2. Pin Assignments in a Null Modem	
Signals	**25-pin connections**
	1 - 1
TD - RD	2 - 3
RD - TD	3 - 2
RTS - DCD	4 - 8
DCD - RTS	8 - 4
CTS & DSR - DTR	5 & 6 - 20
DTR - CTS & DSR	20 - 5 & 6
GND - GND	GND - GND

OPENING AND CONTROLLING A COM PORT

A COM port is opened using the **DosOpen** call, where many of the arguments have no meaning. The standard call has the form

```
err = DosOpen(filename, &handle, &action, size, attribute,
              openflag, mode, reserved);
```

where

filename   The path and name of the file (or device) to be used.

& handle   The address where the file handle is to be returned.

& action   The action taken:

    0x0001 file exists
    0x0002 file created
    0x0003 file replaced

size   The file size in bytes.

attribute   The file attribute bits:

0x0001 read only file
0x0002 hidden file
0x0004 system file
0x0010 subdirectory
0x.0020 file archive

openflag   Action taken if the file exists or does not exist:
If the file exists

xxxx0000 fail
xxxx0001 open file
xxxx0010 replace file

If the file does not exist

0000xxxx fail
0001xxxx create file

mode   Contains the bits D, W, F, I, S, and A mapped to 16 bits as follows:

```
15 14 13 12 11 10 9 8 7 6 5 4 3 2 1 0
 D  W  F  -  -  - - - - I S S S - A A A
```

D 0 means a file and 1 means device is a drive.

I Inheritance flag. If 0 the file handle is inherited by a spawned process and if 1 the handle is private.

W Write-through flag. If 0, the file writes may go through a system buffer cache and if 1 the file I/O is done to disk before the call returns.

F If 0 errors are reported through the system critical error handler and if 1 they are reported to the caller through the return code.

S Sharing mode field. Determines whether a file can be shared.

001   deny read/write access
010   deny write access
011   deny read access
100   allow read/write access

A access mode field

000 read only
001 write only
010 read/write access

reserved   Must be zero.

If the return code is 0 there is no error. If non-zero, some of the errors are

0	no error
2	file not found
3	path not found
4	too many files open
5	access denied
26	not an OS/2 or DOS disk
32	sharing violation
112	disk full

Opening a COM Port

For opening a COM port, only a few arguments are used:

```
err = DosOpen("COM2", &hCom, &action, OL, 0, 1, 0x12, OL);
```

where

"COM2" The port name as a zero-terminated ASCII string.

&hCom The returned handle to the communications port.

&action The action taken. This will always be 0001 = "file exists."

0L The file size is not used.

0 The file attributes are not used.

1 The open flag defines action to take: open it if port exists and fail if it doesn't.

0x12 The open mode. The sharing mode is 001, meaning deny read/write access to any other task, and the access mode is 010, meaning read/write access is requested.

0L   Reserved field.

err   Return value. Should be 0 if the open is successful.

You then write to and read from the COM port using the **DosRead** and **DosWrite** functions

```
DosRead(handle, buffer, buflen, &bytesread);
DosWrite(handle, buffer, buflen, &byteswritten);
```

where

handle   is the file handle returned by **DosOpen**.

buffer   is the address of an array to transfer bytes to or from.

buflen   is the number of bytes to transfer.

bytesread   is the number of bytes actually read.

byteswritten   is the number of bytes actually written.

Once the port has been opened, you can control it using a number of **DosDevIOCtrl** calls, which have the form

```
err = DosDevIOCtrl(data, paramlist, function, category, handle);
```

where

data   is a data value or the address of a data block.

paramlist   is the address of an argument block.

function   is a function code for that device.

category   is the category under which the function code falls.

handle   is the device handle returned from the DosOpen call.

There are 11 categories of functions that this call supports. Category 1 includes the calls to serial devices, so we will define SERIAL as 1.

```
#define SERIAL 1
```

There are a large number of function codes in the serial category: the most important ones are listed in Table 15-3

Table 15-3. Serial Device Function Calls

Code	Description
0x41	Set baud rate
0x42	Set stop, parity, and data bits
0x45	Set break off
0x46	Set modem control signals
0x47	Stop transmitting as if XOFF received
0x48	Start transmitting as if XON received
0x4b	Set break on
0x53	Set Device Control Block
0x61	Return baud rate
0x62	Return stop, parity, data bits
0x64	Return COM control status
0x65	Return transmit status
0x66	Return modem output signals
0x67	Return modem input signals
0x68	Return number of characters in receive queue
0x69	Return number of characters in transmit queue
0x6d	Return COM error
0x72	Return COM event information
0x73	Return Control Block information

Setting the Baud Rate

This function accepts one argument in **data** consisting of the baud rate as an integer. The legal values are 110, 150, 300, 600, 1200, 1800, 2000, 2400, 3600, 4800,7200, 9600, and 19,200.

Setting Line Characteristics

The line characteristics are passed in a 3-byte structure of the form

```
struct LineChar
      begin
      unsigned char databits,
                    parity,
                    stopbits;
      end LineCtrl;
```

where

databits can take on the values 5, 6, 7, or 8, for the number of data bits.

parity can take on the values

  0 no parity
  01 odd parity
  02 even parity
  03 mark parity
  04 null parity

stopbits can take on the values of 0, 1, or 2 for 1, 1.5, or 2 stop bits.

The Device Control Block

The Device Control Block (DCB) is a structure consisting of timeout values, flags, and special characters.

```
struct DCB_info
   begin
      USHORT writetimeout,          /* read timeout in 0.01 seconds
             readtimeout;           /* write timeout in 0.01 seconds
      UBYTE  flags1,                /* DTR, CTS, DSR, DCD control
             flags2,                /* XON/XOFF and RTS control mode
             flags3,                /* timeout processing
             errchar,               /* error replacement character
             breakchar,             /* break replacement character    *
             XONchar                /* XON character
             XOFFchar;              /* XOFF character
   end DCBinfo;
```

Function 0x53 allows you to set the read and write timeouts in the DCB block as well as the settings of the handshaking modes as follows:

flags1   Setting of handshaking modes:

   bits 0-1 DTR control mode
      00 disable
      01 enable
      10 input handshaking
      11 invalid input resulting in general failure
   bit 2   reserved
   bit 3   enable output handshaking using CTS
   bit 4   enable output handshaking using DSR
   bit 5   enable output handshaking using DCD
   bit 6   enable input handshaking using DSR

flags2   XON-XOFF and RTS Control

   bit 0   enable automatic transmit flow control using XON/XOFF
   bit 1   enable automatic receive flow control using XON/XOFF
   bit 2   enable error replacement character
   bit 3   remove null bytes
   bit 4   enable break replacement character
   bit 5   reserved
   bits 6-7   RTS control mode
      00 disable

01 enable

10 input handshaking

11 toggling on transmit

flags3   timeout processing

    bit 0   enable write infinite timeout processing

    bit 1-2 read timeout processing

        00 invalid input resulting in general failure

        01 normal read timeout processing

        10 wait for something read timeout processing

        11 no wait read timeout processing

HANDSHAKING IN SERIAL COMMUNICATION

Handshaking between serial devices is required if data can be sent to a device faster than it can be processed. For example, if you send data to a serial plotter, the plotter will take some time to actually move the pen and draw the line. While the plotter may have some buffer memory, you can eventually fill it up and the plotter must signal the computer not to send any data until it has room to store it. In the case of most serial plotters, the plotter raises the DTR signal when it can accept data and lowers that line when it cannot.

In OS/2, the receive buffer has a length of 1024 bytes and the transmit buffer 128 bytes. Handshaking is necessary to assure that the receive buffer is not overfilled. There are a number of methods of performing handshaking using the signals listed above.

When you open a COM port under OS/2, DTR and RTS are asserted by default, and output handshaking occurs using DSR and CTS. The levels of these signals and the hardware handshaking mode can be adjusted using the SetDCBInfo function 0x53. Exactly which one you choose depends on the handshaking required by the device you are connecting to.

DTR Input Handshaking

In DTR input handshaking mode, the device driver is high when the input queue is less than half full and is lowered if the queue becomes more than half full.

RTS-CTS and DTR-DSR

When a device is ready to transmit a character in this handshaking mode, it asserts (sets high) the RTS (Ready to Send) pin. The receiving device may require that data only be transmitted when it is ready: that is, when it has set CTS (Clear to Send). In the simple transmit-receive sequence supported by DOS, RTS and DTR are both asserted before transmission and the function waits for CTS and DSR before trying to read a character.

XON-XOFF Handshaking

The most common form of software handshaking is accomplished by having the receiving device send an XOFF character (0x13) and send the XON character (0x11) when it is again ready. This can be supported automatically within the COM driver by setting bit 0 of flags2 for transmit flow control and setting bit 1 of flags2 for receive flow control.

A SIMPLE COMMUNICATIONS PROGRAM

The program below sets the baud rate to 9600, enables DTR input handshaking, and reads characters from the COM2 port, printing each on the screen. It also echoes the character back to the sending device, so we can illustrate communications output as well:

```
/********** COMM Port Transmit and Receive Routine********/
#include <cdefs.h>
#define INCL_BASE
#include <os2.h>
#include <stdio.h>
#include <string.h>
```

```
#define SERIAL              1
#define SET_BAUD            0x41
#define SET_PARITY_BITS     0x42
#define SET_MODEM_CONTROL   0x46
#define SET_DCB_INFO        0x53
#define GET_DCB_INFO        0x73

#define BUFLEN 256

void main()
begin
  USHORT hCom, action, baudrate;
  char inbuf[BUFLEN];
  int bytesread, byteswritten, err;

  struct DCB_info
    begin
    USHORT writetimeout, /* read timeout in 0.01 seconds  */
           readtimeout;  /* write timeout in 0.01 seconds */
    BYTE   flags1,       /* DTR, CTS, DSR, DCD control     */
           flags2,       /* XON/XOFF and RTS control mode  */
           flags3,       /* timeout processing             */
           errchar,      /* error replacement character    */
           breakchar,    /* break replacement characater   */
           XONchar,      /* XON character                  */
           XOFFchar;     /* XOFF character                 */
    end DCBinfo;

err=DosOpen("COM2", &hCom, &action,
            0L, 0, 1, 0x12, 0L); /*read-write non shared*/

baudrate = 9600;
err=DosDevIOCtl(0L, &baudrate, SET_BAUD, SERIAL, hCom);
err=DosDevIOCtl(&DCBinfo, 0L, GET_DCB_INFO, SERIAL, hCom);
DCBinfo.writetimeout = 3000;/*30 second write timeout    */
DCBinfo.readtimeout = 3000; /*30 second read timeout     */
DCBinfo.flags1 = 0x02;      /*enable DTR handshaking      */
DCBinfo.flags2 = 0x03;      /*no RTS handshaking          */

err=DosDevIOCtl(0L, &DCBinfo, SET_DCB_INFO, SERIAL, hCom);
```

```
strcpy(inbuf,"");           /*initialize string          */
while (inbuf[0] != 'q')     /*exit if "q" sent           */
  begin
  err = DosRead(hCom, inbuf,
          1, &bytesread);   /*read a char                */
  err = DosWrite(hCom, inbuf,
          1, &byteswritten); /*write a char              */
  inbuf[1]='\0';            /*make a 1-character string  */
  printf("%s",inbuf);       /*print it                   */
  end
end
```

REFERENCES

1. Jeff Prosise, "OS/2 - A Rich Communications Environment," *PC Magazine,* **8,** October 17, 1989, 285.

2. Stephen C. Gates with Jordan Becker, *Laboratory Automation Using the IBM PC.* Prentice-Hall: Englewood Cliffs, NJ, 1989.

3. J. W. Cooper, *Microsoft QuickBASIC for Scientists.* Wiley-Interscience: New York, 1988.

16 Using List Boxes to Get Filenames

LIST BOXES

One of the standard types of dialog box elements is the *list box*, which allows you to select one from a series of listed items. You can also define a list box so that several items can be selected at once. A list box can contain up to 32K of characters in any number of lines of items. When a list box is drawn that contains more items than can be displayed at once time, the scroll bars to the right of the box are activated, and you can scroll through the items by moving the scroll bar *elevator* or by clicking on the up or down arrows at the top and bottom of the scroll bar. A typical list box is shown in Figure 16-1.

Like all dialog box elements, a list box is just a special kind of window that receives and interprets special messages. During the initialization phase of the dialog box procedure, you fill the list box with items by sending it messages as follows:

```
hList =
  WinWindowFromID(hWnd, idList);  /*list box window handle*/

WinSendDlgItemMsg(hWnd,      /*dialog box window handle    */
        idList,              /*id of list box in dialog box*/
        LM_INSERTITEM,       /*tell it to insert an item   */
```

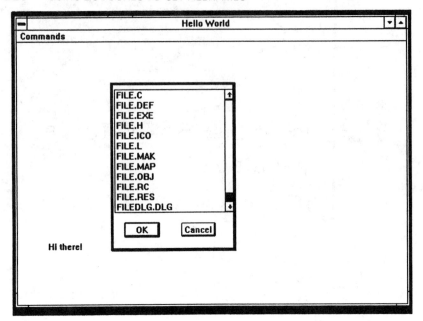

Figure 16-1. A typical list box, displaying filenames

```
(MPARAM)LIT_SORTASCENDING,   /*sort in ascending  */
MPFROMP(text));              /*insert string      */
```

Now, remembering that a dialog box is a window, it is not surprising that we manipulate it by sending it messages. To send them, we must obtain the window handle. In general, we only know the ID value that we assigned during creation of the dialog box using the dialog editor. However, the function **WinWindowFromId** will return the window handle given that ID value.

Similarly, you clear out the list box by sending it the LM_DELETEALL message

```
/* delete all items from list box */
WinSendDlgItemMsg(hWnd, idList, LM_DELETEALL, OL, OL);
```

SELECTING A LINE FROM A LIST BOX

If you point at any list box line with the mouse and click the left button, that line will be highlighted in inverse video. Then, if you select the "OK" button or press Enter (if OK is the default), a **WM_COMMAND** message will be sent to the dialog box window, with **mp1** containing the **DID_OK** message. Then, you can find out the number of the line that was selected by sending the list box the **LM_QUERYSELECTION** message

```
id =                                    /*get the entry number*/
    SHORT1FROMMR( WinSendDlgItemMsg(
                    hWnd,               /*dialog window */
                    FILELIST,           /*list box id   */
                    LM_QUERYSELECTION,/*query          */
                    0L,                 /*no parameters */
                    0L ) );
```

Then you can get the text of that line by sending the list box the **LM_QUERYITMETEXT** message

```
WinSendDlgItemMsg(hWnd,
                FILELIST,               /*get the filename*/
                LM_QUERYITEMTEXT,
                MPFROM2SHORT(id, sizeof(filename)),
                MPFROMP(filename));
```

The other way that a line is often selected in a list box is by *double* clicking on it. In this case the message **WM_CONTROL** is posted to the dialog box, with **mp1** set to **LN_ENTER**. When you receive this message you simply post the **WM_COMMAND** message with **mp1** set to **DID_OK**.

```
case WM_CONTROL:
    switch(SHORT2FROMMP(mp1))    /*look for double click   */
      begin
      case LN_ENTER:              /*comes from a double click*/
        WinPostMsg(hWnd,
                WM_COMMAND, /*post a DID_OK message    */
                MPFROMSHORT(DID_OK),
                0L);
        return((MRESULT)TRUE); /*message processed        */
        break;
      end
```

FILLING A LIST BOX WITH FILENAMES

You can use the **DosFindFirst** and the **DosFindNext** calls to get filenames from the current directory. The **DosFindFirst** call has the form

```
rcode=
    DosFindFirst(filename, &handle, attrib, &rbuf,
                    buflen, &srchcnt, NULL);
```

where

filename   is the filename string to match. You can use the "*" and "?" wildcard characters to specify the name. A path specification may also be part of the name string.

& handle   is a pointer to the handle for this directory operation. If you set the handle to 0xffff, a handle is allocated and returned in this address.

attrib   specifies the file attributes to search for. Each bit set searches for that file type in addition to normal matching filenames.

0x0001	read only files
0x0002	hidden files
0x0004	system files
0x0008	volume labels
0x0010	subdirectories

& rbuf   is the pointer to a result buffer, consisting of the structure FILEFINDBUF shown below.

buflen   is the length of the result buffer.

& srchcnt   is the number of matching entries requested. On return this number of entries is placed in successive **FILEFINDBUF** structures starting at the address specified in **rbuf.**

NULL   is a reserved long argument.

The FILEFINDBUF structure has the form

```
typedef struct _FILEFINDBUF {  /* findbuf             */
    FDATE  fdateCreation;      /*creation date        */
    FTIME  ftimeCreation;      /*creation time        */
    FDATE  fdateLastAccess;    /*last access date     */
    FTIME  ftimeLastAccess;    /*last access time     */
    FDATE  fdateLastWrite;     /*date of last write   */
    FTIME  ftimeLastWrite;     /*time of last write   */
    ULONG  cbFile;             /*file size in bytes   */
    ULONG  cbFileAlloc;        /*allocated file size  */
    USHORT attrFile;           /*file attribute bits  */
    UCHAR  cchName;            /*length of filename   */
    CHAR   achName[13];        /*filename             */
} FILEFINDBUF;
```

Upon return, **rcode** contains 0 if the call was successful, and otherwise contains an error code.

The **DosFindNext** uses the handle returned above to find additional matches to the previously specified filename and attributes:

```
rcode =
    DosFindNext(handle, &rbuf, buflen, &srchcnt);
```

where all the arguments have the same meaning as above. Note that, as before, **rcode** contains 0 if the search is successful and non-zero if no more files can be found that match the filename and attributes.

Getting Subdirectory Names

The DosFind... calls will match all the files that have the path and name specified in the **filename** argument. Thus, to find all files with the .DAT extension, you set the filename to "*.DAT". If you have the subdirectory bit set as well, the subdirectory names in this path will also be found, including the ".." and "." entries for the parent and current directories. While it is easy to tell that a name represents a subdirectory if it is named ".." there is no way to tell whether a name such as DATA is a file or a subdirectory. To distinguish them, we will intercept them and enclose the names in brackets:

```
[..]
[DATA]
```

using the following simple code:

```
if (rbuf.attrFile == SUBDIR) then
   begin                         /*if this is a subdirectory*/
   strcpy(filename, "[");
   strcat(filename, rbuf.achName); /*enclose name in [] */
   strcat(filename, "]");
   end
else
   /*otherwise just put name in list*/
   strcpy(filename, rbuf.achName);
```

The complete routine for filling the list box is shown below

```
void FillListBox(HWND hWnd, int idList, char *filemask)
/*----------------------------------------------------------*/
/* Fills a list box having the id "idList" which is a        */
/* child of the dialog box window "hWnd" with all            */
/* filenames which match the filemask.                       */
/*----------------------------------------------------------*/
begin
   HWND hList;                 /*list box window handle      */
   FILEFINDBUF rbuf;          /*file find buffer structure*/
   USHORT retcode, searchcount,
          attrib;
   HDIR DirHandle;           /*handle to the directory     */
   char filename[80];

hList =
 WinWindowFromID(hWnd, idList);  /*list box window handle*/
WinEnableWindowUpdate(hList,
                   FALSE);    /*no update till filled */
WinSendDlgItemMsg(hWnd,       /*delete all in listbox */
             idList,
             LM_DELETEALL,
             OL, OL);

/*search for matches to filename mask*/
DirHandle = 0xffff;           /*return new handle here */
attrib = SUBDIR;              /*normal files           */
                             /* and subdirectories    */
searchcount = 1;             /*number of matching     */
```

```
                                    /* entries to find        */

retcode =
  DosFindFirst(filemask,          /*find first match         */
               &DirHandle,
               attrib, &rbuf,
               sizeof(FILEFINDBUF),
               &searchcount, NULL);

if (retcode == NULL) then          /*there was one match      */
  begin
    do
      begin
      if (rbuf.attrFile == SUBDIR) then
        begin
        strcpy(filename, "[");  /*if this is a subdir       */
        strcat(filename,
               rbuf.achName);    /*enclose name in brackets*/
        strcat(filename, "]");
        end
      else
        strcpy(filename,
               rbuf.achName); /*else just put name in list*/
      WinSendDlgItemMsg(hWnd,
                        idList,
                        LM_INSERTITEM, /*insert in list box*/
                        (MPARAM)LIT_SORTASCENDING,
                        MPFROMP(filename));
      retcode =
        DosFindNext(DirHandle,
                    &rbuf,    /*look for another match    */
                    sizeof(FILEFINDBUF),
                    &searchcount);
      end
    while(retcode == NULL);   /*loop until none are found */
    end
WinShowWindow(hList, TRUE); /*now display this list box */
end
```

CALLING THE DIALOG BOX

In calling a dialog procedure that will return a filename, we need to use the last argument of the dialog box call to pass the address where the filename will be returned. Then if the call returns TRUE, we know that we have a valid filename in that string; if it returns FALSE, we know there is not a valid filename.

```
rcode =
    WinDlgBox(HWND_DESKTOP,
            hWnd,                /*parent and owner windows   */
            FileDlgProc,         /*address of dialog procedure*/
            NULL,                /*look in the resource file  */
            FILEBOX,             /*id of dlg in resource file */
            (PVOID)mstring); /*address of string to return*/

if (rcode) then
        open_file(mstring); /*open that file if OK pressed*/
```

Recognizing a Subdirectory

If we select a subdirectory, we don't want the dialog box to exit and return that filename. Instead, we want to change to that subdirectory and show the files in it. It's easy to recognize these subdirectories, since we have enclosed them in brackets: we simply see if the first character of the string is a bracket, and if it is, we change to that subdirectory using the **DosChDir** call

```
if (localname[0] ==  '[') then      /*if this is a subdir*/
    begin
    strcpy(filename, localname + 1); /*remove first [     */
    len = strlen(filename);          /*get length         */
    filename[len-1] = '\0';          /*remove last ]      */
    DosChDir(filename, OL);          /*change directory   */
    FillListBox(hWnd, FILELIST, "*.*");  /*refill list box*/
    end
```

The Dialog Box Procedure

```
void FillListBox(HWND hWnd, int idList, char *filemask)
/*-------------------------------------------------------*/
/* Fills a list box having the id "idList" which is a    */
/* child of the dialog box window "hWnd" with all        */
/* filenames which match the filemask                    */
/*-------------------------------------------------------*/
begin
   HWND hList;                  /*list box window handle    */
   FILEFINDBUF rbuf;            /*file find buffer structure*/
   USHORT retcode, searchcount,
          attrib;
   HDIR DirHandle;             /*handle to the directory   */
   char filename[80];

hList = WinWindowFromID(hWnd,
                idList);    /*list box window handle    */
WinEnableWindowUpdate(hList,
                FALSE);    /*no update till filled     */
WinSendDlgItemMsg(hWnd,    /*delete all items from listbox*/
                idList,
                LM_DELETEALL,
                0L, 0L);


/*search for matches to filename mask*/
DirHandle = 0xffff;          /*return a new handle here   */
attrib = SUBDIR;             /*normal files and subdirs   */
searchcount = 1;             /*number of matching entries*/


retcode =
   DosFindFirst(filemask, &DirHandle,
                attrib, &rbuf,
                sizeof(FILEFINDBUF),
                &searchcount, NULL);

if (retcode == NULL) then  /*there was at least one match*/
   begin
     do
       begin
       if (rbuf.attrFile == SUBDIR) then
```

```
            begin
            strcpy(filename, "["); /*if this is a subdir     */
            strcat(filename,
                    rbuf.achName); /*enclose name in brackets*/
            strcat(filename, "]");
            end
         else
            strcpy(filename,
                rbuf.achName);        /*else just put name in list*/
         WinSendDlgItemMsg(hWnd,
                        idList,
                        LM_INSERTITEM, /*insert in list box*/
                        (MPARAM)LIT_SORTASCENDING,
                        MPFROMP(filename));
         retcode =
            DosFindNext(DirHandle,
                        &rbuf,    /*look for another match    */
                        sizeof(FILEFINDBUF),
                        &searchcount);
         end
      while(retcode == NULL);     /*loop til no more found    */
      end
   WinShowWindow(hList, TRUE);   /*now display this list box*/
   end
   /***********************************************************/
   MRESULT EXPENTRY FileDlgProc(HWND hWnd, USHORT msg,
                             MPARAM mp1, MPARAM mp2)
   /*--------------------------------------------------------*/
   /* Dialog box procedure to fill a list box with a         */
   /* filename and return the selected filename in the       */
   /* argument pointer If a subdirectory is selected,        */
   /* the list box is refilled with the files in that        */
   /* subdirectory                                           */
   /*--------------------------------------------------------*/

   begin
     int id, attrib, len;
     static char localname[80], *filename;
```

```
switch (msg)
begin
case WM_INITDLG:
   FillListBox(hWnd,
           FILELIST, "*.*");          /*fill list box       */
   filename = (char *)mp2;            /*pointer to arg      */
   WinPostMsg(hWnd, WM_BUTTON1DOWN,
                       OL, OL);       /*activate window    */
   return((MRESULT)TRUE);            /*message processed*/
   break;

case WM_COMMAND:
  switch(SHORT1FROMMP(mp1))
    begin
    case DID_OK:
      id =
        WinSendDlgItemMsg( hWnd,
                    FILELIST,
                    LM_QUERYSELECTION,
                    OL, OL );
      if (id == LIT_NONE)            /*if no file highlighted*/
         begin
         strcpy(filename, "");        /*set to no length      */
         WinDismissDlg(hWnd,
                    FALSE); /*and return FALSE     */
         return(TRUE);               /*message was processed */
         end
       else
         begin
         WinSendDlgItemMsg(hWnd,
                    FILELIST,  /*get the filename    */
                    LM_QUERYITEMTEXT,
                    MPFROM2SHORT(id, sizeof(localname)),
                    MPFROMP(localname));
         /*copy filename to return it                  */
         strcpy(filename, localname);
         end
       if (localname[0] ==  '[') then    /*if a subdir  */
          begin
          strcpy(filename, localname + 1);/*remove first [*/
          len = strlen(filename);         /*get length    */
```

```
            filename[len-1] = '\0';              /*remove last ] */
            DosChDir(filename, OL);          /*change directory*/
            FillListBox(hWnd,
                     FILELIST, "*.*");     /*refill list box*/
        end
      else
        WinDismissDlg(hWnd, TRUE);    /*return true       */
      return(TRUE);                    /*message processed*/
      break;

   case DID_CANCEL:                    /*Cancel pressed       */
      strcpy(filename, "");            /*set filename to none*/
      WinDismissDlg(hWnd, FALSE);  /*and return false     */
      return(TRUE);
      break;
   end

 case WM_CONTROL:
   switch(SHORT2FROMMP(mp1))        /*look for double click*/
      begin
      case LN_ENTER:                   /*mesg from a dbl click*/
        WinPostMsg(hWnd,
                 WM_COMMAND,        /*post a DID_OK message*/
                 MPFROMSHORT(DID_OK),
                 OL);
        return((MRESULT)TRUE         /*message processed     */
        break;

    default:
      return(WinDefDlgProc(hWnd, msg, mp1, mp2));
    end
  default:
    return(WinDefDlgProc(hWnd, msg, mp1, mp2));
  end
return(FALSE);
end
```

Adding Drive Names to the List Box

You can find out which drives are active in a system by using the **DosQCurDisk** call

```
DosQCurCDisk(&curdisk, &bdisks);
```

where

& curdisks   The drive number of the current drive, where A: is 1, B: is 2, etc.

& bdisks   A bit map of the currently installed drives, where the lowest bit represents an A: drive and the 26th bit a Z: drive.

Then, to insert a drive letter enclosed in hyphens, you write the following:

```
mask = 1L;                          /*set mask to bit 0*/
for (i = 0; i < 26; i++ )           /*loop thru up to Z:*/
  begin
  if (bdisks AND mask) then
    begin
    name[0] = '-';                  /*start string with dash*/
    name[1] = (char)('A' + i);      /*calculate drive letter*/
    name[2] = '-';                  /*terminate with dash   */
    name[3] = '\0';                 /*string null terminator*/
    WinSendDlgItemMsg(hWnd,         /*insert drive name     */
                idList,
                LM_INSERTITEM,
                LIT_SORTASCENDING,
                name);
    mask <<= 1;                     /*shift mask 1 place left*/
    end
  end
```

If you select a drive letter, you must change to that drive using the **DosSelectDisk** call

```
if (localname[0] == '-') then
   begin
   disknum = localname[1] - 'A'; /*calculate drive number*/
   DosSelectDisk(disknum):        /*change to that drive  */
   FillListBox(hWnd,
            FILELIST, "*.*");   /*refill list box       */
   end
```

17 | Graphics Metafiles and Segments

When you issue any of the Gpi calls to draw on the screen or any other device, a series of 16-bit codes called *graphics orders* can be generated that describe these drawing functions in a compact way that can make redrawing very fast. These orders can be stored in a file called a *metafile* or stored in tables associated with a normal presentation space called *graphics segments*.

METAFILES

Graphics metafiles can be used to save and replay complex graphical operations as rapidly as possible. They are device independent and can be interpreted by computers attached to other higher-quality printing and plotting devices to make publication-quality copies. Since metafiles contain a list of graphics orders, they are independent of the resolution of the device and they can be displayed on displays of any convenient resolution.

Once you have saved a metafile on disk, you can use the OS/2 PICPRINT and PICSHOW programs to display and print these metafiles on any plotter or printer supported by OS/2.

You can use metafiles to save and display complex drawings such as 3-dimensional perspective representations, logos, or multiple plots on a single screen. You can save metafiles as actual disk files to read in and display later, or you can just use them as tables of data to display inside your program. This latter approach overlaps with *graphics segments*, which we will discuss later in this chapter.

Creating a Metafile

OS/2 PM considers a metafile to be a device just as a printer or a plotter is a device, and you must create a *device context* for one just as you do for a real device.

```
/*    define a device open structure --              */
/*    only "DISPLAY" is needed*/                     */
DEVOPENSTRUC dop =
         {OL, "DISPLAY", OL, OL, "comments",OL,OL,OL,OL };

hDC =
   DevOpenDC(hAB, OD_METAFILE,
                        "*",   /*open a metafile DC */
                        5L,
                        (PDEVOPENDATA)&dop,
                        NULL);
```

The **DevOpenDC** call creates a device context for a device having the characteristics defined in the DEVOPENSTRUC structure. However, the structure actually expected by this call is a DEVOPENDATA structure, which is the same thing, but must be cast to this type to avoid compilation errors. In this structure, the only relevant field is the device driver name field where we indicate that the driver name is "DISPLAY." This means that the metafile is generated using the current display driver DISPLAY.DLL. The remaining fields are unused.

Once a metafile device context is created, you create a metafile presentation space associating this device context with it. It is also useful to create it using the current window size:

```
WinQueryWindowRect(hWnd, &rc); /*get current window size */
siz.cx = rc.xRight;            /*copy into size structure*/
siz.cy = rc.yTop;
hPSmeta = GpiCreatePS(hAB, hDC,
                      &siz,  /*create a metafile PS    */
                      PU_PELS |
```

GPIA_ASSOC);

Then, you simply do all the drawing you need into this metafile, calling all your drawing routines with the **hPSmeta** presentation space handle.

```
drawscreen(hPSmeta);        /*draw everything into this PS*/
```

Finally, you disassociate the presentation space from any device, and close the device context, which returns the handle to the metafile. Then the **GpiSaveMetaFile** call is used to save the metafile to a disk file. This call will only actually save the file if no file by that name already exists, so it is usual to delete any file of that name before saving it. When you issue the save metafile call, the memory version of this metafile is automatically deleted and the **hMF** handle is no longer valid.

```
GpiAssociate(hPSmeta,
             (HDC)NULL);      /*disassociate from display*/
hMF = DevCloseDC(hDC);        /*here is where the        */
                             /*metafile handle comes in */
strcpy(tname, "META.MET");    /*get a meta file name     */
DosDelete(temp_name, 0L);     /*delete any previous file */
GpiSaveMetaFile(hMF, tname);  /*use it to save metafile  */
```

The complete routine for saving a metafile is show below:

```
void savemeta(HAB hAB, HWND hWnd)
/*----------------------------------------------------------*/
/* This routine creates a metafile, draws into it, and      */
/* saves it as "META.MET". The handle to the current        */
/* anchor block is hAB and the handle to the current        */
/* window is hWnd                                           */
/*----------------------------------------------------------*/

begin
    HDC hDC;                  /*device context           */
    SIZEL siz;                /*size structure           */
    char  tname[80];          /*file name                */
    RECTL rc;                 /*rectangle structure      */
    HPS hPSmeta;              /*metafile PS              */
    HMF hMF;                  /*metafile handle          */
    DEVOPENSTRUC dop;         /*device open structure*/
```

```
WinQueryWindowRect(hWnd, &rc);    /*get current window size*/
siz.cx = rc.xRight;               /*copy into size struct  */
siz.cy = rc.yTop;

dop.pszDriverName = "DISPLAY";    /*display device driver  */
dop.pszComment = "comment";
hDC = DevOpenDC(hAB,
            OD_METAFILE,
            *"",                  /*open a metafile DC     */
            5L,
            (PDEVOPENDATA)&dop,
            NULL);
hPSmeta = GpiCreatePS(hAB, hDC,
            &siz,         /*create a metafile PS   */
            PU_PELS |
            GPIA_ASSOC);

drawscreen(hPSmeta);          /*draw everything into this PS*/
GpiAssociate(hPSmeta,
        (HDC)NULL);      /*disassociate from display   */
hMF = DevCloseDC(hDC);        /*here is where the metafile  */
                             /* handle comes in            */
strcpy(tname, "META.MET");   /*get a meta file name        */
DosDelete(tname, OL);        /*delete any previous file    */
GpiSaveMetaFile(hMF, tname); /*use it to save the metafile*/
GpiDestroyPS(hPSmeta);       /*destroy the meta PS         */
end
```

PLAYING BACK A METAFILE

A metafile stored in memory after a **DevCloseDC** call returns its handle can
be played back immediately using the **GpiPlayMetaFile** call. Playing back a
metafile stored on disk amounts to loading the metafile, which returns the
metafile handle, and then calling the playback function, which has the form

```
GpiPlayMetaFile(hPS, hMF, optionsize,
            options, &segcount, dsize, desc);
```

where

hPS   is the presentation space where the playback is to occur.

hMF   is the handle to the metafile.

optionsize   is the number of entries in the **options** array.

options   is an array of long integers describing the transform-
                   ations transformations, font id's, reset status, playback
                   status, and color tables.

segcount   is the count of any segments in the metafile that are
                   renumbered.

dsize   is the number of bytes in the **desc** string.

desc   is the comment string stored with the metafile.

In this example, we will load the option array with all the default values.

```
void playmeta(HAB hAB, HPS hPS, HWND hWnd)
/*-----------------------------------------------------------*/
/* This routine loads and plays back a metafile              */
/* "META.MET" into the presentation space specified by       */
/* the handle hPS. Boston fans can rename the file if        */
/* desired. The anchor block is hAB and the handle to        */
/* the current window is hWnd.                               */
/*-----------------------------------------------------------*/
begin
        HDC hDC;
        SIZEL siz;
        char *tmppt, desc[256], buf[80];
        RECTL rc;
        HMF hMF;
        int err;
        long options[PMF_COLORREALIZABLE + 1], segcount;

hMF =
  GpiLoadMetaFile(hAB,
            "META.MET");              /*load the metafile  */
options[PMF_SEGBASE] =  0L;           /*set up all defaults*/
options[PMF_LOADTYPE] = LT_DEFAULT;  /*in the option array*/
options[PMF_LCIDS] =    LC_DEFAULT;
options[PMF_RESET] =    RES_DEFAULT;
```

```
options[PMF_SUPPRESS] = SUP_NOSUPPRESS;
options[PMF_COLORTABLES] = CTAB_DEFAULT;
options[PMF_COLORREALIZABLE] = CREA_DEFAULT;

GpiPlayMetaFile(hPS,                    /*now play it in the PS*/
                hMF,
                PMF_COLORREALIZABLE,
                options, &segcount,
                256L, desc);

err = WinGetLastError(hAB);        /*check for error       */
if (err != 0) then
    begin
    sprintf(buf, "Error = %x",err);
    WinMessageBox(HWND_DESKTOP, hWnd, buf,
                  "Metafile error", 1, MB_OK);
    end
end
```

GRAPHICS SEGMENTS

OS/2 provides a way for you to store the same graphics orders generated in metafiles in *graphics segments*, in your presentation space so they can be redrawn rapidly. These segments can only be created and stored in normal presentation spaces, but should in theory provide a way for you to redraw complex graphics quickly. Segments also provide a way for you to select drawing elements with the mouse and see if they have been picked using *correlation* function calls. Whether the segment method is in fact faster is dependent on the type of display you are using and on the version of the OS/2 display device driver.

Graphics segments have a number of attributes that you can use to create and identify them. These include

chained   A chained segment is logically connected to preceding segments. If you do nothing to change it, all segments are chained and can be drawn in a single **GpiDrawChain** call.

fast-chaining   Fast-chaining segments do not reset the graphics attributes to their default values. This is also a default attribute for all segments.

dynamic   Dynamic segments are a group of segments designed to be drawn last and erased and moved as necessary. This is usually done using the segment transform matrix, which we will discuss later.

detectable   If this attribute is set, then this segment can be picked by clicking on it with the mouse. This attribute is usually set to FALSE and must be turned on if you want to be able to pick segments.

visible   Segments with the visibility attribute set to FALSE are not drawn. Normally segments are defined as visible.

propagate visibility   If one segment is made visible then any segments it calls will be visible too.

propagate detectability   If one segment is detectable then any segments it calls will be detectable too.

You can create segments that either are identified with numbers or have zero id's. You number segments if you wish to refer to them again individually, and you leave the identifiers as zero if you will only display them as a group. Segments that you wish to pick out individually using the mouse and the **GpiCorrelate** function must have non-zero identifiers. A simple segment creation routine might be

```
GpiOpenSegment(hPS, segnum);     /*open a segment          */
pt.x = 50; pt.y = 50;
GpiMove(hPS, &pt);               /*move to corner of box */
pt.x = 100; pt.y = 100;
GpiBox(hPS, DRO_OUTLINE, &pt,
                NULL, NULL);     /*draw the box            */
GpiCloseSegment(hPS);            /*and close the segment */
```

Then, any time you wish to draw the items in that segment, you can simply use the call

```
GpiDrawSegment(hPS, segnum);
```

If you create a series of segments having separate numbers or all having zero identifiers, they are by default chained together, and you can draw them all at once using the call

```
GpiDrawChain(hPS);        /*draw all the chained segments*/
```

PICKING (CORRELATING) SEGMENTS

We can find out if the mouse pointer is touching a line belonging to a given segment by using the mouse coordinates as input to the **GpiCorrelateSegment** or the **GpiCorrelateChain** calls

```
hits = GpiCorrelateSegment(hPS, segnum, type, &pt,
                             maxhits, maxdepth, tags);
hits = GpiCorrelateChain  (hPS, type, &pt,
                             maxhits, maxdepth, tags);
```

where

hits   is the number of hits found.

segnum   is the segment number to test for a hit.

type   is either PICKSEL_VISIBLE or PICKSEL_ALL, depending on whether only detectable segments or all segments are to be tested for a hit.

& pt   is the address of the POINTL structure containing the coordinates to be tested for a hit.

maxhits   is the maximum number of hits that may be returned in the **tags** array.

maxdepth   is the maximum number of pairs of segment numbers and tags that may be returned for each hit.

tags is an array of long integers equal in size to **2*maxhits*maxdepth**. For each hit, this array contains a pair of values consisting of the segment number and the segment tag. Each segment may contain one or more segment tags and if several drawing elements having different tags intersect the pick aperture, several hits are produced.

Segment Tags and Labels

You can *tag* each segment with one or more tag values using the

```
GpiSetTag(hPS, tagnum);
```

call. Tags may be any non-zero identifier. A segment initially has a tag of zero and such segments are not picked when the segment is correlated. There can be several tag values within a segment and the latest one is the one returned by the correlate call.

Segment *labels* are set with the

```
GpiLabel(hPS, labelnum);
```

call. Labels need not be unique nor non-zero, and are not returned by the correlation operation. Instead, they are used to search out parts of a segment you wish to edit or delete.

CREATING AND PICKING SEGMENTS

To create and display segments that you can pick, you need to

1. Get a window Device Context.
2. Create a normal Presentation Space.
3. Set the drawing mode to *retain*.
4. Delete any previous segments.
5. Set the segment attributes to *detectable*.
6. Open the segment.
7. Tag the segment with a non-zero value.
8. Do the drawing inside the segment.

9. Close the segment.

You can do all of this at the time the window is created by using

```
case WM_CREATE:
  sz.cx = WinQuerySysValue(HWND_DESKTOP,
                     SV_CXFULLSCREEN);
  sz.cy = WinQuerySysValue(HWND_DESKTOP,
                     SV_CYFULLSCREEN);
  hDC = WinOpenWindowDC(hWnd);          /*get a window DC   */
  hPS = GpiCreatePS(hAB, hDC, &sz, PU_PELS | GPIA_ASSOC);
  GpiSetDrawingMode(hPS, DM_RETAIN); /*retain drawing     */
  GpiDeleteSegments(hPS, 1L, 2L);    /*delete prev. segs */
  segnum =1;                          /*1st nonzero segment*/
  GpiSetInitialSegmentAttrs(hPS,
                     ATTR_DETECTABLE,
                     ATTR_ON);
  GpiOpenSegment(hPS, segnum);         /*open the segment  */
  GpiSetTag(hPS, segnum++);            /*set a segment tag */
                                       /* to nonzero       */
  pt.x = 50; pt.y = 50;                /*lower box corner  */
  GpiMove(hPS, &pt);
  pt.x = 100; pt.y = 100;              /*upper box corner  */
  GpiBox(hPS, DRO_OUTLINE,&pt,
         NULL, NULL);
  GpiCloseSegment(hPS);                /*end of first segment*/
  GpiOpenSegment(hPS, segnum);         /*second segment    */
  GpiSetTag(hPS, segnum++);            /*tag with segment num*/
  pt.x = 150; pt.y = 150;              /*lower box corner  */
  GpiMove(hPS, &pt);
  pt.x = 200; pt.y = 200;              /*upper box corner  */
  GpiBox(hPS, DRO_OUTLINE, &pt,
                     NULL, NULL);
  pt.x = 175; pt.y = 50;               /*also draw a line  */
  GpiSetTag(hPS, 12L);                 /*with another tag value*/
  GpiMove(hPS, &pt);
  pt.x = 250; pt.y =175;               /*end of line       */
  GpiLine(hPS, &pt);
  GpiCloseSegment(hPS);                /*end of 2nd segment */
  break;
```

Then, since the segments are all chained together by default, drawing the screen amounts to a single call plus validating the region when you are done:

```
case WM_PAINT:
    WinQueryWindowRect(hWnd,
                &rc);      /*get current window dimensions*/
    WinFillRect(hPS, &rc,
                CLR_WHITE); /*fill it with white         */
    GpiDrawChain(hPS);      /*draw entire segment chain   */
    WinQueryUpdateRect(hWnd, &rc);
    WinValidateRect(hWnd, &rc,
                TRUE); /*validate entire region          */
    break;
```

Finally, you can simply intercept the **WM_BUTTON1DOWN** messages and see if a segment has been selected by using the correlate chain call

```
case WM_BUTTON1DOWN:            /*when button is pressed*/
    pt.x = SHORT1FROMMP(mp1);    /*get its coordinates   */
    pt.y = SHORT2FROMMP(mp1);
    hits = GpiCorrelateChain(hPS,  /*look for any hits    */
        PICKSEL_VISIBLE, &pt,
        2L, 1L, tags);
    if (hits > 0) then          /*if there are any hits  */
        begin                   /*say so in a message box*/
        sprintf(buf, "Hits = %d",hits);
        sprintf(hitbuf, "Segment = %ld %ld",
                tags[0], tags[1]);
        WinMessageBox(HWND_DESKTOP, hWnd,
                buf, hitbuf, 1, MB_OK);
    end
    break;
```

The Pick Aperture

Normally, the size of the region on the screen that is considered to be picked, called the *pick aperture*, is the size of a character box for that display type. You can make this aperture smaller or larger using the call

```
GpiSetPickApertureSize(hPS, options, &size);
```

where

options   can be either **PICKAP_DEFAULT**, in which case the size parameter is ignored, or **PICKPAP_REC**, where the size value is used.

& size   is the address of the size of the aperture in a SIZEL structure. The members of the structure are the long integers `size.cx` and `size.cy`.

You can also set the pick aperture position without waiting for a mouse click by using the call

```
GpiSetPickAperturePosition(hPS, &pick);
```

where **pick** is the address of a POINTL structure. Once you have set this aperture position yourself, you can actually do any drawing you want with the Gpi functions and examine their return codes. If any Gpi function returns the value **GPIT_HIT** then that drawing passed through the current pick aperture position.

EDITING SEGMENTS

Once you have created a complex graphics segment, you might find it useful to change some small attribute, such as the color or line type, and redraw it without having to reconstruct the entire segment. You can do this if you label the positions in the segment with unique values using the **GpiLabel** call when you create it. Then you can reopen the segent and position the element pointer at that label by making the calls

```
GpiSetElementPointerAtLabel(hPS,
                        label); /*find label and   */
GpiOffsetElementPointer(hPS, 1L);    /*increment pointer*/
```

The first call sets the element pointer to the position containing the label and the second increments to the point just beyond it.

Once you have located the labelled position in a segment, you can insert an element or replace the element at that position by simply making the new function call. Elements are either inserted or replaced depending on the state of the call

```
GpiSetEditMode(hPS, mode);
```

where **mode** can be either **SEGEM_INSERT** or **SEGEM_REPLACE**. The default value is insertion.

GRAPHICS TRANSFORMS

You can draw a segment once using the draw segment or draw chain calls, but it is useful in technical drawing to be able to draw several copies of the same picture when each represents a repeating element of a more complex drawing. OS/2 provides the ability to translate, scale and rotate any segment intwo dimensions by multiplying it by a *transform matrix*. While moving the segment on the screen is actually an addition process, the scaling and rotation operations are multiplication processes. In order that all of the operation be representable in a single matrix operation, the definition of each *x,y* data pair has been expanded to have a third coordinate, which is always 1. For linear translation of data the matrix is

$$[x'\, y'\, 1] = [x\ y\ 1] \begin{bmatrix} 1 & 0 & 0 \\ 0 & 1 & 0 \\ T_x & T_y & 1 \end{bmatrix}$$

for scaling, the multiplication matrix is

$$[x'\, y'\, 1] = [x\ y\ 1] \begin{bmatrix} S_x & 0 & 0 \\ 0 & S_y & 0 \\ 0 & 0 & 1 \end{bmatrix}$$

and for rotation, the matrix is

$$[x'\, y'\, 1] = [x\, y\, 1] \begin{bmatrix} \cos\theta & \sin\theta & 0 \\ -\sin\theta & \cos\theta & 0 \\ 0 & 0 & 1 \end{bmatrix}$$

In general, the equations for scaling, translation, and rotation are

$$x' = Ax + Cy + E$$

$$y' = Bx + Dy + F$$

where

$$[x'\,y'\,1] = [x\,y\,1] \begin{bmatrix} A & B & 0 \\ C & D & 0 \\ E & F & 1 \end{bmatrix}$$

To summarize, the translation values are represented by E and F, the scaling values by A and D, and the rotation values by A, B, C, and D. To make these operations as rapid as possible, they are all carried out in fixed point using a 32-bit representation in which 16 bits represent the integer part of the number and 16 bits the fractional part. Thus, 1.0 is represented as 0001 0000 or 65536L. The matrix has been defined as a 9-element structure of long integers called MATRIXLF and the default matrix with no operations performed can be represented as:

```
#define UNITY 65536L
MATRIXLF mat[] = {UNITY, 0, 0, 0, UNITY, 0, 0, 0, 1};
```

You can embed transform matrices within segments or you can call segments directly or from other segments using the call:

```
GpiCallSegmentMatrix(hPS, segnum, count, mat, options);
```

where

segnum   is the number of the *unchained* segment you want to transform and draw.

count   is the number of elements in the matrix (0-9) that are to be used. Default values are used for any unspecified elements.

mat   is the transform matrix.

options   can be TRANSFORM_PREEMPT if this transform supersedes the existing one on the segment, TRANSFORM_REPLACE if this transform should also replace that one on the segment, and TRANSFORM_ADD if this is in addition to the existing transform.

Drawing and Transforming a Segment

A segment which is to be called and transformed, must be *unchained*, and the default is chained. Therefore you must modify the attribute of any such segments after they are created. The code below draws a simple line in a segment:

```
GpiOpenSegment(hPS, segnum);  /*callable segment          */
GpiSetTag(hPS, segnum);       /*tag with a segment number */
pt.x = 200; pt.y = 200;       /*line origin               */
GpiMove(hPS, &pt);
pt.x = 400; pt.y = 100;       /*line end                  */
GpiLine(hPS, &pt);            /*draw it                   */
GpiCloseSegment(hPS);
GpiSetSegmentAttrs(hPS,
            segnum,           /*set to unchained          */
        ATTR_CHAINED,
          ATTR_OFF);
```

Then, you can draw the segment at PAINT time, once in its original position and once translated by (50, 50) by defining a suitable transform matrix:

```
#define UNITY 65536L

MATRIXLF mat[] = {UNITY, 0, 0, 0, UNITY, 0, 50, 50, 1};

GpiDrawSegment(hPS, segnum);                  /*draw original   */
GpiCallSegmentMatrix(hPS, segnum, 9,   /*draw transformed*/
            mat, TRANSFORM_REPLACE);
```

SUMMARY - USES OF SEGMENTS

The entire segment structure is intended primarily for technical computer-aided drafting and design (CAD-CAM), where a segment is used to build up a very complex structure from a series of elaborate floating point calculations. The point is that in most scientific cases the segment overhead is no less than if you were to calculate the drawing coordinates and pick positions yourself from your knowledge of screen coordinates and the scale of your data on the screen. Thus, if you have only a few drawings or plots and a few places where you might wish to intercept a mouse click, you may not find the segment method any more advantageous than calculating the intersection yourself.

18 Images and Bitmaps

Frequently, scientific data consist of a number of consecutive scans of a sample, either sweeping over it in successive lines or representing scans obtained during different sample perturbations. Examples include scanning electron microscopy (SEM), scanning tunnelling microscopy (STM), and two-dimensional nuclear magnetic resonance (2DNMR). Such scans can be combined to form a raster *image* that can be displayed on a PM screen. Bitmaps can also be used to represent icons and other drawings.

In PM, bitmaps can be 1, 4, 8, or 24 bits per pixel. In a 1-bit bitmap a pixel can only be "on" or "off," while the 4- and 8-bit bitmaps can have 16 or 256 shades or colors per pixel. The 24-bit bitmap assumes that each pixel has a 24-bit RGB value, where 8 bits are used by each of the three primary colors: red, green, and blue.

DISPLAYING AN IMAGE

To display an image in PM, we need to

1. Create a memory Device Context.
2. Create a memory Presentation Space.
3. Create a memory bitmap.
4. Associate the bitmap with the memory PS.
5. Create a color lookup table.
6. Determine the size of the image.

255

7. Read the file into memory a line at a time.
8. Set the bitmap from the file data.
9. Determine the screen area to display the image in.
10. Block transfer the bitmap to the screen area.

The Memory Device Context and Presentation Space

The memory device context is created using a DEVOPENSTRUC structure pointing to the DISPLAY.DLL device driver:

```
DEVOPENSTRUC dop;
hDCmem = DevOpenDC(hAB, OD_MEMORY, "*", 8L,
                   (PDEVOPENDATA)&dop, NULL);
```

Then, we create a *normal* presentation space in memory with a size equal to the maximum possible screen size:

```
sz.cx = WinQuerySysValue(HWND_DESKTOP, SV_CXFULLSCREEN);
sz.cy = WinQuerySysValue(HWND_DESKTOP, SV_CYFULLSCREEN);
hPSmem = GpiCreatePS(hAB, hDCmem, &sz,
        PU_PELS | GPIT_NORMAL | GPIA_ASSOC);
```

Creating a Bitmap

We can then create a bitmap using the **GpiCreateBitmap** call where we tell OS/2 the size of the bitmap and the number of bits per pixel, by putting this information in a bitmap info structure. The **pmgpi.h** file defines a bitmap info structure and a bitmap info header structure, which are identical except for the color lookup table at the end. However, for 8-bit bitmaps, it does not appear that storage for all 256 possible colors is correctly allocated. Therefore, we will create a structure with 256 RGB values already allocated:

```
typedef struct {    /*Bit map header structure definition*/
ULONG cbFix;        /*length of structure              */
USHORT cx, cy,      /*size of bitmap                   */
       cPlanes,     /*number of planes                 */
       cBitCount;   /*bits per pixel                   */
RGB rgb[256];       /*look-up table                    */
} BMAPHEADER;
```

The RGB structure we describe here is a 24-bit or 3-byte entry for each possible intensity, where there is an 8-bit entry for each red, green, and blue color. It is important that you compile this module with the /**Zp** C-compiler option, so that all structures are packed on 8-bit boundaries. Otherwise, the structure members will be aligned on word boundaries and won't be accessed correctly by PM. We initialize the header part of the structure and create the bitmap as follows:

```
/*----------------------------------------*/
/* Create space for a 100 x 100 bitmap */
/* with 8 bits per pixel               */
/*----------------------------------------*/
    binf.cbFix = 12;                  /*length of header    */
    binf.cx = 100;                    /*x size             */
    binf.cy = 100;                    /*y size             */
    binf.cPlanes = 1L;                /*only one plane      */
    binf.cBitCount = 8L;              /*8 bits per pixel    */
    hBmap = GpiCreateBitmap(hPSmem,
                       &binf,  /*create the bitmap   */
              OL, (PBYTE)NULL,
              (PBITMAPINFO)NULL);
    GpiSetBitmap(hPSmem, hBmap);      /*select the bitmap   */
                                      /*   into this PS     */
```

The remaining parameters of the **GpiCreateBitmap** call have to do with initializing special devices and loading the bitmap into device memory. For standard PM displays these are not used.

Initializing the Color Lookup Table

Our bitmap consists of 8-bit numbers from 0 to 255 representing intensities of some measurement, or colors of an image. We can tell PM to render these colors as any RGB value it can select by loading the color lookup table with an RGB value for each of the 256 intensities. In the simplest case we simply make these 256 shades of gray:

```
for (i=0; i<256; i++)
  begin
  binf.rgb[i].bBlue=(BYTE)i;
  binf.rgb[i].bRed=(BYTE)i;
  binf.rgb[i].bGreen=(BYTE)i;
  end
```

where the red, green, and blue values increase at the same rate from 0 to 255.

READING AN IMAGE FILE INTO A BITMAP

One common image file format contains no header information and has 8 bits per pixel of data. When data are in this format, we need to know the number of rows and columns in the file, since there is nothing in the file itself to tell us. In the example below, we read in a row of data at a time into a memory and use the call **GpiSetBitmapBits** to set the values in the actual bitmap. This call has the form

```
GpiSetBitmapBits(hPSmem, linenum, lines,
                 bptr, (PBITMAPINFO)&binf);
```

where

hPSmem   is the handle to the memory PS we created.

linenum   is the line number where we will begin the data transfer.

line   is the number of lines of data to transfer to the bitmap.

bptr   is a pointer to the buffer where those data lines are stored.

& binf   is the pointer to the bitmap info structure describing the bitmap format.

In this example, we read the entire bitmap into memory so we can also manipulate it later, but we only need to read in a line at a time as we are only changing a line after it is read in.

```
bptr = malloc(binf.cx * binf.cy);   /*allocate data space*/
fptr = fopen(pim->filename, "rb");  /*open the file       */
for (i=0; i<binf.cy; i++)            /*read a line at a time*/
    begin
    fread(bptr, binf.cx, 1, fptr);  /*read a line          */
    GpiSetBitmapBits(hPSmem, i, 1,  /*set the bitmap       */
        bptr, (PBITMAPINFO)&binf);
    bptr += binf.cx;                 /*advance the pointer*/
    end
fclose (fptr);                       /*close the file when done*/
```

PAINTING THE BITMAP ON THE SCREEN

Now that we have loaded the bitmap with values, we need only transfer it from the memory bitmap to the actual screen using a bit-block transfer or BitBlt function. The **GpiBitBlt** call also will scale the memory bitmap to a larger or smaller screen bitmap automatically. The call has the form:

```
GpiBitBlt(hPS, hPSmem, count, dims, rop, options);
```

where

hPS   is the destination bitmap, usually the screen.

hPSmem   is the source bitmap, usually a memory bitmap.

count   is the number of point pairs from the **dims** array to inter-
               pret. If it is 3, the destination rectangle is the same size
               as the source rectangle. If it is 4, stretching or com-
               pression is performed on the destination bitmap rec-
               tangle.

dims   is an array of 4 POINTL structures, in the order
               DestBottom, DestTop, SourceBottom, SourceTop, where
               the destination bottom left corner and upper right corner
               are specified in the first two structures and the source
               bottom left and upper right corners are specified in the
               second two structures. These define the sizes of the desti-
               nation and source rectangles.

rop is one of several logical raster operations that can be performed in mixing the source rectangle into the destination rectangle. The more common ones are **ROP_SRCCOPY,** **ROP_SRCINVERT,** **ROP_SRCPAINT,** and **ROP_SRCAND** which replace, XOR, OR, or AND the source with the destination bitmap.

options is **BBO_OR, BBO_AND,** or **BBO_IGNORE,** describing how to merge any eliminated columns if the destination is smaller than the source. For color bitmaps, **BBO_IGNORE** is the preferred method.

In the complete paint procedure, we get the current window size, set it into the **dims** array and bit-blit the bitmap onto the screen:

```
case WM_PAINT:
  WinQueryWindowRect(hWnd, &rc);   /*get window dimensions*/
  dims[0].x =    0;                /*destination dimensions*/
  dims[0].y =    0;
  dims[1].x = rc.xRight;
  dims[1].y = rc.yTop;
  dims[2].x =    0;                /*source dimensions      */
  dims[2].y =    0;
  dims[3].x = binf.cx;
  dims[3].y = binf.cy;
  GpiSetBitmap(hPSmem, hBmap);     /*select bitmap          */
  GpiBitBlt(hPS, hPSmem, 4, p,
        ROP_SRCCOPY, BBO_IGNORE);
  GpiSetBitmap(hPSmem, NULL);      /*deselect bitmap        */
  WinQueryUpdateRect(hWnd, &rc);
  WinValidateRect(hWnd, &rc,
                    TRUE); /*validate entire region*/
  break;
```

THE COLOR LOOKUP TABLE

While we can put any set of RGB values we like into the lookup table, the display and device driver may limit your choices to ones that it can actually produce on the screen. For example, on an EGA or VGA screen, there can only be 16 colors out of a possible 64 at a time, and these are selected by the device driver to be compatible with the historical PC's CGA colors. On the 8514 display (BGA) there are 256 colors selectable out of a possible 256,000 colors, but the selection has been made in the device driver and these colors cannot be changed since they would change the colors in other screen windows as well as the one you are currently working in. Instead, PM uses the closest existing color to the color you requested. This often results in many fewer colors than you may have requested.

Realizing a New Lookup Table

The Gpi calls allow you to create and load new logical color tables, using RGB values to describe the colors you wish to use. However, in OS/2 1.1 none of the display device drivers yet support these calls because of the possible conflict between colors when multiple windows are on the screen. The calls are as follows:

```
GpiCreateLogColorTable(hPS, options, format, start,
                                          count, table);
```

```
GpiRealizeColorTable(hPS);
```

where

hPS   is the presentation space handle.

options   is **LCOL_RESET,   LCOL_REALIZABLE,**   or **LCOL_PURECOLOR,** to reset to the standard color table, realize the current one, and prevent color *dithering* for colors that are not available.

format   is **LCOLF_INDRGB,   LCOLF_CONSECRGB,**   or **LCOLF_RGB.** The first format is a long index value followed by a 32-bit RGB value, the second is a list of 32-bit RGB values, and the third is an array of 24-bit RGB values.

start   is the index of the first value to be replaced.

count   is the length of the table.

table   is the RGB color lookup table in one of the formats described above. If **LCOLF_RGB** is selected, the entire table must be replaced.

The create call loads the table into that presentation space and the realize call loads the table into the devices hardware lookup table.

CHANGING LOOKUP TABLES

If you attempt to display an image on an EGA or VGA display as a series of grayscale tones, you will find that only four shades are displayed: black, dark gray, light gray and white, even though you specified 256 different gray levels in your RGB lookup table. This is clearly unsatisfactory and you must therefore change the lookup table to use more colors to distinguish the various intensity levels in your image. Since we know which RGB levels are actually used in the display, it is fairly simple to construct a new lookup table and reload the bitmap. In the example below, we create an 8-color lookup table:

```
/*---------------------------------------------------------*/
/* reload the color lookup table with 8 primary colors */
/*---------------------------------------------------------*/
void colorlut(UCHAR *image, int *bins, BMAPHEADER *binf,
              HPS hPSmem, HBITMAP hBmap)
begin
        long i;
        UCHAR lut[256], *bptr;
        int err;

 GpiSetBitmap(hPSmem, hBmap);             /*select bitmap*/
 for (i=0; i<32; i++)                     /*black*/
    binf->rgb[i].bBlue=   0;
    binf->rgb[i].bRed=    0;
    binf->rgb[i].bGreen=  0;
 for (i=32; i<64; i++)                    /*blue*/
    binf->rgb[i].bBlue=   0xff;
    binf->rgb[i].bRed=    0;
```

```
      binf->rgb[i].bGreen=  0;
   for (i=64; i<96; i++)                       /*green*/
      binf->rgb[i].bBlue=   0;
      binf->rgb[i].bRed=    0;
      binf->rgb[i].bGreen=  0xff;
   for (i=96; i<128; i++)                      /*cyan*/
      binf->rgb[i].bBlue=   0xff;
      binf->rgb[i].bRed=    0;
      binf->rgb[i].bGreen=  0xff;
   for (i=128; i<160; i++)                     /*red*/
      binf->rgb[i].bBlue=   0;
      binf->rgb[i].bRed=    0xff;
      binf->rgb[i].bGreen=  0;
   for (i=160; i<192; i++)                     /*magenta*/
      binf->rgb[i].bBlue=   0xff;
      binf->rgb[i].bRed=    0xff;
      binf->rgb[i].bGreen=  0;
   for (i=192; i<224; i++)                     /*yellow*/
      binf->rgb[i].bBlue=   0;
      binf->rgb[i].bRed=    0xff;
      binf->rgb[i].bGreen=  0xff;
   for (i=224; i<256; i++)                     /*white*/
      binf->rgb[i].bBlue=   0xff;
      binf->rgb[i].bRed=    0xff;
      binf->rgb[i].bGreen=  0xff;

 bptr = image;                    /*pointer to start of image*/
 for (i=0; i < binf->cy; i++)       /*read a line at a time*/
    begin
    err=GpiSetBitmapBits(hPSmem,   /*set the bitmap        */
                    i, 1,
                    bptr,
                    (PBITMAPINFO)binf);
    bptr += binf->cx;                /*advance the pointer  */
    end

 end
```

PLOTTING AN INTENSITY HISTOGRAM

It is often instructive to view a histogram of the intensities in an 8-bit image, so that you can decide how contrast might best be enhanced. It is obviously not difficult to make a 256-word array and count the number of pixels that have each of these 256 values:

```
kmax = cx * cy;                /*total image size          */
for (i=0; i<256; i++)          /*zero out the array        */
   begin
   bins[i] = 0;
   end
for (k =0; k< kmax; k++)       /*for each byte             */
   begin
   bins[image[k]]++;           /*increment that intensity bin*/
   end
```

Then, you can open a child window and plot these intensities as a series of vertical lines at each of 256 horizontal positions:

```
WinFillRect(hPS, &rc,CLR_BLACK);    /*fill it with black     */
GpiSetColor(hPS, CLR_WHITE);        /*set color to white     */
bin = (int *)WinQueryWindowULong(hWnd, 0);
max = 0;
for (i=0; i<256; i++)
   begin
   if (bin[i] > max) then            /*find maximum count    */
      max = bin[i];
   end
scale = (float)rc.yTop / (float)max; /*get scaling factor*/
for (i=0; i<256; i++)
   begin
   pt.x = i; pt.y = 0;     /*draw each line from the bottom*/
   GpiMove(hPS, &pt);
   pt.y = (int)((float)bin[i]*scale);
   GpiLine(hPS,&pt);                /*to its intensity value*/
   end
```

An image and a window containing the histogram are shown in Figure 18-1.

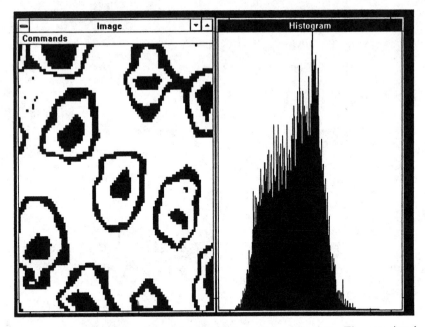

Figure 18-1. An image from scanning tunnelling microscope data. The associated histogram is shown on the right.

HISTOGRAM EQUALIZATION

Once you have examined the histogram of intensities, it often improves the image significantly to spread out the counts over the entire range of intensities, so that the number of counts in each of the intensity bins is more or less equal. This process is known as *histogram equalization*, and the result is that the fraction of pixels below any given grayscale value is roughly equal to the fraction of grayscale below this value. In this procedure, the lookup table remains the same, but once the histogram is calculated, the *image* is changed, byte by byte, so that each new value corresponds to a position in a uniformly distributed histogram.

```
/*------------------------------------------------------------*/
/* Histogram equalization routine                             */
/*------------------------------------------------------------*/
void equalize(UCHAR *image, int *bins, BMAPHEADER *binf,
              HPS hPSmem, HBITMAP hBmap)
begin
        long i;
```

```
        long sum, total;
        UCHAR lut[256], *bptr;
        int err;

total = 0;                              /*initialize running sums*/
sum=0;
GpiSetBitmap(hPSmem, hBmap);        /*select bitmap           */
for (i=0; i<256; i++)
    begin
    total += bins[i];               /*calc total sum of intens*/
    end
for (i=0; i<256; i++)
    begin
    sum += bins[i];                 /*calculate running sum   */
                                    /*set lookup table value  */
    lut[i] = (UCHAR)(256.0*(float)sum/(float)total);
    end

for (i=0; i< binf->cx * binf->cy; i++)
    image[i] = lut[image[i]];       /*set new intensities     */
                                    /* from lookup table      */
bptr = image;
for (i=0; i < binf->cy; i++)        /*read a line at a time   */
    begin
    GpiSetBitmapBits(hPSmem, i, /*set the bitmap             */
                    1, bptr,
                    (PBITMAPINFO)binf);
    bptr += binf->cx;               /*advance the pointer     */
    end
end
```

The equalized image and its histogram are shown in Figure 18-2.

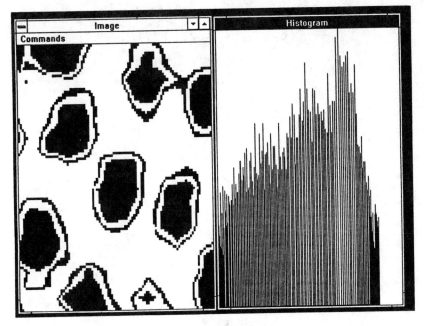

Figure 18-2. The same image as shown in Figure 18-1 after histogram equalization.

19 Multitasking in OS/2

In Chapter 3, we looked at a simple program that started two *threads* of execution that ran simultaneously. We now will look at these features in more detail as used in Presentation Manager programs.

THE MESSAGE QUEUE AND TASKS

One of the standard rules you should follow in PM programming is the *0.1-second rule*: no message should cause processing that lasts longer than about 0.1 second. The reason for this is that such programs will not respond to user commands during that processing period and the program will seem to be locked up. In fact, not only that program, but all windowed programs will be locked up during that processing time. If OS/2 is a multitasking system why is this so? This is not a consequence of the multitasking design, but of the messaging system that windows use to process commands. Each program has a *message queue* associated with its main window. Recall that the main loop of the main routine of any PM program has the form:

```
while ( WinGetMsg( hAB, (PQMSG)&qmsg, (HWND)NULL, 0,0) )
    begin
    WinDispatchMsg(hAB, (PQMSG)&qmsg);
    end
```

Because of this structure, no new messages can be processed until the previous one has been processed and returns from the dispatch message call. In addition, input messages from the keyboard and mouse are *serialized*. This means that keyboard and mouse messages must be processed in the order they are received or their results could be meaningless. Therefore, if a message is received that causes a 30-second computation, no more messages will be processed until the program returns from that message. If you try to switch to a window of some other program, it will not respond either: first because the orginal program can't lose the input focus without receiving a deactivate message and second because input from the user is serialized and no other window can receive messages until the end of the message processing taking place.

This can make a poorly designed program very sluggish and can make all the running programs equally sluggish if your program disobeys this 0.1-second rule. Obviously, however, there must be ways of carrying on long computations without locking up the system, and these are multi-thread programming techniques. There are several possible scenarios where a long calculation is processed in an OS/2 PM environment.

1. A thread carries out a computation and returns a result.

2. A thread prepares a data table to be displayed rapidly when the calculation is completed.

3. A thread performs a slow drawing task in the main window.

4. A thread draws into a separate window.

5. A thread starts an entirely separate program.

Each of these is possible in OS/2 PM and each is handled slightly differently.

THE MULTITHREAD LIBRARY

The IBM C/2 and Microsoft C compilers provide a special version of the C function library LLIBCMT.LIB, which contains the C functions in *reentrant* form. This allows several C threads to be making calls to the same function at the same time without any conflict. Because the reentrant functions must be called using the Pascal calling convention, the include files (.h files) for the reentrant libraries have different declarations. For example, the definition of the **cos** function in the standard library include files is

```
double _CDECL cos(double);
```

while in the multi-thread libraries it is:

```
double far pascal cos(double);
```

To make sure that the correct calling convention is generated when the functions are called, you must be sure to use the multithread include files in the INCLUDE\MT subdirectory. You can cause this to occur by specifically changing the **#include** declarations in your program to

```
#include <mt\math.h>
```

or you can change the environment variable INCLUDE that is set in the CONFIG.SYS file or startup file to

```
SET INCLUDE=c:INCLUDE\MT;c:\INCLUDE;,
```

Since nearly all significant OS/2 programs will in fact have multiple threads, it is probably better to change the environment SET statement as shown above. This is what we have assumed throughout this text.

PROPERTIES OF WINDOWS IN THREADS

You can create a window in a thread, but that thread must then have its own message queue. If you create a thread that only performs computations and does no displaying, no message queue is necessary. Only the thread that creates a window can receive input for that window. A thread can draw into a window created by another window, however, but such a thread must have its own anchor block. Finally, a thread can *post* messages to a window in another thread, but cannot *send* messages to another thread.

USING A SEPARATE THREAD TO DRAW IN THE MAIN WINDOW

In this example, THREAD1, we will create a 4096-point array of random numbers and draw lines between all of them on the screen. On most machines this will take 4-5 seconds: much longer than the recommended 0.1 to 0.5 seconds. We create the array as a global array for simplicity at the same time we create the main window:

```
#include <process.h>    /*where the thread definitions are*/

/*register the Window class*/
WinRegisterClass (hAB,          /*handle to anchor block    */
     "Mainthread",              /*name of window class      */
     HelloWndProc,              /*address of window procedure*/
     CS_SIZEREDRAW |
     CS_SYNCPAINT,              /*use these flags           */
     0 ) ;                      /*number of "extra bytes    */

for (i=0; i<XDIM; i++)     /*generate the array to display*/
   x[i] = (int)((float)rand()*200/32768.0);

flCreate =
    FCF_TITLEBAR | FCF_MINMAX |FCF_SYSMENU |
    FCF_MENU | FCF_SIZEBORDER | FCF_BORDER |
    FCF_SHELLPOSITION | FCF_ICON;

/*create the window */
hFrame =
   WinCreateStdWindow(
        HWND_DESKTOP,           /*child of the desktop window*/
        WS_VISIBLE | FS_ICON,
        &flCreate,              /*control data bits         */
        "Mainthread",           /*this name refers to class */
        "Hello World",          /*title across top bar      */
        WS_VISIBLE,             /*main window visible       */
        NULL,                   /*menu is in resource file  */
        HELLOICON,              /*frame window id-you pick  */
        &hWnd);                 /*client area handle        */
```

The Main Window Procedure

The main window procedure is much like that of previous simple program examples, except that the command DRAWIT is used to create a stack for the thread and start it. A minimum stack size for a new thread is 2000 bytes: threads which use a lot of array space will require larger stacks, since local variable space as well as intermediate computation storage is allocated from that stack. Note that the argument we pass to the thread is the main window handle.

```
MRESULT FAR PASCAL HelloWndProc(HWND hWnd, USHORT msg,
                            MPARAM mp1, MPARAM mp2)
begin
  HPS     hPS;              /*handle to presentation space  */
  RECTL   rc;              /*rectangle definition structure*/
  char *stack;            /*pointer to stack space        */

  switch (msg)            /*interpret messages            */
  begin

  case WM_COMMAND:         /*interpret commands            */
      switch(LOUSHORT(mp1))
          begin
          case DRAWIT:       /*call thread to draw in window*/
              stack = malloc(2000);       /*get stack space   */
              _beginthread(Drawthread,
                      stack, 2000, hWnd); /*start the thread*/
              break;

          default:                        /*else do nothing   */
              return(WinDefWindowProc(hWnd, msg, mp1, mp2));
          end
      WinInvalidateRect(hWnd, NULL, FALSE); /*force repaint   */
      break;

  case WM_PAINT:
      hPS = WinBeginPaint(hWnd,
                      (HPS)NULL, (PWRECT)NULL);
      /*get current window dimensions                      */
      WinQueryWindowRect(hWnd, &rc);
```

```
    WinFillRect(hPS, &rc,CLR_BLACK); /*fill it with black */
    WinEndPaint(hPS);                /*end painting routine*/
    break;

default:                            /*pass on other messages*/
    return( WinDefWindowProc( hWnd, msg, mp1, mp2));;
    break;
end /*switch*/

return(OL);
end
```

The Drawing Thread

In the drawing thread, we will get a presentation space and draw into it. The most important single thing a drawing thread must do is allocate its own anchor block: a thread without one will fail miserably. As before, we calculate the window size so we can scale the drawing appropriately and then begin the drawing process. When the drawing is completed, the PS is released, the anchor block terminated, and the thread ends on exiting the function.

```
void Drawthread(HWND hWndParent)
/* independent thread for drawing the x array into    */
/* the specifed window*/                              */
begin
    long xpos, xinc;
    HPS hPS;                /*local presentation space     */
    RECTL rc;               /*rectangle for window size     */
    POINTL pt;              /*location for each move and draw*/
    int i,err;
    HAB hABtask;            /*local anchor block            */

hBABtask =
    WinInitialize (NULL);       /*init and get anchor handle*/
hPS = WinGetPS(hWndParent);     /*get a cache micro PS      */
GpiSetColor(hPS, CLR_BLUE);     /*set line color to blue    */
/*get current window dimensions                            */
WinQueryWindowRect(hWndParent, &rc);
```

```
xpos = OL;
xinc =                           /*compute x increment      */
   (long)((float)(rc.xRight * 65536L)) / (float) XDIM;
pt.x = 0;
pt.y = x[0];
GpiMove(hPS, &pt);               /*move to first point      */
xpos += xinc;                    /*increment x              */
for (i = 1; i < XDIM; i++)       /*draw remaining points    */
   begin
      pt.x = (int)(xpos >> 16);  /*calculate new x position */
      pt.y = x[i];               /*get new y posn from array*/
      GpiLine(hPS, &pt);         /*draw next line           */
      xpos += xinc;              /*increment x              */
   end
WinReleasePS(hPS);               /*release cached PS        */
WinTerminate(hABtask);           /*end this thread          */
end
```

COMPUTING A DISPLAY BUFFER IN A SECOND THREAD

Another common use for a second thread in producing a display is to calculate the contents of a display buffer that can be displayed rapidly with a **GpiPolyLine** call in the main thread. While the calculation is taking place, the main thread remains active to mouse and keyboard messages and can process other menu items, but the main display will appear after a short calculation interval.

In the example below, we create a window and as soon as its size is known it creates a thread to fill up a display buffer. As soon as the buffer is filled, the thread posts a DRAWREADY message to the main thread and then terminates. As before, for simplicity we will keep both the original x data as a global array and the buffer of POINTL variables and **bufmax** as well.

When our main window first starts up, it will receive a WM_PAINT message. However, our buffer will not be ready yet, so we initialize the first location of the display buffer to 10000 and skip any calls to the **GpiPolyLine** function until the buffer has been filled. When the DRAWREADY message is received, it invalidates the entire window, forcing a new **WM_PAINT** message, which will this time display the data.

```
/* main window procedure for THREAD2 -            */
/* buffer is filled in second thread              */
MRESULT FAR PASCAL MainWndProc(HWND hWnd, USHORT msg,
                              MPARAM mp1, MPARAM mp2)


begin
  HPS      hPS;           /*handle to presentation space  */
  RECTL    rc;            /*rectangle definition structure*/
  char *stack;            /*pointer to stack space        */


switch (msg)                        /*interpret messages       */
begin

 case WM_SIZE:
   /*get current window dimensions                        */
   WinQueryWindowRect(hWnd, &rc);
   buffer[0].x = 10000L;      /*use as flag for completion*/
   stack = malloc(2000);      /*get stack space           */
   _beginthread(Fillthread,  /*start drawing thread       */
           stack, 2000, hWnd);
   break;

 case DRAWREADY:
   WinInvalidateRect(hWnd,
           NULL, TRUE);     /*force paint message          */
   break;

 case WM_PAINT:
   hPS = WinBeginPaint(hWnd, (HPS)NULL, (PWRECT)NULL);
   /*get current window dimensions                        */
   WinQueryWindowRect(hWnd, &rc);
   WinFillRect(hPS, &rc, CLR_BLACK);/*fill it with black*/
   GpiSetColor(hPS, CLR_WHITE);       /*draw white lines  */
   if (buffer[0].x != 10000L) then  /*only if the buffer*/
                                    /*is now filled     */
       GpiPolyLine(hPS, bufmax, buffer);
   WinEndPaint(hPS);                /*end painting routine*/
   break;
```

```
default:                          /*pass on other messages*/
    return( WinDefWindowProc( hWnd, msg,
                              mp1, mp2));

    break;
end /*switch*/

return(0L);
end
```

Our second thread procedure **Fillthread** now needs no message queue or anchor block, because it is processing no messages or doing any drawing. After it has filled the buffer, it posts a message to the main window procedure in the first thread, which causes the screen to be painted:

```
/*---------------------------------------------------------*/
/* independent thread for drawing the x array into the     */
/* specifed window                                         */
/*---------------------------------------------------------*/
void Fillthread(HWND hWnd)
begin
    long xpos, xinc;
    int err, i, j, min, max, oldmin, oldmax, xp;
    float leftpnt, rightpnt, pts_per_bin;
    RECTL rc;
    BOOL up;

/*get current window dimensions                    */
WinQueryWindowRect(hWnd, &rc);
pts_per_bin = (float)XDIM/(float)rc.xRight;
j = 0;
/*   fill the buffer with mins and maxes           */
leftpnt = 0.0;
oldmin = 0;                       /*initialize maxes and mins*/
oldmax = 0;
up = TRUE;                        /*and up flag              */
xp =0;
rightpnt = pts_per_bin;           /*size of one bin          */
while(rightpnt < XDIM)
    begin
    min = 10000;
```

```
    max = -10000;              /*find max and min in each group */
    for (i = (int)leftpnt; i < (int)rightpnt; i++)
      begin
      if (max < x[i]) then max = x[i]; /*look for new max  */
      if (min > x[i]) then min = x[i]; /*and new min       */
      end
    if (min > oldmax) then
          min = oldmax; /*check for overlap with last line*/
    if (max < oldmin) then
          max = oldmin;
    oldmax = max;
    oldmin = min;              /*save for next pass          */
    if (up) then
      begin
      buffer[j].x = xp;
      buffer[j++].y = min;     /*put min and max in buffer  */
      buffer[j].x = xp++;
      buffer[j++].y = max;
      up = FALSE;              /*next one will draw down     */
      end
    else
      begin
      buffer[j].x = xp;
      buffer[j++].y = max;     /*put min and max in buffer  */
      buffer[j].x = xp++;
      buffer[j++].y = min;
      up = TRUE;               /*next one will draw up        */
      end
    leftpnt += pts_per_bin;    /*go on to next grp of points*/
    rightpnt += pts_per_bin;
    end
  bufmax = j - 1;              /*remember how big the buffer is */
  err=                         /*tell other thread ready to draw*/
    WinPostMsg(hWnd, DRAWREADY, OL, OL);
end
```

CREATING A WINDOW IN A SECOND THREAD

Another possibility at first might seem to be the creation of a complete
window for drawing in another thread. It is perfectly possible to create such

a window, but again, it too must obey the 0.1-second rule and not take long periods of time to process messages.

If you create a window in another thread, it must have both its own message queue and anchor block. In the example below, the following code is executed when the second thread is started to create the second window:

```
void Drawthread(HWND hWndParent)
/* opens a window in this thread */
begin
     QMSG qmsg;                    /*defining a message queue*/
     HAB hABtask;
     HMQ hmqChild;
     ULONG flCreate;              /*window create flag bits */
     HWND hFrame, hWnd;

/*init and get anchor handle                              */
hABtask = WinInitialize (NULL);
hmqChild =
  WinCreateMsgQueue(hABtask, 0); /*create msg queue       */
flCreate = FCF_TITLEBAR | FCF_MINMAX |FCF_SYSMENU |
           FCF_SIZEBORDER | FCF_BORDER |FCF_SHELLPOSITION ;
/*create the window */
hFrame = WinCreateStdWindow(
           hWndParent,           /*as child of calling window*/
           NULL,                 /*not yet visible           */
           &flCreate,            /*control data bits         */
           "Child",              /*this name refers to class */
           "Child Window",       /*title across top bar      */
           WS_VISIBLE,           /*child window visible      */
           NULL,                 /*no menu                   */
           2,                    /*frame window id-you pick  */
           &hWnd);               /*client area handle        */

/*now show the window 100 x 100                            */
WinSetWindowPos(hFrame, HWND_TOP,
                100, 100, 100, 100,
                SWP_SIZE | SWP_MOVE|
                SWP_SHOW | SWP_ACTIVATE);

while ( WinGetMsg( hABtask, &qmsg, (HWND)NULL, 0, 0) )
   begin
```

```
WinDispatchMsg(hABtask, &qmsg);
end

/*once the program is over,                         */
/* destroy the window and message queue             */
WinDestroyWindow(hFrame);           /*destroy the window     */
WinDestroyMsgQueue(hmqChild);       /*and the message queue*/
WinTerminate (hABtask);             /* and the anchor block*/
end
```

STARTING A SEPARATE PROCESS

You can also start up completely separate programs from your program. Each is termed a "child process" but executes independently from your program and can continue even if your program terminates. You start separate programs using the **DosExecPgm** call

```
err = DosExecPgm(objname, objlen, flags,
                 argptr, envptr, &rcode, progname);
```

where

objname   is a string where the name of the object that caused the
                     failure of this call is returned.

objlen   is the length of this buffer.

flags   contains information regarding how the program is to be
                     executed:

    0   Program executes synchronously.

    1   Program executes asynchronously and its result
code is discarded.

    2   Program executes asynchronously and its result
code is stored in the first word of the **rcode** structure.

    3   Like value 2, except the program executes under
conditions for debugging.

4   The program executes in the background as a detached process. It should not require any input or output.

5   The program is loaded but not executed until the session manager starts the threads belonging to the process.

6   The program and its descendants execute under conditions for debugging.

argptr   is a pointer to block of argument strings passed to the program. These are discussed below.

envptr   is a pointer to a block of text strings like the SET environment variable strings.

rcode   is a pointer to a RESULTCODES structure shown below.

progname   is the name of the file to be executed. This name must include the extension and may include a path name.

err   is zero if no error occurred.

The RESULTCODES structure has the form

```
typedef struct _RESULTCODES {
    USHORT codeTerminate; /*Termination Code or Process ID*/
    USHORT codeResult;    /* Exit Code                    */
} RESULTCODES;
```

The Argument String

The convention in both DOS and OS/2 is that the string **argptr** passed to this function contains as its first component the program name, then a null byte, then the arguments, and then two null bytes. Thus, if you wanted to execute the command

        c:\adc\acquire.exe data.txt

you would create a name string as follows:

```
char name[80], *s, objbuf[80];
RESULTCODE rcode;

strcpy(name, path);              /*contains "c:\adc\"    */
strcat(name, "Acquire.exe"):     /*add the program name   */
s = name + strlen(name) +1;      /*point beyond null byte */
strcpy(s, "data.txt");           /*add argument string    */

DosExecPgm(objbuf, 80, 1, name,
           NULL, &rcode, name); /*asychronous start      */
```

Once you have another program running, you can communicate with it through semaphores, pipes, queues, or shared memory as described in the following chapter.

20 | Communicating between OS/2 Processes and Threads

Since OS/2 is a multitasking system, it is often necessary to have one process or thread wait until a task being performed by another thread has completed. There are three ways of communicating between processes and threads: semaphores, pipes, and queues. In addition, as we have seen earlier, timers can be used to trigger processing after a specified interval.

SEMAPHORES

A semaphore is a flag that can be either 1 or 0 and can be tested and set by one or more entities. There are two kinds of semaphores: *system semaphores* and *RAM semaphores*. System semaphores have names like filenames and maintain a *use count* so they can be accessed by recursive routines. RAM semaphores are just double words of storage within a program that have no ownership or use count and cannot be accessed recursively. A special *fast-safe* RAM semaphore structure can also be created so that ownership can be tracked.

SYSTEM SEMAPHORES

A system semaphore is a named resource like a file, and always has the "subdirectory" \SEM\. You create a system semaphore with

```
DosCreateSem(noexcl, &hSem, name);
```

where

noexcl   is a flag indicating whether the creating process wants
                     exclusive ownership of the semaphore. If it is 0 the cre-
                     ating process has exclusive ownership, and if it is 1 then
                     other processes can modify it.

& hSem   is the address where the handle to the semaphore is
                     returned.

name   is the semaphore's name. It must have the prefix or
                     "subdirectory" of \SEM\.

Once you have created a semaphore, you can use the following calls to
clear, set, and test it:

```
DosSemClear(hSem);          /* clear a semaphore         */
DosSemSet(hSem);            /* set a semaphore           */
DosSemWait(hSem, timeout);  /* block thread
                            /* until semaphore clears    */
DosSemSetWait(hSem, timeout); /* block thread until sem  */
                            /* clears, then set it       */
DosSemRequest(hSem, timeout); /* block thread until      */
                            /* ownership available       */
DosMuxSemWait(&index,
           list, timeout);  /* block until one of sems   */
                            /* in list clears            */
```

In all cases **timeout** is the number of milliseconds to wait. If it is -1, the wait
is indefinite.

Semaphore Ownership

A semaphore is *owned* by the thread that sets it. If the semaphore is created
as exclusive (**noexcl** flag set to 0) then no other *process* can set or clear it.
Thus, the **DosSemRequest** blocks the current thread until it can *set* a
semaphore or, in other words, until it has been *cleared* by another thread. By
contrast, the **DosSemSetWait** call does *not* establish semaphore ownership,
since it waits *until* the semaphore can be set, but does not set it.

The following example creates a semaphore, sets it, and waits for it to be cleared by a second thread. The second thread simply issues a **DosSleep** for 2 seconds and then clears the semaphore. Note that the system semaphore name string includes double backslashes, since backslashes themselves indicate that a special character follows in C strings.

```
/*Simple program to set and wait for a semaphore to clear*/
void main()
begin
     unsigned char  *stack;
     HSEM hSem ;

DosCreateSem(1, &hSem,
          "\\SEM\\TIMER.TIM");   /*create a system semaphore*/
DosSemSet(hSem);              /*set the semaphore high    */

/*Create a semaphore clearing thread */
stack = malloc(2000);         /*get stack space           */
_beginthread(SemClr, stack,
          2000, &hSem) ;      /*pass address of semaphore*/
DosSemRequest(hSem, -1L);     /*block thread              */
                              /*until we can set sem      */
printf("Exiting \n");         /*exit message              */
DosExit(1, 0);                /*end all threads           */
end
/*-----------------------------------------------------*/
/* waits 2 seconds and clears sem                       */
/*-----------------------------------------------------*/
void SemClr( HSEM *hSem)
begin
DosSleep(2000L);              /*wait 2 seconds            */
DosSemClear(*hSem);           /*and clear the semaphore   */
end
```

Sharing Semaphores between Processes

If you want to access a system semaphore in a totally separate program or process, you will have to open the semaphore and obtain its handle using the **DosOpenSem** call

```
DosOpenSem(&hSem, name); /*open existing system semaphore*/
```

This gives you the handle of that semaphore if **hSem** is not null on return, but does not establish semaphore ownership. Once you have the handle all of the above calls are valid.

RAM SEMAPHORES

A RAM semaphore is simply a double-word of storage. You can simply address the word as a global variable, and you can use the above calls to operate on it. While it is possible for another process to get access to the address of a RAM semaphore, you should not use RAM semaphores between processes, but only between threads of the same process. Since a RAM semaphore is just a word in your program's memory, there is no possibility of tracking semaphore ownership, and your program must use it as a local flag with whatever meaning it wants to define for it. Note, however, that you can use the DosSem functions to clear, set, and wait for a RAM semaphore to clear. The only changes we need to make in the above program are the use of the *address* of the RAM semaphore instead of the handle of a system semaphore:

```
ULONG ramsem;                    /*RAM semaphore             */
/*-------------------------------------------------------------*/
void main()
begin
    unsigned char  *stack;
    HSEM hSem ;

ramsem = 0;                      /*initialize RAM semaphore*/
DosSemSet(&ramsem);              /*set the semaphore high  */

/*Create a semaphore clearing thread */
stack = malloc(2000);            /*get stack space         */
_beginthread(SemClr, stack,
             2000, &ramsem); /*pass address of semaphore*/
DosSemRequest(&ramsem, -1L);  /*block thread            */
                                 /*until we can set sem    */
printf("Exiting \n");            /*exit message            */
DosExit(1, 0);                   /*end all threads         */
```

```
end
/*-----------------------------------------------------------*/
/* waits 2 seconds and clears sem                          */
/*-----------------------------------------------------------*/
void SemClr( HSEM *hSem)
begin
DosSleep(2000L);                    /*wait 2 seconds          */
DosSemClear(hSem);                   /*and clear the semaphore */
end
```

RAM semaphores provide a small performance advantage since the program operates directly on the *address* of the semaphore rather than a handle which must be resolved into an address.

Fast-Safe RAM Semaphores

A Fast-Safe RAM semaphore is a compromise between the system semaphore, where ownership is tracked and the standard RAM semaphore where it is not. The FS RAM semaphore is a 14-byte structure of type DOSFSRSEM which contains fields for ownership. It also includes a count field, so that it can be accessed recursively. It can be accessed by threads of different processes, but it is located in the memory of one of those processes. Thus, the only way that this can be accomplished is if the FS RAM semaphore structure is placed in a shared memory segment. Shared memory is discussed later in this chapter. FS RAM semaphores have only two allowed calls:

```
DosFSRamSemClear(&fsram);    /*clear an FS RAM semaphore*/

DosFSRamSemRequest(&fsram,
                timeout);    /*request ownership of FS RAM */
```

where the structure of the **fsram** semaphore is DOSFSRSEM:

```
typedef struct _DOSFSRSEM {
    USHORT cb;              /* length of this structure        */
    PID    pid;            /*Process ID of the owner or zero*/
    TID    tid;            /* Thread ID of the owner or zero*/
    USHORT cUsage;         /* Reference count                 */
    USHORT client;         /* 16 bit field for use by owner */
```

```
    ULONG  sem;          /* OS/2 Ram Semaphore              */
} DOSFSRSEM;
```

Purposes of Various Semaphores

RAM semaphores are designed primarily for signalling one process that another has completed some task, while system semaphores are designed for resource control: to indicate that some resource is now available. When a semaphore is used for signalling, the semaphore is never owned, and any thread can clear or set it at will. If two processes control access to a resource, such as an interface card, using system semaphores, then if one process terminates, the other *will* be able to access the semaphore and gain access to the resource. This is not true of FS RAM semaphores, where termination of one process could leave the other hanging indefinitely waiting for the semaphore to clear.

COMMUNICATING WITH PIPES

OS/2 allows you to pass data between threads using both unnamed and named pipes. An unnamed pipe is like a file that can be written into by one thread and read back by another thread. Unnamed pipes can only be used within one process as a substitute for intermediate file I/O, but named pipes can be used between processes. Pipes are limited in size to 64K bytes, although they are frequently as small as a single line of characters.

Unnamed Pipes

Unnamed pipes are used primarily for sending file information between threads without actually writing to disk. You create an unnamed pipe using the call

```
/*create an unnamed pipe                                   */
DosMakePipe(&hRead, &hWrite, MAXLEN);
```

where **hRead** and **hWrite** are the returned read and write handles and **MAXLEN** is the size of the pipe. Then, you write into the pipe using **DosWrite** and read from it using **DosRead**. You can also use the asynchro-

nous read and write commands that do not wait until data are available. The
following simple program illustrates the use of unnamed pipes:

```
void main()
begin
  unsigned char  *stack, buf[MAXLEN];
  HFILE hRead, hWrite;
  int read;

DosMakePipe(&hRead, &hWrite,
            MAXLEN);              /*create an unnamed pipe*/
stack = malloc(2000);            /*get stack space        */
_beginthread(PipeWrite, stack,
            2000, hWrite); /*pass address of write hnd*/
DosRead(hRead, buf,
            MAXLEN, &read);      /*wait for read          */
printf("%s", buf);               /*print out text read    */
DosClose(hRead);                 /*close the pipe         */
DosExit(1, 0);                   /*end all threads        */
end
/*-----------------------------------------------------*/
/* writes text into a pipe and returns                 */
/*-----------------------------------------------------*/
void PipeWrite( HFILE hWrite)
begin
  int written;
  char buf[MAXLEN];
strcpy(buf, "Writing to a Pipe\n");    /*message to write*/
DosWrite(hWrite, buf,
            strlen(buf), &written);   /*write to pipe   */
DosClose(hWrite)                       /*close pipe      */
end                                    /*and end thread  */
```

Named Pipes

Named pipes are designed for more sophisticated communication between processes, although they can be used within threads as well. A named pipe must be created using **DosMakeNmPipe** having the subdirectory prefix \PIPE\ followed by a normal filename. Once a pipe is created, you can block the current thread waiting for another thread or process to connect to it with **DosConnectNmPipe**.

Named pipes can send data as *byte streams* or as *messages*. A message pipe has a header associated with it that contains the length of the message that follows. These headers are added by **DosWrite** and removed by **DosRead** so you needn't manage them yourself. Byte stream pipes send bytes without any associated size information. Pipes can be one-way or full duplex, and reading and writing then takes place using the same handle.

To create a named pipe, you use the function

```
DosMakeNmPipe(name, &handle, openmode, pipemode,
                        osize, isize, timeout);
```

where

name   is the name of the pipe. It must be prefixed with \PIPE\.

& handle is the location where the pipe handle is returned.

openmode contains the open mode bits

```
15 14 13 12 11 10 9 8 7 6 5 4 3 2 1
0  W  -- -- -- -- - - I 0 0 0 A A A
```

where **W** is 1 if network buffering is not allowed and 0 if network buffering is allowed; **I** is **0** if spawned processes *can* inherit the pipe handle and **1** if they cannot; and **AAA** controls the access to the pipe.

000   read only pipe

001   write only pipe

010   duplex pipe

pipemode controls the pipe transmission mode:

```
15 14 13 12 11 10 9 8 7 6 5 4 3 2 1
B  -- -- --   T   T R R  |-- count --|
```

B   is 0 if the pipe is to be blocked if no data are available and 1 if the pipe is to return immediately if no data are available.

TT   write mode: is **00** if this is a byte stream pipe and **01** if this is a message stream pipe.

RR   read mode: is **00** if the pipe is to be read as a byte stream and **01** if the pipe is to be read as a message stream.

count is the number of instances of that pipe that can be created.

osize   is the number of bytes recommended for the outgoing buffer.

isize   is the number of bytes allowed in the incoming buffer.

timeout   is the number of milliseconds to wait for **DosWaitNmPipe**. If this is zero the system default of 50 msec is chosen.

When the pipe has been created, you can then wait for the other thread or process to connect to it with the call

```
err = DosConnectNmPipe(hPipe);
```

This call will block the current thread until a connection is made if blocking mode is set, or returns immediately with **err** non-zero if blocking is not set. The following simple program illustrates the named pipe calling sequence:

```
/*----- connect 2 threads using a named pipe ------------*/
void main()
begin
    unsigned char  *stack, buf[MAXLEN];
    HPIPE hPipe;
    int read, err;

DosMakeNmPipe("\\PIPE\\dream.pip",   /*open a named pipe */
            &hPipe,                  /*return handle here*/
            0x2,                     /*duplex pipe       */
            0x0001,                  /*byte pipe         */
            MAXLEN, MAXLEN,          /*size of buffers   */
```

```
                  0);                        /*default timeout    */

/*Create a semaphore clearing thread */
stack = malloc(2000);                       /*get stack space    */
_beginthread(PipeWrite, stack,
                 2000, OL) ;  /*pass address of semaphore*/

err = DosConnectNmPipe(hPipe); /*wait for pipe connection*/
DosRead(hPipe, buf,
              MAXLEN, &read); /*read a message from the pipe*/
printf("%s", buf);            /*print it out               */
DosClose(hPipe);              /*and close it               */
DosExit(1, 0);                /*end all threads            */
end
/*-----------------------------------------------------------*/
void PipeWrite()
begin
   int written, action, err;
   char buf[MAXLEN];
   HPIPE hPipe;

err = DosOpen("\\PIPE\\dream.pip",
                 &hPipe,        /*open same named pipe*/
                 &action,       /*action taken        */
                 80L,           /*size               */
                 0,             /*attributes         */
                 1,             /*open flag          */
                 0x2012,        /*open mode          */
                 OL);           /*reserved           */
strcpy(buf, "Writing to a Pipe\n");/*copy message         */
DosWrite(hPipe, buf,
         strlen(buf), &written); /*write it to pipe    */
DosClose(hPipe);                 /*then close it       */
end                              /*end thread          */
```

SHARING MEMORY SEGMENTS

Memory segments (up to 64K) can be allocated and shared between processes in two ways: as shared segments and as named shared segments.

Shared segments can be addressed by any created child processes, and named segments can be shared by processes created in any session.

Shared Memory Segments

The following calls are used to allocate and share segments with child processes:

```
DosGiveSeg(callseg, pid,       /*give access to segment    */
              &recipseg);      /*as recipseg               */

DosGetSeg(seg);                /*get access to segment     */
DosGetPID(&pidinfo);           /*get proc id               */
DosGetPPID(pid, &parpid);      /*get parent's process id   */
DosAllocSeg(size, &seg,        /*allocate memory;          */
                flags);        /*return selector           */
DosFreeSeg(seg);               /*deallocate memory segment */
```

Memory segments allocated with **DosAllocSeg** can be shared by calling **DosGiveSeg** and obtaining the selector for the child process. Then, this selector is passed to the child process using a named pipe or queue. The child process then calls **DosGetSeg** and the memory is then sharable between the two processes. The memory is only released when **DosFreeSeg** has been called by *both* processes, or when both have terminated.

Named Shared Memory Segments

Analogous to named pipes and semaphores is the concept of named shared memory segments. Such segments are allocated with **DosAllocShrSeg** and are accessed by other processes using **DosGetShrSeg.**:

```
DosAllocShrSeg(size, name, &sel);
DosGetShrSeg(name, &sel);
```

where

size   is the number of bytes (<64K) to allocate.

name   is the name of the shared segment. This must have the
                        subdirectory prefix \SHAREMEM\ and be followed by
                        a standard filename.

& sel   is the selector value allocated or shared.

QUEUES

A queue is a named buffer that has data put in by one or more processes and
that can only be read out by the owning process. The purpose of a queue is to
send information to the owning process for action, such as requesting the
services of a device.

Queue Ownership

The process that creates the queue is considered the owner, and can execute
any of the following calls:

```
DosCreateQueue(&hQ, priority, name);
DosPeekQueue(hQ, &req, length, address,
                      elementcode, nowait, priority, hSem);
DosReadQueue(hQ, &req, length, address,
                      elementcode, nowait, priority, hSem);
DosPurgeQueue(hQ);
DosQueryQueue(hQ, &size);
DosWriteQueue(hQ, req, length, address, priority);
DosCloseQueue(hQ);
```

Writing to a Queue

A thread of the owning process or any other process can write to a queue
using the calls

```
DosWriteQueue(hQ, req, length, address, priority);
DosQueryQueue(hQ, &size);
DosOpenQueue(ownerpid, &hQ, name);
DosCloseQueue(hQ);
```

Any process other than the owning process must first call **DosOpenQueue**. The queue name must include the \QUEUES\ prefix. The semaphore used in **DosReadQueue** is cleared when data are placed in the address specified. It can be either a system or a RAM semaphore. The priority defined in **DosCreateQueue** determines whether a queue is read first-in first-out (FIFO = 0), last first (=1) or by individual element priority (2).

THREADS AND MESSAGE QUEUES

The communication techniques we have illustrated in this chapter can be used to communicate with threads that do *not* have a message queue. A thread with a message queue is usually one that supports windows and receives messages. Such threads must obey the 0.1-second rule and cannot spend a lot of time performing calculations. Therefore, such threads cannot "hang" waiting on a semaphore or pipe data value, since this will block the thread and prevent messages from being processed quickly. Instead, you should post messages to such threads as we did in the previous chapter.

21 | Elements of Assembly Language Programming

The fundamental reason for writing a routine in assembly language is to handle bit and address manipulation when it dominates over numeric calculation, as is usually the case in system and interrupt routines. Such manipulations may be faster in assembly language because you can select the minimum number of integer instructions to get the job done without having the overhead that the compiler may impose on such calculations. For example, you can keep all the important values in registers and never store them back into memory unless they are actually needed later. In addition, interrupt service of device registers may not be possible any other way while still preserving rapid interrupt response.

THE 80X86 MICROPROCESSOR FAMILY

The original IBM PC was built around the 8088 microprocessor, which has the instruction set we will be discussing here and an 8-bit data path to and from the chip. The 8086 microprocessor is a somewhat more efficient implementation of the same instruction set and has a 16-bit data path to and from the chip.

The 80286 microprocessor is the chip used in the Personal Computer AT (PC/AT) and and the PS/2 Models 30-286, 50 and 60. It has the same instruction set as the 8088 in *real* address mode, but with a few enhancements, considerably faster operating speeds, a 16-bit data path, and in *protected* address mode the ability to address up to 16 megabytes of memory.

The 80386 microprocessor is the chip used in the PS/2 Models 70 and 80 as well as in a number of machines with the "386" designation in their names. It runs even faster than the previous generation and has much more sophisticated additional processor modes. It has a 32-bit data path and can address up to 2^{48} bytes or four *gigabytes* of memory. It also will operate as a very fast 8088 processor in real address mode.

INSTRUCTIONS AND DATA

Memory in the 80x86 family is organized into 8-bit *bytes*. Two bytes make up a 16-bit word, and most integer operations take place on 16-bit words. In digital computers, an instruction pointer (IP) register is set to contain the address of some memory location where numbers called *instructions* are stored. Locations that contain instructions are no different than locations that contain other numbers except that the programmer tells the computer to begin executing the numbers at some address and continue executing from that point. Obviously, if a computer begins executing locations containing data values, it will probably behave strangely, usually resulting in a "crash."

ORGANIZATION OF THE 8088 INSTRUCTIONS

The 8088 microprocessor is fundamentally an *accumulator machine* in which the four registers AX, BX, CX, and DX can be used as places to put values and carry out calculations. Each of these registers is 16 bits wide and can be broken into two 8-bit registers:

16-bit	8-bit
AX	AH, AL
BX	BH, BL
CX	CH, CL
DX	DH, DL

These "general" registers also have special purposes inherent in their names:

AX   Accumulator register

BX   Base register

CX   Counter register

DX   Data register

You can carry out 8- or 16-bit operations depending on whether the instruction refers to the 8- or 16-bit register name.

As noted earlier, the 80xxx has a segmented address scheme in which a 16-bit address can refer to 65,536 bytes of memory relative to a *segment register*. These registers are assumed to point to the code, the data, the stack, and to another "extra" data set:

CS   Code segment register

DS   Data segment register

ES   Extra segment register

SS   Stack segment register

Thus, while the basic 8088 instruction set can only address 65,536 bytes directly, you can change a segment register so that you can address 1 megabyte of memory or 1,048,586 bytes. This 1-megabyte limit is enforced by a 20-bit internal address bus: the 80286 and 80386 have much larger potential address spaces, but not when running the instruction set and addressing modes of the 8088 chip. It is this 20-bit limit that leads to the 640K limit on a PC's memory running in real mode, where the upper 384K of the 1 megabyte are reserved for the addresses of the video screens and the read-only memory, which make up the basic input/output system (BIOS) code of the PC. This 640K limit applies only under DOS, however, since OS/2 runs in the 80286 protected mode.

The actual address of any memory location is made up of a segment register value and an offset. A *segment address* is simply the absolute 20-bit address with the lowest 4 bits dropped. Therefore the address of the EGA screen memory is $A0000_{16}$ and the segment address is just 0xA000. Thus, only every 16th address can be described directly by a segment register value, and these addresses are called *paragraph* addresses. In the protected mode, these registers actually refer to descriptor table locations and offsets.

If we want to refer to a given location relative to a segment address, we usually write a 32-bit number with a colon between the upper and lower 16 bits: a000:0123 means address a0123.

The other registers in the basic 80x86 are two index registers and two pointer registers:

SP   Stack pointer

BP   Base pointer

SI   Source index

DI   Destination index

Each of these has special purposes, as we will see in the examples that follow.

FUNDAMENTAL MACHINE INSTRUCTIONS

There are a number of instructions for carrying out arithmetic and logical operations in the 80xxx microprocessor, but we will only mention a few common ones here. Most are *dual operand instructions:* they have two parts, a *source operand* and a *destination operand.* The source operand is never changed and the destination operand is almost always changed. The syntax of these two operand instructions is

```
opr dest, source        ;perform operation on source
                        ; and put in destination
```

Note that unlike some other instruction syntaxes, the destination operand is written *first,* followed by the source operand. Note that *comments* in assembly language always start with *semicolons,* unlike in C where "/*" or "//" symbols were used.

CAPITALIZATION IN ASSEMBLY LANGUAGE

The MASM assembler program recognizes instructions in either uppercase or lowercase as being equivalent. We will follow Microsoft's recommended convention and write all of our instructions in lowercase and all of the *directives* that tell the assembler how to carry out the assembly in uppercase.

DUAL OPERAND INSTRUCTIONS

Some of the most common dual operand instructions include:

```
mov  b, a            ;move A to B
add  b, a            ;add A to B
sub  b, a            ;subtract A from B
xchg b, a            ;swap A and B
and  b, a            ;AND A with B
or   b, a            ;OR A with B
xor  b, a            ;exclusive OR A with B

cmp  b, a            ;subtract A from B and set
                     ; the condition flags

test b, a            ;AND A with B and set
                     ; the condition flags
```

In each case the source A and the destination B may be registers or memory addresses, but both cannot be memory addresses. To move a value from one address to another, you must first move it to a register and then move the register to another memory address. There are also multiplication and division instructions, but they are seldom necessary since such operations are usually better written in C.

SINGLE OPERAND INSTRUCTIONS

Some of the most common *single operand instructions* include

```
inc a            ;add 1 to A
dec a            ;subtract 1 from A
neg a            ;negate A
not a            ;take ones complement of A
jmp x            ;jump to location named "x"
```

SHIFT INSTRUCTIONS

Shift instructions move the bits in a register to the right and left. The bits on the end fall off and are lost in the chronosynclastic infundibulum. A *logical shift* causes the bits on the source end to be filled with zeroes.

A right *arithmetic shift* causes the sign bit (bit 15) to be copied into each of the vacated leftmost bits.

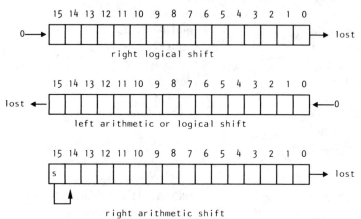

The shift instructions have the syntax

```
sal a, 1        ;shift A 1 place left
sal a, cl       ;shift A left the number of place
                ;contained in register CL

shr a, 1        ;logical shift A right 1 place
shr a, cl       ;logical shift A right by CL

sar a, 1        ;arithmetic shift A right 1 place
sar a, cl       ;arithmetic shift A right by CL
```

ROTATE INSTRUCTIONS

There are also four rotate instructions in which the data are rotated out of one end of the register and into the other. Two of them also include the carry flag register in the rotation.

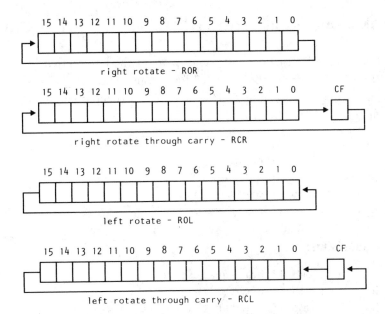

right rotate - ROR

right rotate through carry - RCR

left rotate - ROL

left rotate through carry - RCL

THE FLAG REGISTERS

The 8088 processor has a set of six 1-bit flags that are used to monitor the result of the last executed operation. These flags can be tested as part of conditional jump instructions to make decisions that control the flow of the program.

CF   Carry flag. Set if there is a carry out or borrow in.

ZF   Zero flag. Set if the result is zero.

SF   Sign flag. Set if the result is negative.

OF   Overflow flag. Set if the signed result is out of range.

PF   Parity flag. Set if the result has an even number of bits set to 1.

AF   Aux carry flag. Set if there is a carry out from the low 4 bits to the high 4 bits of the lowest byte of the operand.

DECISION-MAKING INSTRUCTIONS

The conditional jump instructions test one or more of the flag register bits and jump if and only if the condition tested for is true. These flag bits are set by arithmetic operations and by CMP and TEST instructions, but *not* by MOV instructions.

```
jmp x      ; jump always
jc         ; jump if carry
jnc        ; jump if not carry
je         ; jump if equal zero
jcxz       ; jump if cx is zero
```

Signed comparisons:

```
jne        ; jump if not equal to zero
jg         ; jump if greater than
jge        ; jump if greater than or equal to zero
jle        ; jump if less than or equal to zero
jl         ; jump if less than
```

Unsigned comparisons:

```
ja         ; jump if above
jae        ; jump if above or equal
jbe        ; jump if below or equal
jb         ; jump if below
```

THE LOOP INSTRUCTION

The LOOP instruction is used to loop through a small section of code extremely quickly. Each time the loop instruction is encountered, it decrements CX by 1 and loops back to the specified address if CX is non-zero. When CX becomes zero, the loop is completed and the next instruction is executed:

```
        mov cx, 5           ;set counter
c10:    mov dx, ax          ;copy AX into DX, for instance
        ; :                 ;other instructions
        loop c10            ;go back until CX is 0
```

There are also two special forms of the LOOP instruction that are useful for searching a table for the first zero or non-zero element:

```
    LOOPE   addr    ;loop until ZF is set or CX is zero
    LOOPNE  addr    ;loop until ZF is clear or CX is zero
```

ADDRESSING MODES IN THE 8088

Thus far we have discussed the various 8088 registers and the condition flags, but have not discussed how we can address memory locations using the previous instructions. The 8088 has seven basic addressing modes:

```
    mov ax, bx          ;register addressing

    mov ax, 5           ;immediate addressing

    mov ax, fred        ;direct addressing
    mov ax, ds:010h

    mov ax, [di]        ;indexed indirect addressing
    mov ax, [si]
    mov ax, [bx]        ;based indirect addressing
    mov ax, [bp]

    mov ax, [bp+6]      ;base relative (6 off BP)
    mov ax, 6[bp]       ;base relative also 6 off BP
    mov ax, [bx-12]     ;base relative
    mov ax, [di+20]     ;direct indexed
    mov ax, [si+33]     ;direct indexed

    mov ax, [bx][di]    ;based indexed
    mov ax, [bp][di]
    mov ax, [bx][si]
    mov ax, [bp][si]
```

```
mov ax, 12[bx][di] ;based index with displacement
mov ax, 25[bp][di]
mov ax, 42[bp][si]
```

In all of these addressing modes, the segment register is assumed to be the DS register unless the BP register is used in the instruction. Using the BP register always implies that the SS register is used. In most cases, these registers are loaded for you by the calling program and you seldom have to load them or be aware of their contents when writing subroutines to be called from C.

Register Addressing

In this mode, the data are in one of the registers. In the first example above, the BX register is the source, and in all of the examples, the AX register is the destination.

Immediate Addressing

In this mode, a 16-bit constant is moved into a register. The constant is actually stored in a second location just after the instruction. Obviously, these constants can only be used as source operands.

Direct Addressing

Direct addressing is almost always used when a program wishes to move data to or from a memory location nearby. This could occur for local constants that are accessed from a number of places or when a routine uses local data storage for temporary results. In MASM syntax, a named or labelled location must start with an alphabetic character or with an underscore (_), a question mark (?), a dollar sign ($), or an "at" sign (@), and the label may be up to 31 characters long. You define a location as having a name by placing the name on a line followed by a colon. You use a name by simply referring to it as an address:

```
        mov bx, tem32    ;get contents of location TEM32
                         ;and put in the BX register
                ;:
tem32:  03456h           ;address containing a constant
```

Usually, such labelled addresses are nearby in the code and are referred to as NEAR, meaning that they are addressed as part of the code segment pointed to by the CS register. This will always be true in the simple examples in this chapter, but it is possible to refer to FAR labels where another segment register is implied or used specifically.

Based and Indexed Indirect Addressing

In both of these addressing modes, a register contains the *address* of the memory location of interest. Unless a segment register is specified, the assembler assumes that the segment is pointed to by DS and the register contains an offset relative to this segment address for addresses pointed to by BX, SI, or DI. If BP is used, the stack segment register SS is assumed. The purpose of these modes is to calculate a pointer address that can be used to refer to a data location. Often these addresses are incremented or decremented in a loop so that a table of addresses can be referred to sequentially. This provides a way of stepping sequentially through an array.

Base Relative and Direct Indexed Addressing

In both of these modes, a register contains a fixed address and an offset is specified that is added to this register to calculate the final address. Several slightly different syntaxes have evolved over the history of the 80xxx processors, and all are accepted by the current MASM assembler as identical:

```
mov cx, 6[bp]        ;all refer to the same operation:
mov cx, [bp + 6]     ;get contents of address 6 off bp
mov cx, [bp] + 6     ;and put it in cx
```

In each of these examples, 6 is added to the contents of the BP register to form a new address. This address is the one used to retrieve the data. Since BP is used, the stack segment (SS) register is implied. The purpose of these modes is usually to fetch a value from a table of values passed to a subroutine, where the start of this table is pointed to by the base register.

Based Indexed Addressing

In this mode, the contents of a base register BX or BP are added to the contents of an index register SI or DI and a specified constant offset is added to this to form the effective address of the data. If BX is used, DS is implied, and if BP is used, SS is implied. As above, there are a number of equivalent syntaxes:

```
mov dx, [bp] [si] + 12      ;equivalent syntaxes
mov dx, 12 [bp] [si]        ; for based index addressing
mov dx, [bp + si +12]
mov dx, [bp][si + 12]
```

The main purpose of this mode is really to access elements in a table of fixed-length records. If BP contains the address of an array of records and SI contains the offset to a given record in the table, then the displacement (12) is the number of bytes to the address of a given element in that record.

THE STACK

The stack is an array of numbers pointed to by the stack pointer register. It is used for temporary storage of data passed to subroutines and for the return addresses from subroutine. The stack pointer always starts at a high memory location and grows toward low memory (address 0). The SP register always contains the address of the last value pushed onto the stack. For each value pushed onto the stack, the stack pointer is *decremented* by 2, and a value is put in the location whose address is represented by SS:SP. For each value popped off the stack, a value is moved from the address SS:SP and put into a destination register; then the stack pointer is *incremented* by 2.

```
push ax              ;put the contents of AX onto the stack
push bp              ;put the contents of BP onto the stack
  .
  :
pop bp               ;retrieve old value of BP from the stack
pop ax               ;get old AX value from the stack
```

The address in SS and SP is usually controlled by the calling program and does not need to be calculated in your subroutines. However, if you push values onto the stack, you must retrieve them before exiting so that the stack pointer has the same value when you leave a subroutine as it did when you entered it.

CALLING SUBROUTINES IN ASSEMBLY LANGUAGE

The CALL instruction is used to call subroutines in assembly language. This instruction saves the address following the call on the stack and then jumps to the address named in the instruction:

```
      call ztest         ;call ZTEST subroutine
```

This has the effect of

```
      push IP            ;save the instruction pointer
      jump ztest         ;jump to address "ztest"
```

The reason why this instruction is so powerful is that it gives us a way to call a routine from many places and return to those locations after executing the subroutine, since the address we came from is saved on the stack.

Of course, there must be a complementary instruction to return to the address following the call

```
      ret                ;return to the address on the stack
```

The RET instruction pops the address of the stack and puts it into the IP, so that the next instruction fetched is that at the new address in the IP, thus causing a return from the subroutine to the address after the original CALL statement.

NEAR AND FAR PROCEDURES

Since the 80xxx addresses are always made up of a segment value and an offset value, the "true" address of any procedure is also 32 bits long, made up of a segment and offset. Therefore, if you call a procedure, it may be in the current segment or in a different 64K segment of memory. We call a procedure in the same segment a NEAR procedure and one in another segment a FAR procedure. To call a FAR procedure, we need to save both the code segment register CS and the current address offset in IP on the stack, and load new values into the CS and IP. Likewise, to return from a FAR procedure, we need to pop both of these values off the stack.

The MASM assembler has NEAR and FAR directives to be used with each subroutine so that it can decide whether to generate a near or a far call and return for each procedure:

```
ztest: PROC NEAR        ;the near subroutine starts here
         .
         :
       ret              ;return from a near procedure
       ENDP             ;tell MASM this is the end of ZTEST

ftest: PROC FAR         ;start of far procedure
         .
         :
       ret              ;this will be a far return
       ENDP             ;tell MASM this is the end of FTEST
```

We will see the uses of the stack and PROC directives in the following chapter.

THE STRING INSTRUCTIONS

The 8088 series also has a set of instructions for transferring blocks of data from one location to another. These instructions are very efficient ways of moving, comparing, and scanning strings of up to 64K bytes in length. Actually we refer to "strings" for these instructions, although the compilers often use these instructions for moving many types of numbers from one place to another. We will not use them in our programming examples but merely list them here for completeness:

```
movsb      ;move string of bytes
movsw      ;move string of words

cmpsb      ;compare string of bytes
cmpsw      ;compare string of words

scasb      ;scan string of bytes
scasw      ;scan string of words
```

Each time one of these instructions is executed, one element of the string is moved, compared, or scanned, and SI and DI are changed by 1 or 2. The entire operation can be carried out in a single pair of instructions by adding the REP prefix to the instructions:

```
rep movsw      ;move entire word string
repne cmpsb    ;repeat while not equal (zf=0)
repe cmpsb     ;repeat while equal (zf=1)
```

In each of these instructions, the length of the strings is contained in CX, the address of the source string in DS:SI, and the address of the destination string in ES:DI. The strings can be scanned from low memory to high memory or vice versa, depending on the state of a special flag called the *direction flag*. If the direction flag is 0, the SI and DI registers increment after each use, and if DF is 1, they decrement.

```
CLD      ;clear direction flag
STD      ;set direction flag
```

MULTIPLE REGISTER LOAD INSTRUCTIONS

Two instructions are commonly used to load a segment and an offset register simultaneously:

```
LDS reg, ea      ;load data segment
LES reg, ea      ;load extra segment
```

Both of these instructions get 4 bytes from the effective address: two that go into the segment register and two that are loaded into the specified destination register.

This concludes our brief summary of the 80xxx assembly language. In the following chapters we will show how C and assembly language can be interfaced in device drivers.

22 | Sending I/O Commands to Devices

OPERATING MODES OF THE 80286

The 80286 microprocessor runs in two modes: real mode (8086 mode) and protected mode (80286 mode). In real mode, the processor runs as if it were an 8086, limited to addressing a single 1-megabyte address space. In protected mode, the microprocessor can address a 16-megabyte address space and has a substantial number of features to allow multitasking. It further allows complete protection of each job's code and data space from interference by other jobs.

This protected mode is actually divided into four *rings* numbered from 0 to 3, with successively more protection. Most programs run at ring 3, where they have no I/O or interrupt privileges, and the OS/2 kernel and device drivers run at ring 0, with both interrupt and I/O privileges. If you want to access a device using IN and OUT instructions, but do not need to use interrupts, you can write code in a special segment with I/O privileges, which runs in ring 2. OS/2 makes no use of ring 1. Because of this protection scheme, you must write a device driver if you want to access the device at interrupt level.

313

WRITING AN IOPL SEGMENT PROGRAM

If you only need occasional access to the ports of your device and do not need to control or respond to interrupts, you can write a program that contains an *IOPL segment*. Such a routine can be written entirely in C except for the routine that actually accesses the ports of the device. This routine must be written in assembly language, although it may be quite short and simple. You cannot write a routine that uses the C library functions **inp** and **outp** to access the ports since these routines lie in a segment linked to your program that does not have IOPL privileges and does not run at ring 2.

To illustrate how we can write such a routine, we will use the example of the Metrabyte ucDAS-8PGA card which is normally set so that the I/O ports have the following definitions:

Address	Read Function	Write Function
300	A/D Low byte	Start 8-bit conversion
301	A/D High byte	Start 12-bit conversion
302	Status register	Control register

To start a 12-bit A/D conversion, we write any value to port 301. To see if the conversion is done, we look at bit 7 of the status register. If it is 1 the conversion is still in progress and if it is zero the conversion is complete. The converted data can then be read from ports 301 and 300. Port 301 contains the top 8 bits and port 300 the bottom 4 bits. A simple assembly routine for starting the ADC and reading the result into the AX register is shown below.

```
        TITLE       READADC
        .286p
.MODEL LARGE
.CODE

; int readadc()
; define bytes for port access
        PORT1           EQU         300h
        PORT2           EQU         310h

        PUBLIC  _readadc            ;reads one value from adc
```

```
_readadc PROC       FAR
            mov     dx, PORT1+1     ;adc start location
                                    ;sending any byte
            out     dx, al          ;will start the adc
            inc     dx              ;port+2 is status byte
wait1:      in      al,  dx         ;check status
            test    al, 080h        ;is ADC busy bit set?
            jne     wait1           ;wait until it goes low
            mov     dx, PORT1+1     ;now read upper byte of
            in      al, dx          ;converted result
            mov     ah, al          ;save in ah
            dec     dx              ;port to read lower byte from
            in      al, dx          ;get lower byte
            shr     ax, 4           ;shift both 4 bits right
            ret                     ;and exit
_readadc        ENDP

END
```

The C-language routine that calls READADC is the simple

```
#include <cdefs.h>
#define INCL_BASE
#define INCL_DOSDEVICES
#include <os2.h>
#include <stdio.h>

void main();
int readadc();            /*assembly language routine     */
                          /*in IOPL segment               */
/*--------------------------------------------------------*/
/* illustrates reading from a device port using OS/2      */
/* and an IOPL segment                                    */
/*--------------------------------------------------------*/
void main()
begin
    int result;
    result = readadc();         /*read one value from the adc*/
    printf("val=%d\n", result); /* and print it out          */
end
```

SPECIFYING AN IOPL SEGMENT

Thus far there is nothing particularly difficult about this process. We have simply illustrated the calling of a simple assembly language function from C. The one significant difference in writing a program having a segment running at ring 2 is in the .DEF file. Here we must specify that the routine READADC is to run as an IOPL segment. This is done as follows:

```
NAME ADPORT
PROTMODE
SEGMENTS readadc_TEXT CLASS 'CODE' IOPL
```

The PROTMODE statement specifies that the program will run in OS/2 mode and the SEGMENTS statement lists any segments with special properties: here the READADC segment is given IOPL privileges. Linking this in the usual way produces a running program that will allow you to access the ports and print out the value read from the A/D converter. The link command is

```
link @adport.1 /NOD;
```

and the link command file is

```
adport.obj readadc.obj
adport.exe
adport.map
llibce.lib+
os2.lib
adport.def
```

GAINING ACCESS TO THE PORTS

While OS/2 1.2 does not require it, for upward compatibility your IOPL segment routines should request access to the port numbers they plan to use. This is done using the DosPortAccess call, which has the form

```
DosPortAccess(0, access, firstport, lastport);
```

where

0	is a reserved short integer.
access	is 0 to request access and 1 to release access.
firstport	is the address of the first port you wish to address.
lastport	is the address of the last port you wish to address.

However, you must make this call directly from your **IOPL** segment, which means it must be made in assembly language:

```
EXTRN    DosPortAccess:FAR

PORTLO        EQU      300h
PORTHI        EQU      310h
ACCESSREQ     EQU      0        ; request access to port(s)
ACCESSREL     EQU      1        ; release access to port(s)

PUBLIC  _readadc                ; reads adc

_readadc      PROC     FAR
              push     0        ; reserved integer
              push     ACCESSREQ   ; request access to port(s)
              push     PORTLO
              push     PORTHI
              call     DosPortAccess   ; request access to ports
                                ;  PORTLO-PORTHI
```

23 | Writing Device Drivers

A device driver contains a series of subroutines that control some device and that can be called from application programs. In OS/2, these drivers are resident programs that are installed when the system is initialized. You communicate with them by *opening* the device by name. OS/2 returns a device handle that you can use to refer to the device until you close it. Device drivers run at ring 0 and do not need to be linked as IOPL segments or to request access to ports.

THE METRABYTE 8PGA CARD

In this chapter we will write at device driver for the Metrabyte ucDAS-8PGA card, where we set up the card so that it' clock causes an interrupt each time it is to obtain a data point. This driver reserves a shared data segment where the data points accumulate and clears a semaphore when the total specified number of points has beena acquired. Then the calling program can read and store these points from that memory block.

The Metrabyte card we describe here is a low cost PS/2 card that can acquire data a point at a time on command or can acquire data at regular intervals based on a clock pulse and interrupt. The registers for this card start at the port base address (usually 0x300) and have the functions shown in Table 23-1

Table 23-1. Metrabyte 8PGA Registers

Address Offset from Base	Read Function	Write Function
0	A/D Low byte	Start 8 bit conversion
1	A/D High byte	Start 12 bit conversion
2	Status register	Control register
3	Status/Gain	Gain register
4	Read counter 0	Load counter 0
5	Read counter 1	Load counter 1
6	Read counter 2	Load counter 2
7		Counter control

Reading Data Points

There are several ways to acquire an array of data points from the 8PGA card and ones like it.

1. Start a conversion and wait for the result.
2. Have a clock start conversions and check for whether a conversion is done.
3. Have a clock cause interrupts and start conversions when interrupts occur.

Methods 1 and 2 require that your program "hang" waiting for a result, and this wastes computing time unnecessarily. Instead, it is best to have data points acquired each time an interrupt occurs. As we have seen, you can initiate a single 12-bit conversion by writing any value to port 0x301, and can check whether the conversion has been completed by checking bit 7 of the status register. If bit 7 is set, the conversion has completed. Here, however, we will use the clocks to trigger the ADC repetitively and acquire data at uniformly spaced time intervals.

Because the 8PGA board is designed to be flexible, yet inexpensive, you make some of the choices about how it is to be used by connecting pins on a *jumper block* connected to the rear connecter on the board. The most important pins on this connector are shown in Table 23-2.

Pin	Function
Table 23-2. Metrabyte 8PGA I/O Connector Pins	
2	Clock 0 input
3	Clock 0 output
4	Clock 1 input
5	Clock 1 output
6	Clock 2 output
19	Analog channel 0 input (-)
24	Interrupt input
37	Analog channel 0 input (+)

Note that while there are several clock inputs and an interrupt input, there is no pin to start an A/D conversion. Therefore, in our device driver we will cause an interrupt at regular intervals and start and A/D conversion by writing to port 0x301. At the next interrupt, we will read the result of the previous conversion and begin another. Other, more expensive A/D boards from a number of manufacturers, including Metrabyte, allow a clock to initiate an A/D conversion directly and cause an interrupt when the conversion is complete.

The 8PGA Clocks

There are 3 clocks in the 8PGA board, numbered 0, 1 and 2. The input of clock 2 is permanently connected to a 1 MHz clock and by loading this counter with a value between 100 and 65535, you can get interrupts every 100 microseconds down to every 65.5 milliseconds. While the A/D can convert a data point every 35 μsec, OS/2 cannot respond to interrupts much faster than every 100 μsec. If slower rates are necessary, you can cascade together 2 or more of the clocks by connecting the output of clock 2 into the input of clock 1, etc.

The Control and Status Registers

The 8PGA board Control register selects which of 8 multiplexed analog inputs is converted, and is used to turn on the board's interrupt capability by setting the INTE flip-flop. You can read this same register (0x302) to find out if a conversion is in progress and whether an interrupt has been requested. The bits assignments are shown in Table 23-3.

Pin	Control (write)	Status (read)
	Table 23-3. Metrabyte 8PGA Control and Status Register	
7	1 = adc busy 0 = adc done	OP4
6	IP3	OP3
5	IP2	OP2
4	IP1	OP1
3	Interrupt request	Interrupt on
2	MUX2	MUX2
1	MUX1	MUX1
0	MUX0	MUX0

Signals OP1 - OP4 are 4 digital output lines that you can set or clear and signals IP1 - IP3 are three digital input lines that you can read. The three MUX lines allow you to select 8 input channels from 000 to 111, and bit 7 inidicates whether a conversion is in progress (1) or not (0). If you want the interrupt input from the connector to cause an interrupt, you must set bit 3 of the control register, and you can see if an interrupt has been requested by reading bit 3. While you are processing an interrupt you should clear bit 3 and reset it when you have finished.

PARTS OF A DEVICE DRIVER

Like any other program, there are two major sections to a device driver: the data area and the code area. Since device drivers have a specific format for OS/2 to recognize them, the data area comes first, starting with an 11-word (22-byte) *header*, followed by local constants, variables, and, if written in assembly language, a command table.

The code area consists of three sections: the strategy routine, the interrupt service routine, and the driver initialization routine. Since the initialization routine is called only when the driver is first loaded, it is placed at the end of the code segment so that its memory can be released when initialization is complete.

MEMORY MODELS

Device drivers are generally written using the Small memory model: with a single code segment and a single data segment. While it is possible to write a device driver primarily in C, there are certain sections that must be written in assembly language. These include the interrupt service routine, the beginning of the strategy routine, and an interface to call the Dev_help subroutine. In addition, it may be necessary to write parts of the initialization routine in assembly language, depending on the nature of the device. In our first example, we will write the entire driver in assembly language. We will illustrate how to write much of the driver in C in the following chapter.

THE DEVICE DRIVER HEADER

The header for a device driver contains 22 bytes of information and MUST be the first data in the driver executable file. These data are as follows:

```
; device driver header bytes
point_to_next   dw   0ffffh
                dw   -1              ;32-bit -1 means loadable
device_attr     dw   8880h          ;device attribute bits
offst           dw   dcode:strategy ;offset to strat. routine
reserved        dw   -1             ;reserved
dev_name        db   'device$ '     ;8-char device name
res2            dw   4 dup (0)       ;reserved

; local data storage starts here
; --saved at initialization time
base_address    dw   ?              ;I/O port base address
intrpt_lvl      dw   ?              ;interrupt level
device_help     dd   ?              ;address of device help entry
mbuf_selector   dw   ?              ;GDT selector slot
Handle          dw   ?              ;handle returned on open
bufsize         dw   ?              ;size of acquisition buffer
bufcnt          dw   ?              ;count of acquire points
bufhi           dw   ?              ;high address of buffer
buflo           dw   ?              ;low address of buffer
bufpnt          dw   ?              ;pointer to current data pt
sem_hi          dw   ?              ;high key to semaphore
sem_lo          dw   ?              ;low key to semaphore
```

point_to_next A pointer that will be linked to the next chained device driver. The 32-bit -1 means the driver is loadable.

attributes The device attribute bits have the following meanings:

15 Set if this is a character device driver.

14 Set if device driver participates in interdriver communication.

13 If character device, set for output until busy support. If block device, set if non-IBM block format.

12	Set if file system sharing rules apply (character only).
11	For character devices, if set the device must receive Open and Close commands. For block devices, if set the driver handles removable media.
10	Unused.
9-7	Function level, where 001 means OS/2 device driver.
6-4	Unused.
3	Clock device bit. If set the character device is the system clock device.
2	If set, the character device is the NULL device.
1-0	For character devices, set bit 1 if this is the new stdout device and set bit 0 if this is the new stdin device.
strategy	This is the offset in bytes to the strategy routine entry point.
dev_name	This is an 8-character ASCII character device name. IBM recommends that your device name end in a $ sign. For a block device, place the number of units in the first byte.

Following this data header, you should place all the variable and constant storage locations you will need for data storage while your driver is executing. We will see later that we need to save the DevHelp routine address, and we may need to save some device-dependent parameters as well.

Character and Block Devices

Character devices are ones that have names like "LPT1:" and can have one or more bytes of information sent to or received from them. Block devices have names like "d:" and are devices like disk drives. A character device is not restricted to single characters and is the usual choice for data acquisition cards that process large "blocks" of data.

THE STRATEGY ROUTINE

The strategy routine is the "command interpreter" entry point for the device driver. All requests for the device pass through this routine and are dispatched to various routines within the driver. Upon entry to the strategy routine, the registers ES and BX point to a structure called a *request packet*. The request packet has a variable length depending on what data is being passed to the driver, but always includes

```
Packet          struc
PktLen     db   ?       ; Length in bytes of packet
PktUnit    db   ?       ; Subunit number of block device
PktCmd     db   ?       ; Command to device driver
PktStatus  dw   ?       ; Status word -status returns here
PktDOSLink dd   ?       ; Reserved
PktDevLink dd   ?       ; Device multiple-request link
PktData    db   PktMax dup (?) ; Data words
Packet          ends
```

The most important byte in this packet is the PktCmd byte, which describes the action the driver is to take. The data words at the end vary depending on the action.

Commands to the Strategy Routine

The strategy routine must be able to process any commands it receives and return errors for the ones that it cannot deal with. The most common commands it receives are

0h	INIT Initialize the device. Sent when the driver is loaded.
4	READ
6h	INPUT STATUS
7h	INPUT FLUSH
8h	WRITE
Ah	OUTPUT STATUS
Bh	OUTPUT FLUSH
Dh	OPEN
Eh	CLOSE

| **10h** | GENIOCTRL |
| **14h** | DEINSTALL |

In this chapter we will deal with INIT, OPEN, CLOSE, and GENIOCTRL. The remainder are discussed in the *I/O Subsystems and Device Drivers* OS/2 manual.

Returning Status and Errors

The PktStatus byte of the request packet has the form:

15	14	13 - 10	9	8	7 - 0
err	derr	reserved	busy	done	err code

If the driver detects an error, it must set bit 15, the error bit, and return an error code in bits 7-0. Bit 14 may be used by the driver for its own assigned meaning along with bit 15. Regardless of whether the driver detects an error or completes the command successfully, it *must* set the Done bit. If this bit is not set, the driver may crash. If an error is detected, both the Done and Error bits are set, and bits 0-7 are set to the error code. The error codes that can be returned are

0	Write protect violation
0x1	Unknown unit
0x2	Device not ready
0x3	Unknown command
0x4	CRC error
0x5	Bad drive request structure length
0x6	Seek error
0x7	Unknown media
0x8	Sector not found
0x9	Printer out of paper
0xA	Write fault
0xB	Read fault
0xC	General failure
0xD	Change disk
0x10	Uncertain media (like in a close election?)

0x11   Character I/O call interrupted
0x12   Monitors not supported
0x13   Invalid parameter

The errors you will most commonly return are 0x3, 0xC, and 0x13.

THE COMMAND DISPATCH TABLE

The simplest way to check for legal commands is simply to set up a command table starting at 0 (for the INIT command) and going up as high as the largest number command you will process. For each command in the list that you will process, simply indicate the address of the routine that the program is to call. For each command you will not process, give the address of an illegal command handler routine. You also need to have a maximum check to see that no command is greater than the maximum in the table.

The example code in this chapter follows closely that provided in the OS/2 Programmer's Toolkit sample driver DEMODD.ASM.

```
;------------------------------------------------------------
;       Command table for commands to driver

last_command   equ    16        ;Command codes >16 are illegal
command_table  dw     INIT      ;0 calls INIT Subroutine
               dw     BAD       ;1 to 7   are
               dw     BAD       ;not supported
               dw     BAD       ;3
               dw     BAD       ;4
               dw     BAD       ;5
               dw     BAD       ;6
               dw     BAD       ;7
               dw     BAD       ;8   calls WRITE subroutine
               dw     BAD       ;9   is unsupported
               dw     BAD       ;10 calls STATUS Subroutine
               dw     FLUSH     ;11 calls FLUSH Subroutine
               dw     BAD       ;12 is unsupported
               dw     OPEN      ;13 calls OPEN Subroutine
               dw     CLOSE     ;14 calls CLOSE Subroutine
               dw     BAD       ;15 is unsupported
```

```
          dw    GENIOCTL ;16 calls GENIOCTL Subroutine
;-----------------------------------------------------------
;
```

Then, interpreting the command table amounts to simply calculating the offset from 0 to the command in words, doubling to make the byte offset and making a near call to the address pointed to.

```
;-----------------------------------------------------------
;
ERROR_BIT          equ    8000h ;Word indicating error
DONE_BIT           equ    0100h ;Bit indicating command done
GENERAL_FAILURE    equ    000ch ;General failure error code
UNKNOWN_COMMAND    equ    0003h ;Unknown command error code
INVALID_PARAMETER  equ    0013h ;invalid parameter code

STRATEGY PROC FAR
;The code below calls the appropriate subroutine based
;on the call table in the data segment

    mov    al,byte ptr es:[bx].PktCmd  ;get command code
    cmp    al,last_command      ;Is this one in range?
    ja     UNSUPPORTED          ;no, go to error routine
    cbw                         ;convert byte in al to word
    mov    di,ax                ;move it to di
    shl    di,1                 ;multiply by 2 for bytes
    call   word ptr command_table[di] ;and call routine
    or     es:[bx].PktStatus, DONE_BIT   ;set done bit
    ret                         ;and exit


UNSUPPORTED:
        call   BAD              ;command is not supported
        ret

STRATEGY ENDP
;-----------------------------------------------------------
;
BAD PROC NEAR          ;set error bit and unknown command code
        mov es:[bx].PktStatus,  ERROR_BIT + UNKNOWN_COMMAND
        ret
BAD ENDP
;-----------------------------------------------------------
;
```

The BAD subroutine simply sets the error bit and the unknown command error code and returns. The UNSUPPORTED label is used so that a call to the BAD routine can be made from both places. If a match is found, on the other hand, the routine pointed to by

`command_table[di]`

is called and, upon exit, the command interpreter sets the DONE bit.

INITIALIZING THE DEVICE DRIVER

When the OS/2 system is loaded at power-up or bootstrap time, the OS/2 scans the CONFIG.SYS file and loads any device drivers whose names are specified using the DEVICE= statement in that file. When the drivers are loaded, they are sent an INIT command packet containing the following information:

```
InitPacket      struc
IPktLen      db    24 ; Length in bytes of packet
IPktUnit     db    ?  ; Subunit number of block device
IPktCmd      db    ?  ; Command to device driver
IPktStatus   dw    ?  ; Status word -status returns here
IPktDOSLink  dd    ?  ; Reserved
IPktDevLink  dd    ?  ; Device multiple-request link
InitData1    db    ?  ; return number of devices here
InitPtr1     dd    ?  ; pointer to DevHlp entry point
InitPtr2     dd    ?  ; pointer to INIT arguments
InitData2    db    ?  ; driver num for first block dev unit
InitPacket           ends
```

Note that the first 13 bytes are just like the request packet described above. The only difference is the assignment of the bytes after the first 13. The most important argument here is InitPtr1, which contains the address of the DeviceHlp routine. This routine can be used to request a number of complex system services such as registering interrupts and requesting a memory buffer that can be accessible to both the driver and the user's calling program. The other argument you may choose to process is InitPtr2 which points to the string of arguments that can be passed after the DEVICE= command in the CONFIG.SYS file. The interpretation of this string is entirely up to you.

INITIALIZING THE DEVICE DRIVER

The minimum that you must do, then, when processing the INIT command is to save the address of the DevHelp routine in your driver's data segment. This can be done by the following simple code:

```
;----------------------------------------------------------
;
END_OF_CODE   equ $         ;define last used location
;----------------------------------------------------------
;
INIT PROC NEAR              ;device initialization

;--------
; Save the first word of the pointer to the DevHlp routine
;--------
 mov ax, word ptr es:[bx].InitPtr1
 mov word ptr device_hlp, ax
;--------
; Save the second word of the pointer to the DevHlp routine
;--------
 mov ax, word ptr es:[bx].InitPtr1+2
 mov word ptr device_hlp+2, ax
 ;     :
 ;
```

Upon returning from the INIT command, you must set the value of the pointer following the basic request packet to contain the 16-bit offset to the end of the code and the 16-bit offset to the end of the data segment. You must also set the second long pointer to zero for character devices. Since the INIT routine is called only once during the life of your device driver, it is not unreasonable to release that memory after the code is executed. You do this by returning in **InitPtr1** the word offset to the end of the code segment. You generally put the INIT code last in your device driver and return the offset to the location where INIT starts so that memory can be reused.

```
;set done bit to show that initialization is done
 mov es:[bx].PktStatus, DONE_BIT

;copy end of code address to request packet
 lea ax, END_OF_CODE
 mov word ptr es:[bx].InitpEnd, ax

;copy end of data segment to request packet
 lea ax, END_OF_DATA
```

```
mov word ptr es:[bx].InitpEnd+2, ax

xor ax, ax                        ;set ax to 0
mov word ptr es:[bx].InitpEnd+4,ax  ;zero out 2nd pointer
mov word ptr es:[bx].InitpEnd+6,ax  ;
ret
```

INTERROGATING THE PROGRAMMABLE OPTIONS

All PS/2's running on the Microchannel architecture allow the user to con-
figure the boards' I/O port addresses and interrupt levels by software
command. This obviously makes the system more flexible when a number of
different kinds of cards are present in a system. However, it does mean that
you cannot be sure that the board in your system will respond to the same
I/O ports and interrupt levels as in another system. For you to find out how
the boards are configured, each has been assigned a unique id number. If
you know the id number of the board, you can search each slot for it and, if
it is found, ask it how it is configured.

To make this query, you start by interrogating slots 8 - 15 for board id's.
If your board id is 0x6029, you start by sending the slot number to port 0x96
and then read the low byte of the board id from port 100. If it matches, you
check the id of the upper byte from port 101. If that matches, you begin
querying the board-specific parameters from ports 102, 103, and higher as
specified in the board documentation. In the case of the Metrabyte
ucDAS-8PGA board, port 0x102 returns a byte containing the lower bits of
the port base address, interrupt level, and whether the board is currently
enabled:

7 - 5   port base address, bits 7-5
4 - 1   interrupt level
0   board is enabled if this bit is 1.

Port 0x103 contains the upper byte of the base port address. We refer to the
"base address" because such boards usually use a block of I/O ports starting
at a defined base address. In the case of the ucDAS-8PGA card, eight
sequential ports are used. After querying the board's I/O port base address
and interrupt level, you should save them in the driver's data area so you can
use them when the driver is asked to access the board.

THE DEVICE HELP ROUTINE

The DeviceHlp routine is a system routine you can call with a series of arguments to access OS/2 system services. OS/2 version 1.2 defines 38 such service routines that you may access. We list the most common ones in Table 23-4 All of these functions are called with arguments in the registers and return with results in the registers.

VIRTUAL AND PHYSICAL ADDRESSES

In protected mode OS/2 does not refer to addresses directly. Instead, the segment registers are loaded with *selectors* from a *descriptor table*. These selectors point to either a local descriptor table (LDT) or a global descriptor table (GDT), which in turn contains the offsets of the actual physical addresses. The purpose of this is to allow memory protection and the movement of data in physical memory during memory management without requiring a change in the addressing of the program. An address constructed of a selector and an offset is referred to as a *virtual address* since the actual address calculation is performed by the hardware. In real mode, however, the segment registers do contain the addresses of actual segments in memory, and these are referred to as *physical addresses.*

A number of the functions provided as DevHelp calls allow you to manipulate memory address representations between physical and virtual addresses, so you can use physical addresses for hardware-dependent functions such as DMA buffers and virtual addresses to refer to the locations in protected mode. The other implication of these functions is the ability to run an OS/2-style device driver in DOS mode. This is provided primarily for compatibility and is of little interest to new program development and will not be covered in detail here.

RESERVING A MEMORY BUFFER

A number of kinds of cards that you may write device drivers for are used to acquire data of some sort into a table or memory buffer. These data may be samples from an analog-to-digital converter or characters from some communication device. In either case, you will need a memory buffer where you

Table 23-4. Common Device Help Calls

Service	Code	Description
SemRequest	6	Claim a semaphore
SemClear	7	Clear a semaphore
SemHandle	8	Get a semaphore handle
PhysToVirt	0x15	Convert physical to virtual address
VirtToPhys	0x16	Convert virtual to physical address
PhysToUVirt	0x17	Convert physical to user virtual address
AllocPhys	0x18	Allocate physical memory
FreePhys	0x19	Free physical memory
SetIRQ	0x1B	Set interrupt handler
UnSetIRQ	0x1C	Reset interrupt handler
AllocGDTSelector	0x2D	Allocate GDT descriptors
PhysToGDTSelector	0x2E	Convert physical to virtual GDT address
RealToProt	0x2F	Switch from real to protected mode
ProtToReal	0x30	Switch from protected to real mode
EOI	0x31	Issue an End of Interrupt
UnPhysToVirt	0x32	Mark PhysToVirt complete
ABIOSCall	0x36	Invoke advanced BIOS function

can store these data and pass the array back to the calling program. While the acquisition of these data is a topic to be discussed as part of GenIOCtrl functions, you must reserve the place in the Global Descriptor Table (GDT) at initialization time. Note that you do not actually reserve any memory yet, but only a place in the descriptor table.

```
; reserve one GDT selector - offset left in mbuf_selector
; symbols are defined in this file:
;-----------------------------------
include driver.inc
;-----------------------------------
;
push    ds                        ;copy GDT selector into es
pop     es                        ;es contains GDT selector
mov     di, offset mbuf_sel       ;offset to this data location
mov     cx, 1                     ;number to reserve
mov     dl, DevHlp_AllocGDTSel    ;number of function
call    [device_help]             ;call function
jc      init_err                  ;error if carry set
```

THE OPEN COMMAND

An OPEN command is really intended primarily for file I/O handling, so that future commands to that file need not carry so much information regarding filename and location. It is also possible to use the OPEN command as a check to make sure that your device isn't in use by another task and to set up interrupt processing closer to the time that you will need to use it.

The OPEN command is passed to the driver when you make a DosOpen call from your main program. This has the form

```
DosOpen(szDevName, &handle, &action, 1L,
        attr, openflag, openmode, 0L);
```

where

szDevName   is a string containing the device's name, such as "pga8$."

& handle   is the location where the device handle is returned.

& action returns 1 if the file exists, 2 if it was created, and 3 if replaced. For a device, this should always return 1.

1L is the file size, and any value will do.

attr is the file attribute word. Should be 0 for a device.

openflag specifies the action to take if the "file" exists.

xxxx0000	fail if file exists
xxxx0001	open file if it exists
xxxx0010	replace file if it exists
0000xxxx	fail if file does not exist
0001xxxx	create file if it does not exist

The correct value for opening a device is 0x01.

openmode This is a 16-bit word whose flag bits are set as

DWFxxxxxISSSxAAA

where

D D=0 means open normal file, D=1 means this is a block device.

W Writes to the file through the system buffer cache if this is 0, and if 1 the actual physical write is performed before the write call returns.

I Inheritance flag. If 0 the file handle is inherited from a calling process, if 1 the file handle is private.

F If 0, errors are reported to the system error handler, and if 1, errors are returned to the caller by a return code.

S Sharing mode. Defines action other processes can take with this file/device:
001 deny read-write access
010 deny write access
011 deny read access
100 allow read and write access

x reserved.

0L   reserved.

Receiving the OPEN Command

When an open command is passed to your device driver, OS/2 has already
assigned a device handle to this call to the device. This handle is in the first
data byte after the packet. You need only check to see that the device currently is not in use and save the handle to indicate that it is now in use.

```
OPEN PROC NEAR
   test    Handle, 0ffffH       ;see if handle is currently 0
   jne     open_err             ;device already opened!
   mov     ax, word ptr es:[bx].PktData   ;get file handle
   mov     Handle, ax           ;save locally
```

REGISTERING AN INTERRUPT

One common task that may be performed at Open time is telling OS/2 that
your device will expect interrupts on a given level and want to have those
interrupts sent to a particular interrupt service routine. You already know
the interrupt priority level from the INIT command, where it was either set
permanently or interrogated from the POS routine. The SetIRQ call is used
to register the fact that this device can now generate interrupts. The arguments include the request level, whether the interrupt can be shared, and the
address of the interrupt handler. Note that bx is used and must be saved
and restored:

```
   push bx                              ;save bx
   mov     ax, OFFSET cs:inthandler     ;address of handler,
   mov     bx, intrpt_lvl               ;interrupt request 3
   mov     dh, 0                        ;dis-allow sharing
   mov     dl, DevHlp_SetIRQ            ;device help func #
   CALL    [device_hlp]                 ;call it
   jc      open_err                     ;error if carry set
   pop bx                               ;restore bx
   mov     es:[bx].PktStatus, DONE_BIT  ;and set done bit
   ret
```

THE INTERRUPT HANDLER

When an interrupt occurs, it is intercepted by the OS/2 kernel, and all the registers are saved. Then your interrupt service routine is called by a far call and you must return using a far return. Your service routine does not need to save or restore any registers.

The main strategy of an interrupt service routine is to respond to the interrupt as quickly as possible, obtain the data point, and return to the interrupted program. If you have set up your device to allow interrupt sharing, then you must be sure that this interrupt is from your device. If it is *not* from your device, you should return from the interrupt as quickly as possible with carry set, so that OS/2 can continue polling other devices on that level. If it *is* from your device, you should process the interrupt as quickly as possible and return with carry clear. Note that you return from the service routine with a RET instruction, since the final interrupt handling is carried out by OS/2.

The interrupt service routine that follows is for acquiring an array of data points from the 8PGA board: one each time the clock ticks. When the total number specified is collected, the interrupt flag on the board is disabled, and a semaphore is sent to the calling program indicating that the data are collected.

```
;-----------------------------------------------------------
;       Interrupt Handler
; In the 8PGA ADC board, interrupts are caused by the clock
; and the ADC must be started manually. In order to do
; this efficiently the handler reads the ready ADC value
; and starts the next conversion going thereafter.
;-----------------------------------------------------------
INTHANDLER PROC FAR
        mov     dx, adc_status  ;see if this belongs to us
        in      al, dx          ;check status bit
        test    al, 8h          ;if high it is ours
        jne     int_ours        ;yes it is
        stc                     ;this says it is NOT ours
        ret                     ;exit to Colonel

;interrupt is ours, process it ASAP
int_ours:
```

```
        mov     dx, adc_status
        xor     al, al
        out     dx, al          ;disable interrupt flag
        mov     ax, int_level   ;set interrupt level
;       mov     dl, DevHlp_EOI  ;official way to send EOI
;       call    [device_hlp]    ;send EOI to intrpt ctrlr
        add     ax, 060h        ;add spec EOI bits for 8259
        mov     dx, 020h
        out dx, al              ;set int levl spec EOI
        mov     dx, adc_hibyte  ;don't bother to
                                ;check status bit

        in      al, dx
        mov     ah, al          ;put it in high bit
        dec     dx              ;address of lower byte port
        in      al, dx          ;get lower byte
        shr     ax, 4           ;shift to 12 bits
        mov     dx, adc_hibyte  ;writing to port
                                ;starts next conversion
        out     dx, al          ;contents unimportant

;store current data point in buffer
        smsw    bx              ;get machine status word
        push    bx              ;copy it onto stack
        rcr     bx, 1           ;puts processor state in cf
        jc      protmode        ;already in protect mode
        mov     dl, DevHlp_RealToProt   ;else switch
        call    [device_hlp]

protmode:
        mov     bx, mbuf_selector ;get GDT selector
        mov     es, bx          ;and set as es seelctor
        mov     bx, bufpnt      ;get buffer pointer
        mov     es:[bx], ax     ;store data point
        add     bx, 2           ;increment buf pointer
        mov     bufpnt, bx      ;and restore
        mov     cx, bufcnt      ;see if we're done
        dec     cx              ;decrement counter
        mov     bufcnt, cx      ;put it back
        jg      intexit         ;if not continue
;turn off ADC now
        xor     al, al          ;set ax=0
```

```
        mov     dx, adc_status  ;Stop getting points
        out     dx, al          ;INTE flop is disabled
;send the main program a semaphore that the data is done
        mov     ax,sem_hi
        mov     bx,sem_lo
        mov     dl,DevHlp_SemClear
        call    device_hlp
; now release semaphore
        mov     ax,sem_hi
        mov     bx,sem_lo
        mov     dh,0    ;not in use
        mov     dl,DevHlp_SemHandle
        call    device_hlp
        jmp intdone

intexit:
        mov     ax, mux_value   ;select mux and INTE flag
        add     ax, IREQ_bit
        mov     dx, adc_status
        out     dx, al          ;turn INTE on in 8PGA


;restore interrupts and exit
intdone:
        sti                     ;turn interrupt on
        pop     ax              ;restore processor status
        rcr     ax, 1           ;check protected mode
        jc      protex              ;yes, do nothing
        mov     dl, DevHlp_ProtToReal   ;no, put it back
        call    [device_hlp]
protex:
        clc                     ;interrupt was ours
        ret                     ;and exit

INTHANDLER ENDP
```

Sending an End of Interrupt to the Controller

All of the PC's and PS/2's use an 8259 interrupt controller chip that must be reset as soon as you are sure that you are acknowledging your own interrupt. This allows interrupts to continue to occur at the same or higher levels. If you are sharing interrupts with other devices on the same level, you must use the DevHlp call to reset the interrupt controller:

```
mov     ax, intrpt_lvl    ;get interrupt level
mov     dl, DevHlp_EOI    ;get function number
call    [device_hlp]      ;send EOI to interrupt controller
```

If your interrupt is not shared, you can usually manipulate the controller chip yourself by sending 0x60 plus the interrupt level number to port 0x20.

```
mov     ax, int_level     ;set interrupt level
add     ax, 060h          ;add spec EOI bits for 8259
mov     dx, 020h          ;send this to IO port 0x20
out     dx, al            ;set int levl spec EOI
```

While this is some 80 microseconds faster than making the call to DevHlp, it is not technically recommended for multitasking systems and cannot be used when an interrupt level is shared.

Real versus Protected Mode

If the interrupt is yours, you must be sure that the cpu is running in protected mode before trying to address the data array using the global descriptor table and offset. To do this you use the SMSW instruction to copy the machine status word into a register. If bit 0 is one, the processor is running in protected mode, and if it is zero, the processor is running in real mode. If the processor is indeed in real mode, you must call the DevHelp function to switch it to protected mode before getting the data point. You must also restore the processor to its original mode when you are finished:

```
smsw    bx                      ;get machine status word
push    bx                      ;copy it onto stack
rcr     bx, 1                   ;puts processor state into carry
jc      protmode                ;already in protect mode
mov     dl, DevHlp_RealToProt   ;else switch into protect mode
```

Changing machine states is very slow on 80286 machines, which must essentially be "rebooted," but quite fast on 80386 and later machines. If your OS/2 machine has an 80286 microprocessor, modify your CONFIG.SYS file to include the statement

PROTECTONLY=YES

This will prevent the "DOS box" from appearing, and the machine will run only in protected mode.

Processing the Interrupt

Once you are in the correct mode, you can address the data buffer using the selector allocated at INIT time and loaded at ADCGO time. The offset into the buffer must be stored locally in the data segment and loaded into an index register. Then, it must be incremented and re-stored and the counter decremented. If the number of data points is not completed, you simply exit with a RET instruction. If it is, you turn off whatever continues to cause the interrupt.

```
protmode:
     mov bx, mbuf_selector        ;get GDT selector
     mov es, bx                   ;and set as es selector
     mov bx, bufpnt               ;get buffer pointer
     mov es:[bx], ax              ;store data point
     add bx, 2                    ;increment buf pointer
     mov bufpnt, bx               ;and restore
     mov cx, bufcnt               ;see if we're done
     dec cx                       ;decrement counter
     mov bufcnt, cx               ;put it back
     jle intstop                  ;if not continue getting points
     mov ax, mux_value            ;select mux and INTE flag
     add ax, IREQ_bit             ;re-enable interrupt to board
     mov dx, adc_status
     out dx, al                   ;turn INTE on in 8PGA
;restore interrupts and exit
     sti                          ;turn interrupt on
     pop ax                       ;restore processor status
     rcr ax, 1                    ;see if it was in protect mode
     jc  protex                   ;yes, do nothing
```

```
   mov dl, DevHlp_ProtToReal ;no, put it back
   call [device_hlp]
protex:
   clc                          ;interrupt was ours
   ret                          ;and exit
INTHANDLER ENDP
```

THE GENIOCTRL COMMANDS

The generic I/O control command category is intended to be used to communicate any special type of information specific to the device. For example, you could set timing parameters, data rates, numbers of data points, and multiplexer information using these commands. You also use one of these commands to actually begin data acquisition or other communication with the board.

The function call from C has the form

```
DosDevIOCtl( &data, &parms, function, category, handle);
```

where

& data   is a long pointer to a structure that will receive data from the call.

& parms   is a long pointer to a structure that will send data to the device.

function   is a function code, usually 11 for general I/O commands.

category   is the category within the function.

handle   is the device handle returned by the DosOpen call.

When a GenIOCtrl command is received by the driver, the structure pointed to by ES:BX has the form

```
GIOPacket      struc
GPktLen    db  20   ; Length in bytes of packet
GPktUnit   db  ?    ; Subunit number of block device
GPktCmd    db  ?    ; Command to device driver
GPktStatus dw  ?    ; Status word -status returns here
GPktDOSLink dd ?    ; Reserved
GPktDevLink dd ?    ; Device multiple-request link
```

```
GIOCategory  db   ?   ; function category
GIOCode      db   ?   ; function code
GIOParm      dd   ?   ; pointer to parameters
GIOData      dd   ?   ; pointer to data returned
GIOSysFile   dw   ?   ; System file number
GIOPacket         ends
```

The function categories and codes have been defined so that only some are available for your use. Categories 1-11 have specific meanings, and category 11 has been defined as General Device Control. Within the category, only codes 1, 2, and 0x60 have been defined:

1   Flush input buffer

2   Flush output buffer

0x60 Query monitor support

As before, you must respond to each command by either processing it or returning an error. If your device driver does not support device monitors, as few data acquisition cards would, you must return the error 0x12: no monitors supported.

While it might appear that you can use any function codes under category 11 that you wish, it turns out that individual bits of the function code have special definitions:

Bit   **Meaning**

7   0 - return error if unsupported; 1 - ignore error.

6   0 - intercepted by OS/2; 1 - passed to driver.

5   0 - sends data and commands to device; 1 - queries data and information from device.

The state of bit 5 is merely a convention, but you *must* set bit 6 to 1 in order for your function command to be passed to the driver from the calling program. Therefore, all user-defined function codes must have bit 6 set (0x40).

Defining Commands to GenIOCtrl

You can use any of these commands with bit 6 set to perform any device specific tasks you wish to define. You can pass arguments to the call by setting the pointer **& parms** to point to a structure containing any values you need to use to set up your device. Likewise, the driver can return any data values in a structure pointed to by **& data**.

Interpreting GenIOCtrl Commands

The easiest way to detect which of several GenIOCtrl commands has been sent is to scan another table just like the main command table. For a data acquisition card, this table might include

```
; Command table for GenericIOCtl commands
; -- all have bit 6 set
MinFuncCode       equ       40h
                  even
GenCmdTable       label     word
                  dw        offset SetClock      ;40h
                  dw        offset SetGain       ;41h
                  dw        offset ADCGo         ;42h
                  dw        offset SetMux        ;43h
                  dw        offset GetCount      ;44h

EndGenCmdTable    equ       $-GenCmdTable
```

Then this table can be used to call the correct subroutine by

```
GENIOCTL PROC NEAR
    mov al, es:[bx].GIOCategory      ;get the category
    mov ah, es:[bx].GIOFunc          ;put fn and cat in ah-al
    cmp     es:[bx].GIOCategory, GENDEV ;genl device IO Ctrl
    je      GenCategoryOK            ;category ok, go on

;If not allowable category, set the error bit
GenIOCtlBad:
    or es:[bx].PktStatus, ERR_BIT + UNKNOWN_COMMAND ;
    ret                              ;and exit
```

```
GenCategoryOK:            ;Verify range of Function Code
    xor     ah,ah                     ;set ah = 0
    mov     al,es:[bx].GIOFunction    ;Get fn code from packet
    sub     al,MinFuncCode            ;Make rel. to table start
    jl      GenIOCtlBad               ;illegal if < 0
    shl     ax,1                      ;convert to table offset
    cmp     ax,EndGenCmdTable         ;Beyond end of table ?
    jae     GenIOCtlBad               ;yes, error
    mov     di,ax                     ;Save table offset
    call    word ptr GenCmdTable.[di]  ;and call routine
    ret                               ;exit
```

BEGINNING DATA ACQUISITION

Interrupt-driven data acquisition presents two special problems unlike those found in classical interface cards. Since data may be arriving at a fairly high rate of speed, you need to be able to store it without waiting for the main program to respond. Therefore there must be a memory region where these data can be stored that is accessible to both the device driver and the calling program. Second, such data usually arrive in bursts or *scans*, followed by a pause sufficient to process or store the data. Therefore the calling program must have some way of discovering when the scan is complete so that it can move the data from the buffer to long-term storage elsewhere.

Allocating a Memory Buffer

Since the data will arrive under interrupt control, the device driver must allocate the memory and then pass the address of that memory to the user's calling routine. This takes place in the following steps:

1. Fetch the desired memory size.
2. Allocate physical memory.
3. Convert this memory address to a GDT selector for the driver.
4. Convert the memory address to a user selector. Pass the pointer back to the user.

Let us assume that the number of points to acquire is sent to the driver as part of the parameter structure, along with a pointer to a semaphore handle.

```
struct ADCParms
    begin
    int point_count;          /* number of data points */
    unsigned long far *sem;   /* semaphore handle      */
    end adcp;
```

Then we can access these parameters by making DS-SI point to the structure:

```
push    ds                          ;this is destroyed right here
lds     si, es:[bx].GIOParm    ;pointer to parameters
mov     cx, ds:word ptr [si]   ;count of points to acquire
mov     bx, ds:word ptr [si+2];high sem handle
                                    ;bx is lost here
mov     ax, ds:word ptr [si+4];low sem handle
pop ds                              ;here we put ds back
mov     bufcnt, cx             ;save count
```

We then allocate physical memory using the DevHlp call AllocPhys. This has the parameters

ax:bx   size of data area in bytes.

dh   If 0, look above 1 meg boundary, if 1 look below 1 meg.

dl   Value of AllocPhys function code.

```
mov     bx, bufcnt          ;set size
shl     bx, 1               ;*2 for bytes
mov     ax, 0               ;high part of size
mov     dh, 0               ;look above 1 meg
mov     dl, DevHlp_AllocPhys
call    [device_hlp]        ;allocate memory
jnc     gotsome             ;OK if carry clear

; as a last resort, try below 1 meg
mov     bx, BUFSIZE         ;set size
mov     ax, 0               ;high part of size
mov     dh, 1               ;look below 1 meg
mov     dl, DevHlp_AllocPhys
```

```
        call    [device_hlp]            ;allocate memory
        jnc     ADC_Err                 ;give up if no bufs
                                        ; available

gotsome:
        mov     bufhi, ax               ;save physical address
        mov     buflo, bx               ;returned in ax:bx
```

Setting a GDT Selector

Recall that we allocated a GDT selector at initialization time, so that we could use it to point to memory that we will be using in data acquisition. We now need to take the physical address of the memory buffer we just allocated and convert it to a GDT selector. Then we can quickly respond to acquisition requirements at interrupt time. This is done using the **PhysToGDTSelector** function.

```
;convert physical address of buffer to GDT
        mov     ax, bufhi               ;get physical address
        mov     bx, buflo               ;high and low words
        mov     cx, bufsize             ;set the size needed
        mov     si, mbuf_selector       ;here is where it is returned
        mov     dl, DevHlp_PhysToGDTSelector
        call    [device_hlp]            ;now the GDT points to buffer
        jc ADC_Err                      ;else deep yogurt
```

Converting Buffer Address to a User Virtual Address

We also need to represent the buffer address such that the user can get at the buffer. This is done by converting this same address to one that the user's local descriptor table (LDT) can access:

```
        push    es                      ;save es:bx, destroyed by call
        push    bx
        mov     ax,bufhi                ;get physical addresses again
        mov     bx,buflo
        mov     cx,bufsize              ;and size
        mov     dh,1                    ;segment read/writable
        mov     dl,DevHlp_PhysToUVirt
```

```
    call    device_hlp          ;convert for user
    jc      ADC_Err             ; error if can't convert
; now supply the user with the virtual address
phys1:
    mov     ax,es               ;answer returned in es:bx
    mov     cx,bx               ;copy to ax:cx
    pop     bx                  ;restore ptrs to packet
    pop     es                  ;restore both again here
    push    ds                  ;and save ds
    lds     si, es:[bx].GIOData ;get address of data
    mov     ds:word ptr [si],cx ;copy address descriptor in
    mov     ds:word ptr [si+2],ax
    pop     ds                  ;restore ds again
```

TELLING THE CALLING PROGRAM THAT ACQUISITION IS DONE

When we start data acquisition, we pass the device driver a number of points to acquire, and the pointer to a semaphore handle that we will set, and wait to have cleared, indicating that one scan is completed.

```
        unsigned long far *SemHandle; /* system Semaphore */

/* set up a semaphore to see when scan is done */
DosCreateSem((USHORT)1,          /*not exclusive ownership*/
     (PHSYSSEM)&SemHandle,       /*location of handle      */
     "\\SEM\\ADDONE.ADC");       /*name of semaphore       */
DosSemSet(SemHandle);            /*set the semaphore       */
adcp.point_count = 200;          /*take 200 points         */
adcp.semhandle = SemHandle;      /*pass semaphore handle   */
                                 /* to driver              */

DosDevIOCtl((PVOID)&dataword,    /*start ADC for 200 pts   */
     (PVOID)&adcp, ADCGO,
     DeviceIO, handle);

DosSemWait(SemHandle, 32768L); /*wait for semaphore to clr*/
DosCloseSem(SemHandle);        /*then delete it           */
```

Clearing the Semaphore from the Driver

Recall that we save the pointer to the semaphore when we saved the number of data points above. Since we are operating in a different protection ring and using different descriptor tables in the driver, we must convert the address of the semaphore to a *semaphore key* we can use within the driver:

```
;remainder of call at start of ADCGO - get semaphore handle
   mov      bx,ds:word ptr [si+2]   ;high sem handle
                                    ;--bx is lost here
   mov      ax,ds:word ptr [si+4]   ;low sem handle
   pop ds                          ;here we put ds back
   mov      bufcnt, cx              ;save count
;convert to semaphore key usable by driver
;-returns in ax-bx(bx is lost)
   mov      dh,1                    ;semaphore in use
   mov      dl,DevHlp_SemHandle
   call     device_hlp             ;converts to semaphore key
   mov      sem_hi,ax               ;save system "key"
   mov      sem_lo,bx
```

Then, when acquisition is complete, you simply clear that semaphore using the analogous DevHlp call, and then release the semaphore:

```
;send the main program a semaphore
;indicating that the data are gathered
   mov      ax,sem_hi               ;get the semaphore key
   mov      bx,sem_lo               ;from local storage
   mov      dl,DevHlp_SemClear      ;clear it
   call     device_hlp
; now release semaphore
   mov      ax,sem_hi               ;reload ax and bx
   mov      bx,sem_lo               ;with the semaphore key
   mov      dh,0                    ;indicate release it
   mov      dl,DevHlp_SemHandle
   call     device_hlp
```

ASSEMBLING AND LINKING YOUR DEVICE DRIVER

The assembly process is completely straightforward: simply use the MASM assembler to assemble the driver. Then link it as

```
link aiodrvr.obj,aiodrvr.sys,aiodrvr.map/map,\
     os2.lib,aiodrvr.def;
```

where the .DEF file contains the following:

```
;**** Module Definition File for the Device Driver  ****

LIBRARY AIODRVR    ;Specifies AIODRVR as dynamic link module
PROTMODE           ;Runs only in protect mode
CODE    PRELOAD    ;Device driver - preload
DATA    PRELOAD    ;Device driver - preload
```

24 | Writing a Device Driver in C

Since much of the job of a device driver is interpreting commands and calling the appropriate routine, it seems as if it might be unnecessary to write the entire driver in assembly language. It is in fact possible to write most of a device driver in the C language with only a small assembly language wrapper program that remains unchanged from one driver to the next.

OVERALL C-DRIVER STRATEGY

Just as we wrote our assembly language driver in the small model, where there is only one code and one data segment, we will do the same in the C program case. The main difference is that we must convince the linker to link the segments in a particular order, with the data segment containing the driver header block coming first in the file.

Communication from Assembly to C

The assembly language header will contain a pointer to a small assembly language strategy routine, which will move the pointers to the request packet from ES and BX to the stack, and then call the C strategy routine. The interrupt service routine should generally remain in assembly language so it can run as fast as possible and the only communication necessary is that its address must be declared PUBLIC so it can be registered and deregistered within the C part of the device driver.

Communication from C to Assembly

The main parts of the communication back to assembly language are the calls to the DevHelp routine, which is called with all of the arguments in the registers and all results returned in the registers. This is done by creating a structure containing the registers that is passed to the assembly language calling routine, which loads the registers with these values and calls the DevHelp routines directly. This is entirely analogous to the method DOS programmers use to call advanced DOS programs from C.

We will also simplify the error code return procedure by making our assembly language wrapper return the error (1 or 0) in the AX register, making the wrapper an integer function whose return code indicates whether an error occurred or not.

In addition, it is necessary to provide assembly routines to access the I/O ports directly. We are essentially replacing the **inp** and **outp** routines that would normally be called as library routines, since these routines would be in a different segment and won't work from the device driver level.

POINTERS IN A C DEVICE DRIVER

Even though this is a small model C program, you must be careful to make all pointers you pass between the C code and the assembly header into FAR pointers. This is required because you can not in general be sure whether the variable will be located in stack space or pointed to by the data segment register. This single point is the most troublesome: nearly every bug uncovered during development of this device driver sample turned out to be a near pointer that should have been a far pointer. Again, if you declare that a variable is a pointer, make sure you include the keyword **far**.

THE ASSEMBLY LANGUAGE HEADER PROGRAM

The declarations in the assembly language program are critical and they must be exactly those shown below:

```
.SEQ                ;Use the segments in the order listed
.286p               ;Use 286 instructions

;group the segments into the correct order
DGROUP  group   NULL, _DATA, CONST, _BSS, LAST_D
CGROUP  group   _TEXT, END_TEXT
```

These segment names are not arbitrarily chosen, and are in fact those that the C compiler uses. By declaring them all here, we are saying that all of them will be part of either the code (CGROUP) or the data segment (DGROUP).

The Device Driver Header

All device drivers must start with a particular 22-byte header block and this block must be first in the NULL data segment. In this example, we will describe a device called FRED$, which will be opened and used from a C program, and which has the same characteristics as the previously described Metrabyte ucDAS-8PGA Analog-to-Digital converter.

```
NULL SEGMENT word public 'BEGDATA'
        public dev_header
        public _devhelp
;Device driver header for the FRED$ driver
dev_header    equ $
ptr_to_next   dd  0ffffffffh     ;means loadable
device_attr   dw  8880h          ;option bits
offst         dw  _text:strategy ;assembly strategy routine
reserved      dw  -1
dev_name      db  'FRED$   '     ;device name
res2          dw  4 dup (0)
```

```
;-------------end of actual device header----------------
;             data needed for device follows

_devhelp        dd      ?          ;This is the entry pt to
                                   ; the device help routine
_mbuf_selector  dw      ?          ;gdt selector goes here
_int_level      dw      3          ;interrupt level- could
                                   ;be changed by POS
NULL ENDS
```

Then the following segments must be listed, empty, in this order to tell the linker they should be linked in this order

```
_DATA   segment word public    'DATA'
_DATA ends

CONST   segment word public    'CONST'
CONST ends

_BSS    segment word public    'BSS'
_BSS ends

;Dummy segment symbol so we can tell OS/2 the end of our data
    LAST_D  segment word public     'LAST_DATA'
    _last_d equ     $           ;address of last data
    LAST_D ends
public  _last_d                 ;addr of end of data segment
```

The LAST_D segment is used to generate a constant indicating where the last word in the data segment is located.

THE STRATEGY ROUTINE

The assembly language strategy routine is pointed to by the **strategy** offset in the device driver header. It merely serves as a wrapper to call the C strategy routine that does all the work. All it does is push the ES and BX registers onto the stack so that they can be retrieved by the C strategy routine as arguments in the form of a long pointer to the request packet structure

```
;===============================================================
;          Code segment starts below
;          Entry point to Strategy routine
;===============================================================

_TEXT    SEGMENT word public 'code'
         assume cs:_TEXT, ds:DGROUP, es:nothing


STRATEGY PROC FAR
;      INT 3                ;debugging
       push es              ;on entry es:bx pnts to request packet
       push bx              ;put them on stack for C-call
       call _strategy_c     ;call C strategy routine
       pop  bx              ;restore registers
       pop  es
       ret
STRATEGY ENDP
```

The C strategy routine must, of course, be declared as EXTRN within the assembly language header so that it can be resolved by the linker:

```
         extrn _strategy_c:near   ;C-strategy routine
```

Note that the C routine is declared as NEAR so that a near call is made, since all of the code will be in the same segment.

THE C STRATEGY ROUTINE

The C strategy routine receives the long pointer to the request packet as an argument to the function and simply implements a switch statement to decide which command to act on. The **lpreq** structure is simply the C definition of the request packet

```
typedef struct Request_packet
  begin
  BYTE    reqlength,          /*length of request packet      */
          devunit,            /*device unit code              */
          reqcommand;         /*command passed to driver      */
  USHORT  reqstatus;          /*return status bits here        */
  ULONG   reqreserved,        /*resrved                        */
          quelink;            /*queue linkage                  */
  BYTE    fcategory,          /*IO function category           */
          fcode;              /*IO function code               */
  LONG    far *GioParams,     /*data passed to driver          */
          *GioData;           /*data returned from the driver*/
  end far *lpRequest;
```

It is also convenient to define the structure of the packet used at initialization time with its own structure

```
typedef struct Init_packet /*bytes are aligned              */
                           /*differently in this packet     */
  begin
  BYTE    reqlength,          /*length of request packet      */
          devunit,            /*device unit code              */
          reqcommand;         /*command passed to driver       */
  USHORT  reqstatus;          /*return status bits here        */
  ULONG   reqreserved,        /*reserved                       */
          quelink;            /*queue linkage                  */
  BYTE    fcategory;          /*IO function category           */
  ULONG   lpDevHlp,           /*address of dev help routine */
          InitArgs;           /*initialization arguments       */
  BYTE    drivenum;           /* drive number for 1st          */
                              /*  block device unit            */
  end far *lpInit_Packet;
```

The actual routine simply calls other routines based on the **reqcommand** value:

```
/*--------- device driver strategy routine--------------*/
void strategy_c(lpreq)
        lpRequest lpreq;

begin
```

```
/*interpret the command to the driver                    */
switch(lpreq->reqcommand)
  begin
  case INIT:
    initdevice(lpreq);        /*initialize the device     */
    break;

  case OPEN:
    devopen(lpreq);           /* open the device           */
    break;

  case CLOSE:
    devclose(lpreq);          /*close the device          */
    break;

  case GENIO:                 /*generic I/O Control cmnds */
    GenIOCtrl(lpreq);
    break;

  default:                    /*otherwise set error bits  */
    lpreq->reqstatus = GEN_ERR +
                  ERR_UNKNOWNCOMMAND + DONE_BIT;
    break;
  end /*switch*/
end
```

THE INITIALIZATION ROUTINE

The device initialization is now done at the C level and amounts to saving
the pointer to the DeviceHelp routine and requesting a slot in the global
descriptor table. Both of these values are stored in the data segment list just
after the device driver header, and the locations are thus declared **extern** in
the C program and PUBLIC in the assembly language program.

```
/*--------device initialization routine----------------*/
extern ULONG devhelp;         /*address of device help */
                              /*routine set at init     */

void initdevice(lpreq)
```

```
        lpRequest lpreq;
begin
    lpInit_Packet lpi;
    union REGS reg;                 /*used to load registers  */
    union REGS far *preg;           /* for devhelp calls      */
    int errnum, far *mbuf, lc, ld;

preg = &reg;                        /*to pass args to Dev Help*/
lpi = (lpInit_Packet)lpreq;         /*cast ptr to structure   */
devhelp = lpi->lpDevHlp;            /*save device help address*/
```

Returning the End Addresses

It is critical that you return the end addresses of the data and code segments as part of the exit from the initialization routine. These are actually compile-time constants, but you must return them as addresses. In the assembly language header, they are declared as PUBLIC:

```
        public   _last_d ;offset to end of data segment
        public   _last_c ;offset to end of code segment
```

In order that they be treated as addresses by C, we declare them as if they were *functions*.

```
/* dummy routines -actually pointers                        */
extern void near last_c();  /* to code                      */
extern void near last_d();  /* and data                     */
```

Then, to pass these addresses back at exit time, we simply put them in the upper and lower parts of the pointer to the DeviceHelp function. Recall that the second pointer must be returned as zero for all character drivers:

```
lc = (int)last_c;               /*offset to end of code segment*/
ld = (int)last_d;               /*offset to end of data segment*/
lpi->lpDevHlp =
    MAKEULONG(lc, ld);          /*return these in parms in pkt */
lpi->InitArgs = 0L;             /*must be zero for char driver */
```

To reserve a GDT selector, we must see how to make calls to the **devhelp** routine from C.

CALL DEVHELP FROM C

Since all calls to the DeviceHelp routine are made with all the arguments in the registers, we must create a structure into which we can place the arguments and from which we can retrieve results. This is much like the register structure used in DOS programming, except that we have included the ES register for simplicity. Note that in protected mode you *must* put either a valid value or NULL in ES at all times.

```
struct WORDREGS {
  unsigned int ax;
  unsigned int bx;
  unsigned int cx;
  unsigned int dx;
  unsigned int si;
  unsigned int di;
  unsigned int cflag;
  unsigned int es;             /* note ADDITION of ES to this */
  };
/* byte registers */
struct BYTEREGS {
    unsigned char al, ah;
    unsigned char bl, bh;
    unsigned char cl, ch;
    unsigned char dl, dh;
    };

union REGS {                   /* overlays two structures    */
    struct WORDREGS x;
    struct BYTEREGS h;
    };
```

Allocating a GDT Selector

The procedure for allocating a GDT selector amounts to passing the far address of the location where the selector is to be returned to the DeviceHelp routine. This is done by breaking the 32-bit address into two parts and putting them in the ES and DI registers:

```
/*------------allocate a GDT selector----------------*/
mbuf = &mbuf_selector;             /*address where selector */
                                   /*will be returned       */
reg.x.di = (int)&mbuf_selector; /*offset part of address */
reg.x.es =
    (int)((long)mbuf >> 16);     /*segment part of address*/
reg.x.cx = 1;                      /* get only 1 GDT selctr */
reg.h.dl =
    DevHlp_AllocGDTSel;            /*number of DevHlp func  */

errnum = CDevHelp( preg);          /*call C dev helper routn*/
```

CALLING IN AND OUT ROUTINES

In order for your initialization routine or any other part of your driver to be able to access the I/O ports of your device from C, you must write your own **inp** and **outp** routines in the assembly header. Fortunately these are extremely simple to write:

```
        public _inp             ;C-call to in-port routine
        public _outp            ;C-call to out-port routine

;===============================================================
;       INP routine to be called from C
;===============================================================
;       int inp(int port);
;
_INP    PROC    NEAR
        push    bp
        mov     bp, sp          ;set frame
        mov     dx, [bp + 4]    ;get port address
        xor     ax, ax          ;set ax = 0
        in      al, dx          ;return argument in ax
        pop     bp              ;and base pointer
        ret

_INP    ENDP
;===============================================================
;       OUTP routine to be called from C
;===============================================================
```

```
;           void outp(int port, int value)
;
_OUTP    PROC     NEAR
         push     bp                ;save base pointer
         mov      bp, sp            ;set frame
         mov      dx, [bp + 4]      ;get port address
         mov      ax, [bp+6]        ;and value to send out
         out      dx, al            ;send value out
         pop      bp                ;and base pointer
         ret
_OUTP    ENDP
```

They must be declared as **extern** in C and PUBLIC in the assembly module. In addition, you must specify that the default libraries are not to be linked, so that the C-library versions of these routines are not linked instead.

```
extern int  near inp();
extern void near outp();
```

THE DEVICE OPEN ROUTINE

Whenever we open our device, we will register its interrupt. This means that we need to tell OS/2 the interrupt level, whether the interrupt is shared, and the address of the interrupt service routine. The service routine itself will be written in assembly language and declared PUBLIC, and declared **extern** in C.

We also obtain the device's current handle from the OPEN call, and only open the device if the handle value is currently zero:

```
/*------------device open routine---------------------*/
void devopen(lpreq)
    lpRequest lpreq;

begin
    union REGS reg;             /*used to load registers */
    union REGS far *preg;       /*for devhelp calls       */
    int err;

    preg = &reg;                /*to pass args to Dev Helper  */
    if (handle == 0 ) then      /*open only if not already open*/
```

```
begin
handle = lpreq->devunit;          /* copy handle number  */
lpreq->reqstatus = DONE_BIT;      /* set done bit         */

/*------ set up request to use interrupt --------------*/
reg.x.ax = (int)inthandler;  /*addr of interrupt handler*/
reg.x.bx = int_level;        /*set interrupt level       */
reg.h.dh = 0;                /*no interrupt sharing      */
reg.h.dl = DevHlp_SetIRQ;    /*set interrupt request     */
reg.x.es = NULL;             /*es not used, set to NULL  */
err = CDevHelp(preg);
if (err) then
    lpreq->reqstatus = GEN_ERR+
                    ERR_GENERALFAILURE + DONE_BIT:
end
else
    lpreq->reqstatus = GEN_ERR+
                    ERR_GENERALFAILURE + DONE_BIT;
end
```

GENERIC I/O CONTROL CALLS

The generic I/O control calls are handled with a second switch statement. In our routine we first check to see that it is category 11 (general device I/O) and second that it is one of the expected user-defined function codes.

```
/*---------------Generic I/O Control-------------------*/
void GenIOCtrl(lpreq)
    lpRequest lpreq;

begin

if (lpreq->fcategory == GENDEV) then
    begin
    switch(lpreq->fcode)
        begin
        case SETGAIN:                /*set the gain for the ADC*/
            SetGain(lpreq);
            break;
```

```
          case SETMUX:            /*set the number of       */
            SetMux(lpreq);        /*multiplexer channels    */
            break;

          default:
            lpreq->reqstatus = GEN_ERR+
                              ERR_UNKNOWNCOMMAND + DONE_BIT;
          end /* switch*/
      end      /* if */
else
      lpreq->reqstatus = GEN_ERR+
                        ERR_UNKNOWNCOMMAND + DONE_BIT;

end
```

DEVICE ACCESS FROM GENIOCTRL COMMANDS

There are two ways to command the actual device: either store the parameters and load them all when data acquisition is initiated, or have them take effect immediately. The SetMux routine simply stores the multiplexer value in a global static variable **adcmux** and the SetGain routine actually changes the hardware setting using calls to the **outp** routine.

```
/*-------------Set Multiplexer----------------------------*/
void SetMux(lpreq)
   lpRequest lpreq;

begin
          long far *muxadd;       /*address of mux value      */
          int muxval;

muxadd = lpreq->GioParams;    /*get address of mux value */
muxval = (int)*muxadd;        /*get actual value          */
if ((0 <= muxval) AND (muxval <= 7)) then
     adcmux = muxval;         /* copy into global parm     */
lpreq->reqstatus = DONE_BIT;  /* set done bit              */
end
/*-----------Set Gain----------------------------------*/
void SetGain(lpreq)
   lpRequest lpreq;
```

```
begin
   int gainval=0;
   long far *gainadd;

gainadd =lpreq->GioParams;      /*address of gain value    */
gainval = (int)*gainadd;        /*actual gain value        */

/* set the gain value now */
outp(PORT_BASE + ADC_GAIN, gainval); /*send the value out*/
lpreq->reqstatus = DONE_BIT;         /*set done flag     */
end
```

CLOSING THE DEVICE

When the user is finished accessing your device, he should issue a CLOSE command, which your driver should interpret by just de-registering the interrupt.

```
/*--------------Device CLose Routine--------------------*/
void devclose(lpreq)
    lpRequest lpreq;

begin
    union REGS reg;            /*used to load registers     */
    union REGS far *preg;      /*for devhelp calls          */
    int err;

preg = &reg;
handle = 0;                    /* release handle */
reg.x.bx = int_level;
reg.h.dl = DevHlp_UnSetIRQ; /* release interrupt request */
err = CDevHelp(preg);
if (err) then
    lpreq->reqstatus = GEN_ERR+ ERR_GENERALFAILURE;
else
    lpreq->reqstatus = DONE_BIT; /*set done bit*/

end
```

COMPILING AND LINKING YOUR DRIVER

The C part of your driver must be compiled using the Small memory model

```
cl /c /Gs /Asnw /Zpe /Fc driver.c
```

where

/c	means compile and do not link.
/Gs	means remove stack checking.
/Asnw	is the memory model specification:

          As   Small model C.
          n   Use near pointers. This is overridden for each one.
          w   Don't load DS on entry to routines.

/Zpe	packs structures and enables language extensions.
/Fc	generates a .COD file with assembly language listing to assist in debugging.

Assembling the Header File

The MASM call is

```
masm -Mx drivhead,,drivhead.lst;
```

where -Mx indicates that all public variables are to be case sensitive to be consistent with C conventions.

Linking the Resulting File

The statement in the driver MAKE file is just

```
driver.sys: driver.obj drivhead.obj driver.def
    link @driver.l
```

where the response file contains

```
drivhead.obj + driver.obj /A:16 /NOD /MAP
driver.sys
driver.map
slibce.lib+
os2.lib
driver.def
```

and the DEF file contains

```
LIBRARY DRIVER      ;Specifies DRIVER as a dynamic link module
PROTMODE            ;Runs only in protect mode
CODE     PRELOAD    ;Device driver - preload
DATA     PRELOAD    ;Device driver - preload
```

as before.

CALLING THE DRIVER FROM C

The following simple program opens the driver, sets a couple of parameters, and closes it.

```
/*driver calling test program */
#include <cdefs.h>
#define INCL_BASE
#include <os2.h>
#include <stdio.h>

#define SETCLOCK        0x40
#define SETGAIN         0x41
#define ADCGO           0x42
#define SETMUX          0x43
#define GETCOUNT        0x44

#define DeviceIO         11

void main();
/****************************************************************/
void main()
begin
  int  clockword, i, count;
  HFILE handle;
```

```
    USHORT result, attr, oflag, omode,action;
    ULONG fsize, reserved, muxword, gainword;
    unsigned long far *SemHandle;
    long dataword;
    int *p;

fsize = 0L;
attr = 0;
oflag = 1;
omode = 0x0012;
dataword = 0;
muxword = 0;

/* open the "FRED$" device                              */
result =DosOpen("fred$", &handle, &action, fsize,
                attr, oflag, omode, reserved);

/* set the multiplexer                                  */
        muxword = 0;
result = DosDevIOCtl((PVOID)(long far *)&dataword,
                     (long far *)&muxword,
                     SETMUX, DeviceIO, handle);

/* set the gain to +/- 5v                               */
gainword = 0x0;
result = DosDevIOCtl((PVOID)&dataword, (PVOID)&gainword,
                     SETGAIN, DeviceIO, handle);

/* close the device                                     */
DosClose(handle);
end
```

THE DRIVER ASSEMBLY LANGUAGE HEADER PROGRAM

The amount of assembly language is now minimal and amounts to wrappers
for the strategy routine, device helper routine, and in and out routines.

```
;***** Assembly language minimum module for device drivers*
    .SEQ                ;Use the segments in the order listed
    .286p
page , 132
    extrn _strategy_c:near    ;C-strategy routine
    public _inp               ;C-call to in-port routine
    public _outp              ;C-call to out-port routine
    public _CDevHelp          ;C-call to device helper
    public _mbuf_selector
    public _inthandler
    public _int_level         ;level of interrupt


;group the segments into the correct order
DGROUP  group   NULL, _DATA, CONST, _BSS, LAST_D
CGROUP  group   _TEXT, END_TEXT


;============================================================
;        Start of the Data Segment
;        Must start with the device header information
;============================================================
;
NULL SEGMENT word public 'BEGDATA'
        public dev_header
        public _devhelp
;Device driver header for the PGA8$ driver
dev_header      equ     $
ptr_to_next     dw      0ffffh          ;-means loadable
                dw      -1
device_attr     dw      8880h   ;
offst           dw      _text:strategy  ;strategy routine
reserved        dw      -1
dev_name        db      'FRED$  '       ;device name
res2            dw      4 dup (0)


;-------------end of actual device header----------------
;               data needed for device follows

_devhelp        dd ?    ;entry pt to the device help routine
_mbuf_selector  dw ?    ;gdt selector goes here
_int_level      dw 3    ;could be changed by POS routine
NULL ENDS
```

```
;==============================================================
;      Other segments are listed below in order to be linked
;==============================================================
         _DATA    segment word public      'DATA'
         _DATA ends

         CONST    segment word public      'CONST'
         CONST ends

         _BSS     segment word public      'BSS'
         _BSS ends

;=====Dummy segment symbol so we can
;=====tell OS/2 the end of our data
         LAST_D   segment word public      'LAST_DATA'
                  public  _last_d
         _last_d equ       $                ;address of last data
         LAST_D ends


;==========================================================
;Structure of a request packet
;
PKTMAX              equ    18               ;Maximum size of packet

Packet        struc
PktLen     db   ?         ; Length in bytes of packet
PktUnit    db   ?         ; Subunit number of block device
PktCmd     db   ?         ; Command code
PktStatus  dw   ?         ; Status word
PktDOSLink dd   ?         ; Reserved
PktDevLink dd   ?         ; Device multiple-request link
PktData    db   PKTMAX dup (?) ;specific packet data
Packet              ends
;==========================================================
;       Code segment starts below
;       Entry point to Strategy routine
;==========================================================

_TEXT   SEGMENT word public 'code'
        assume cs:_TEXT, ds:DGROUP, es:nothing
```

```
STRATEGY PROC FAR
;     INT 3               ;debugging
      push es             ;on entry es:bx pnt to request packet
      push bx             ;put them on stack for C-call
      call _strategy_c    ;call C strategy routine
      pop  bx             ;restore registers
      pop  es
      ret
STRATEGY ENDP
;==========================================================
;         INP routine to be called from C
;==========================================================
;         int inp(int port);
;
_INP     PROC     NEAR
         push     bp
         mov      bp, sp          ;set frame
         mov      dx, [bp + 4]    ;get port address
         xor      ax, ax
         in       al, dx          ;return argument in ax
         pop      bp              ;and base pointer
         ret

_INP     ENDP
;==========================================================
;         OUTP routine to be called from C
;==========================================================
;         void outp(int port, int value)
;
_OUTP    PROC     NEAR
         push     bp              ;save base pointer
         mov      bp, sp          ;set frame
         mov      dx, [bp + 4]    ;get port address
         mov      ax, [bp+6]      ;and value to send out
         out      dx, al          ;send value out
         pop      bp              ;and base pointer
         ret
_OUTP    ENDP


;==========================================================
;Device Helper interface routine to C
```

```
;This wrapper copies the values into the registers from the
;Registers structure, calls the DevHelp system routine
;and puts the results back into the structure on exit.
;Note that the CX register is not used on exit, and that
;the error indicator returned in the C-flag is returned as
;a result of the function in the actual AX register
;(not in the structure's AX register)
;============================================================
;         #include <dos.h>
;         BOOL devhelper(struct WORDREGS *w);
;============================================================
; structure of registers passed to devhelper call
;============================================================
Registers struc
         axo     dw      ?       ;ax register
         bxo     dw      ?       ;bx register
         cxo     dw      ?       ;cx register
         dxo     dw      ?       ;dx register
         sio     dw      ?       ;si register
         dio     dw      ?       ;di register
         cflag   dw      ?       ;flags register
         eso     dw      ?       ;es register-must be NULL
                                 ;or real value
Registers ends

_CDevHelp        PROC NEAR
;------------------------------------------------------------
devhelpstack struc
    oldbp dw ?              ;saved bp
    retadr dw ?            ;short return address
    regadd dd ?           ;long pointer to seg structure
devhelpstack ENDS
;------------------------------------------------------------
;   INT 3                  ;debugging
    push     bp
    mov      bp, sp        ;set frame
    push     di            ;save index regs
    push     si

; get values from addresses
    les      di, [bp + regadd] ;get address of start
```

```
                                    ;of structure
    mov     ax, es:[di].sio
    push    ax                      ;save es and si for last
    mov     ax, es:[di].eso
    push    ax                      ;save es and si for last
    mov     ax, es:[di].axo         ;ax-value
    mov     cx, es:[di].cxo         ;copy all values from struct
    mov     dx, es:[di].dxo         ;to the actual registers
    mov     bx, es:[di].bxo         ;before making the call
    mov     di, es:[di].dio
    pop     es
    pop     si                      ;restore registers for call
    call    [_devhelp]              ;call the dev-helper routn

;return the values to the calling program
    push    ax                  ;save ax
    lahf                        ;copy flags into ah register
    mov     cl, ah              ;copy to cl
    xor     ch, ch              ;zero upper byte
    pop     ax                  ;restore ax
    push    es                  ;save these
    push    di                  ;for last loading
    les     di, [bp + 4]        ;get address of
                                ;start of structure
    mov     es:[di].cflag, cx   ;return carryflag value
    mov     es:[di].axo, ax     ;return value of ax
    mov     es:[di].bxo, bx     ;return bx-value
    mov     es:[di].dxo, dx     ;return dx-value
    pop     ax
    mov     es:[di].dio, ax     ;return di
    pop     ax                  ;and es
    mov     es:[di].eso, ax
    mov     ax, cx              ;get carry flag into
                                ;AX for return
    and     ax, 1               ;only carry bit is returned

    pop     si                  ;restore real si and di
    pop     di
    pop     bp                  ;and base pointer
    ret
_CDevHelp   ENDP
```

```
;===========================================================
;         Interrupt Handler
;===========================================================
_INTHANDLER PROC FAR
        clc                              ;interrupt was ours
        ret                              ;and exit

_INTHANDLER ENDP

_TEXT ENDS
;===========================================================
;     Dummy routine to generate symbol marking end of C-Code
;===========================================================
END_TEXT          segment word public 'CODE'
        public _last_c               ;last word of c-code
_last_c equ       $
END_TEXT ENDS


;     End of CODE segment
;
;===========================================================
      END
```

THE DRIVER C PROGRAM

All of the actual functions are interpreted and carried out in the C part of
the program:

```
/****************** C- device driver ******************/
#include <cdefs.h>
#define   INCL_BASE
#include <os2.h>

#define INIT 0
#define READ 4
#define OPEN 0xd
```

```
#define CLOSE 0xe
#define GENIO 0x10

#define PORT_BASE   0x300
#define ADC_GAIN 3

#define DONE_BIT 0x100
#define GEN_ERR 0x8000
#define ERR_UNKNOWNCOMMAND 3
#define ERR_GENERALFAILURE 0xc

#define DevHlp_AllocGDTSelector 0x2d
#define DevHlp_SetIRQ 0x1b
#define DevHlp_UnSetIRQ 0x1c

/**************************************************************/
/* entry points in the assembly language header file        */
/*----------------------------------------------------------*/
extern ULONG devhelp;                /*address of device help */
                                     /*routine set at init     */
extern void near inthandler();  /*entry to intrpt handler*/
extern int near CDevHelp(void far *);  /*wrapper to call */
                                     /*device help routine     */
extern int  mbuf_selector;        /*gdt allocated goes here*/
extern int  near inp();
extern void near outp();
extern int int_level;                /*interrupt level used    */
/**************************************************************/
/* pointers to tne end of the code and data segments        */
/*----------------------------------------------------------*/
extern  void near last_c(); /* dummy routines            */
extern  void near last_d(); /* actually pointers to code*/
/**************************************************************/
/* global variables used within the C program               */
/*----------------------------------------------------------*/
unsigned handle;            /*device handle returned on open */
int adcmux;                /*multiplexer value saved here    */
/**************************************************************/
/* These structures are used to pass information to the     */
/* Device Helper routine. Note they are like the DOS        */
/* definitions except that ES is added.  You must ALWAYS    */
```

```
/* set ES to NULL or a legal value                              */
/*------------------------------------------------------------*/
struct WORDREGS {
   unsigned int ax;
   unsigned int bx;
   unsigned int cx;
   unsigned int dx;
   unsigned int si;
   unsigned int di;
   unsigned int cflag;
   unsigned int es;    /* note the ADDITION of ES to this */
   };
/* byte registers */
struct BYTEREGS {
        unsigned char al, ah;
        unsigned char bl, bh;
        unsigned char cl, ch;
        unsigned char dl, dh;
        };

/* general purpose registers union -                           */
/*  overlays the corresponding word and byte registers.   */

union REGS {
        struct WORDREGS x;
        struct BYTEREGS h;
        };

/****************************************************************/
/*       Definition of the Request Packet structure           */
/*------------------------------------------------------------*/
typedef struct Request_packet
   begin
   BYTE    reqlength,        /*length of request packet    */
           devunit,          /*device unit code            */
           reqcommand;       /*command passed to driver     */
   USHORT  reqstatus;        /*return status bits here       */
   ULONG   reqreserved,      /*reserved                      */
           quelink;          /*queue linkage                 */
   BYTE    fcategory,        /*IO function category          */
           fcode;            /*IO function code              */
```

```
    LONG  far *GioParams,   /*data passed to driver      */
          *GioData;         /*data returned from the driver*/
    end far *lpRequest;
/***********************************************************/
/* Definition of the request packet structure used at     */
/* initialization time                                    */
/*-------------------------------------------------------*/
typedef struct Init_packet  /*bytes are aligned           */
                            /*differently in this packet  */
    begin
    BYTE    reqlength,      /*length of request packet    */
            devunit,        /*device unit code            */
            reqcommand;     /*command passed to driver    */
    USHORT  reqstatus;      /*return status bits here      */
    ULONG   reqreserved,    /*resrved                      */
            quelink;        /*queue linkage                */
    BYTE    fcategory;      /*IO function category         */
    ULONG   lpDevHlp,       /*address of device            */
                            /*helper routine               */
            InitArgs;       /*initialization arguments     */
    BYTE    drivenum;       /*drive number for 1st         */
                            /*block device unit            */
    end far *lpInit_Packet;
/***********************************************************/
/* Strategy routine called by device driver               */
/* assembly header                                        */
/* to interpret commands to the driver and execute them   */
/* After command execution is complete the reqstatus bits */
/* are set in the request packet                          */
/*-------------------------------------------------------*/
void strategy_c(lpreq)
        lpRequest lpreq;

begin
/*interpret the command to the driver                     */
switch(lpreq->reqcommand)
    begin
    case INIT:
        initdevice(lpreq);  /*initialize the device        */
        break;
```

```
    case OPEN:
        devopen(lpreq);       /* open the device            */
        break;

    case CLOSE:
        devclose(lpreq);      /*close the device            */
        break;

    case GENIO:               /*generic I/O Control commands*/
        GenIOCtrl(lpreq);
        break;

    default:                  /*otherwise set error bits    */
        lpreq->reqstatus = GEN_ERR +
                           ERR_UNKNOWNCOMMAND+ DONE_BIT;

        break;
    end /*switch*/
end
/**********************************************************/
/*       Device Driver Initialization Routine            */
/*------------------------------------------------------*/
void initdevice(lpreq)
        lpRequest lpreq;
begin
    lpInit_Packet lpi;
    union REGS reg;           /*used to load registers      */
    union REGS far *preg;     /*for devhelp calls           */
    int errnum, far *mbuf, lc, ld;

    preg = &reg;                          /*to pass args to Dev Helper*/
    lpi = (lpInit_Packet)lpreq;  /*cast pointer to structure */
    devhelp = lpi->lpDevHlp;     /*get device help address   */
                                 /*  and save it             */

    /*allocate a GDT selector                               */
    mbuf =  &mbuf_selector;      /*address where selector    */
                                 /*will be returned          */
    reg.x.di = (int)&mbuf_selector;   /* pass in es:di */
    reg.x.es =(int)((long)mbuf >> 16);
    reg.x.cx = 1;                     /*get only 1 */
    reg.h.dl = DevHlp_AllocGDTSel; /*number of DevHlp functn*/
```

```
errnum = CDevHelp( preg);        /*call system device      */
                                 /*helper routine          */

lc = (int)last_c;                /*offset to end of code segment*/
ld = (int)last_d;                /*offset to end of data segment*/
lpi->lpDevHlp =
    MAKEULONG(lc, ld);    /*return these in parms in pkt */
lpi->InitArgs = 0L;        /* must be zero for char driver*/
if (errnum) then              /*set if error              */
    lpreq->reqstatus = DONE_BIT +
                       GEN_ERR+ ERR_GENERALFAILURE;
else
    lpreq->reqstatus = DONE_BIT; /*set done bit if no err*/

handle = 0;                  /*device handle initialized:  */
                             /*not in use                  */
end
/***************************************************************/
/*        Open the Device                                    */
/***************************************************************/
void devopen(lpreq)
        lpRequest lpreq;

begin
  union REGS reg;            /*used to load registers      */
  union REGS far *preg;      /*for devhelp calls           */
  int err;

preg = &reg;                 /*used to pass args to Dev Helper*/
if (handle == 0 ) then       /*only open if not already open  */
  begin
  handle = lpreq->devunit;         /* copy handle number    */
  lpreq->reqstatus = DONE_BIT;     /* set done bit          */

  /* set up request to use interrupt */
  reg.x.ax = (int)inthandler; /*addr of intrpt handler     */
  reg.x.bx = int_level;        /*set interrupt level        */
  reg.h.dh = 0;                /*not allow interrupt sharing*/
  reg.h.dl = DevHlp_SetIRQ;    /*set interrupt request      */
  reg.x.es = NULL;             /*es not used, set to NULL   */
```

```
    err = CDevHelp(preg);
    if (err) then
        lpreq->reqstatus = GEN_ERR+
                        ERR_GENERALFAILURE + DONE_BIT:
    end
else
        lpreq->reqstatus = GEN_ERR+
                        ERR_GENERALFAILURE + DONE_BIT;
end
/**********************************************************/
/* Generic IO Control Handler --                         */
/* Interprets Device Specific Commands                   */
/* This routine interprets specific functions in specific*/
/* categories In this case, only the category GENDEV-11  */
/* General Device Control is interpreted. All others are */
/* treated as errors                                     */
/**********************************************************/
/* Device specific commands -all must have bit 6 set     */
/* to be passed to handler                               */
#define         SETCLOCK        0x40
#define         SETGAIN         0x41
#define         ADCGO           0x42
#define         SETMUX          0x43
#define         GETCOUNT        0x44

/* Only category to be checked for legal commands        */
#define         GENDEV          11
/*======================================================*/
void GenIOCtrl(lpreq)
        lpRequest lpreq;


begin

if (lpreq->fcategory == GENDEV) then
    begin
    switch(lpreq->fcode)
        begin
        case SETGAIN:                   /*set the gain for the ADC*/
            SetGain(lpreq);
            break;
```

```
            case SETMUX:                  /*set the number of        */
              SetMux(lpreq);              /*multiplexer channels     */
              break;

            default:
              lpreq->reqstatus = GEN_ERR+
                                 ERR_UNKNOWNCOMMAND + DONE_BIT;
           end /* switch*/
       end     /* if */
else
    lpreq->reqstatus = GEN_ERR+
                       ERR_UNKNOWNCOMMAND + DONE_BIT;

end
/*=========================================================*/
void SetMux(lpreq)
       lpRequest lpreq;

begin
          long far *muxadd;        /*address of mux value       */
          int muxval;

muxadd = lpreq->GioParams;     /*get address of mux value */
muxval = (int)*muxadd;         /*get actual value           */
if ((0 <= muxval) AND (muxval <= 7)) then
     adcmux = muxval;          /*copy into global parm      */
lpreq->reqstatus = DONE_BIT;   /* set done bit              */
end
/*=========================================================*/
void SetGain(lpreq)
       lpRequest lpreq;

begin
          int gainval=0;
          long far *gainadd;
gainadd =lpreq->GioParams;      /*address of gain value     */
gainval = (int)*gainadd;        /*actual gain value         */

/* set the gain value now */
outp(PORT_BASE + ADC_GAIN, gainval); /*send the value out*/
lpreq->reqstatus = DONE_BIT;         /*set done flag       */
```

```
end
/*=============================================================*/
void devclose(lpreq)
        lpRequest lpreq;

begin
    union REGS reg;            /*used to load registers      */
    union REGS far *preg;      /*for devhelp calls           */
    int err;

preg = &reg;
handle = 0;                                /* release handle        */
reg.x.bx = int_level;
reg.h.dl = DevHlp_UnSetIRQ;        /*release interrupt req  */
err = CDevHelp(preg);
if (err) then
    lpreq->reqstatus = GEN_ERR+ ERR_GENERALFAILURE;
else
    lpreq->reqstatus = DONE_BIT; /*set done bit              */

end
```

COMMUNICATING WITH DMA CHANNELS

Many data acquisition boards allow data to be transferred to memory directly without intervention of the processor. Such boards are called "DMA boards" and utilize the Direct Memory Access channel of the PC or PS/2 to transfer data. This DMA approach is also commonly used by disk drive interfaces as well as a number of LAN communication cards, so the DMA controller is not totally free for your exclusive use.

From the point of view of data acquisition, however, a DMA card is an ideal choice for high data rates in a multitasking system such as OS/2, since there is no point-by-point overhead in acquiring data and hoping that the interrupt can be serviced before the next point is ready. DMA acquisition cards simply put the entire array of data points in memory without interrupting the processor, and then cause a single interrupt when all points have been acquired.

The DMA controller consists of a number of *channels* or *arbitration levels*

ABIOS functions are called through the DevHelp interface and are extremely simple to use. Each DMA device must have a logical ID or LID to communicate with ABIOS. This is obtained with the **GetLIDEntry** call. Then, all calls to ABIOS are made using the **ABIOSCall** function with the **si** register pointing to an ABIOS request block.

A great deal of information on call ABIOS routines and on DMA control is given in the *IBM Personal System/2 BIOS Interface Technical Reference Manual*, part number 15F0306. We summarize here the most generally useful functions for control of data acquisition hardware.

Getting a Logical ID

This is accomplished by simply loading the registers with the DMA device ID and calling the DEVHELP routine

```
/* get logical ID for communicating with ABIOS */
reg.h.al = DMA_Device_ID;
reg.h.bl = 0;                      /*get first unclaimed LID*/
reg.h.dh = 1;                      /*DMA is a shared device */
reg.h.dl = DevHlp_GetLIDEntry;     /*function code          */
reg.x.es = 0;                      /*must be 0 to avoid      */
                                   /*protection exceptions  */

err = CDevHelp(preg);
```

where **DMA■Device_ID** has the value **0xf** indicating that the device is a DMA device. The remaining values of this argument are for internal devices such as keyboard, clock, video, etc., and are listed in the BIOS technical reference manual. None of the remaining values are useful in writing device drivers for laboratory data acquisition cards.

Allocating Physical Memory

For a DMA device to work, you must allocate physical memory and pass the address of that block to ABIOS, using the **AllocPhys** DevHelp call

```
reg.x.ax =
     HIUSHORT(bufsize);    /*get high part of 32-bit size*/
reg.x.bx =
     LOUSHORT(bufsize);    /*get low  part of 32-bit size*/
reg.h.dh = 0;                  /*above 1 Mbyte boundary     */
reg.h.dl = DevHlp_AllocPhys;   /*function code             */
reg.x.es = 0;                  /*required                  */

err = CDevHelp(preg);

physptr =                      /*ax:bx is 32-bit physical address*/
   MAKEULONG(reg.x.bx, reg.x.ax);
```

While this DevHelp call will return a pointer to any size memory block, the DMA controller is limited to handling blocks of 64K *words* or 128K bytes at a time.

If you want this data block to be accessible by the user program while it is being filled with data by the DMA controller and ADC card, you need to convert the physical address to a user virtual address as we did before:

```
reg.x.ax = HIUSHORT(physptr);  /*high part of address  */
reg.x.bx = LOUSHORT(physptr);  /*low part             */
reg.x.cx = bufsize;            /*size of buffer       */
reg.h.dh = 1;                  /*readable and writeable*/
reg.h.dl = DevHlp_AllocPhys;   /*function code        */
reg.x.es = 0;                  /*required             */

err = CDevHelp(preg);
lpreg->GioData =
   MAKEP(reg.x.es, reg.x.bx); /*return address        */
```

Making Calls to ABIOS

ABIOS calls are made using the DevHelp call with SI pointing to the ABIOS request block, which has the form

```
struct abios_request
        begin
        int blocklen,            /*length of request block */
            logid,               /*logical ID              */
            unit,                /*unit number             */
            function,            /*input functio number    */
            res1,                /*reserved                */
            res2,                /*reserved                */
            retcode,             /*return code             */
            timeout;             /*time out in seconds x 16*/
/*call-specific parameters for DMA calls           */
/* start at offset 0x10                            */
            int res3;            /*reserved                */
            long dataptr1,       /*pointer to input data   */
                 res4,           /*reserved 4 bytes         */
                 dataptr2,       /*2nd pointer to input    */
                 params;         /*whatever follows to end */
        end;
```

Some of the most common ABIOS calls you might use are listed below. The left column is the function code. The indented values are the call-specific offsets into the ABIOS request packet.

0x3 Read DMA parameters.

> **0x10 word** maximum address under 1MB
> **0x12 word** maximum DMA transfer size
> **0x14 byte** number of arbitration levels
> **0x15 byte** number of DMA channels

0xb Allocate arbitration level

> **0x1f byte** arbitration level to allocate

0xc Deallocate arbitration level

> **0x1f byte** arbitration level to deallocate

0xe Get DMA transfer count

> **0x1f byte** arbitration level to check
> **0x18 long** number of bytes left to transfer

OXf   Abort transfer

0x1f byte   arbitration level to abort
0x18 long   number of bytes not transferred

0x10   ReadMemoryWriteIO

0x10 long   physical address of memory
0x14 long   physical address of I/O
0x18 long   number of bytes to transfer
0x1c   Mode control
   bits 7-3   reserved
   bit 2   programmable I/O
   bit 1   reserved
   bit 0   auto initialization
0x1d   transfer control 1
   bit 2   0=increment, 1=decrement
   bit 0   device size 0=8 bit, 1=16 bit
0x1e   transfer control 2
   bit 0   device size 0=8 bit, 1=16 bit

0x11   ReadIOWriteMemory- Same offsets as 0x10

Structures for ABIOS Calls

Since the arguments from offset 0x10 up vary with the call, it is often useful
to set up some equivalent structures that are then overlaid as UNIONs with
the base abios_request structure

```
struct abios_DMA_10
        begin
        int blocklen,           /*length of request block */
            logid,              /*logical ID             */
            unit,               /*unit number            */
            function,           /*input functio number   */
            res1,               /*reserved               */
            res2,               /*reserved               */
            retcode,            /*return code            */
```

```
              timeout;            /*time out in seconds x 16*/
/*call-specific parameters for DMA calls                  */
/* start at offset 0x10                                    */
        long memoryadd,          /*physical memory address */
             IOaddr,             /*physical I/O address     */
             count;              /*words to transfer        */
        char mode,               /*mode control            */
             control1,           /*count and device size   */
             control2,           /*device size 2           */
             arblevel;           /*arbitration level       */
        end;
```

Setting up the Arbitration Level

Each board is set up in a PS/2 using the installation diskette, and its arbitration level can be selected at that time. Before using this level, you must tell ABIOS to allocate it using the AllocArbLevel ABIOS function.

```
struct abios_DMA_IO ab;

ab.blocklen = sizeof(abios_request); /*set packet size   */
ab.logid = LID;                       /*set logical id    */
ab.unit = 0;                          /*unit=0            */
ab.function = 0xb;                    /*allocate arb level*/
ab.retcode = 0xffff;                  /*must initialize    */
ab.timeout = 0;                       /*infinite wait     */
ab.res1 = 0;
ab.arblevel = arblevel;               /*from POS on board */

reg.x.ax = LID;                       /*set logical ID    */
reg.x.si = LOUSHORT(ab);              /*offset of packet  */
                                      /*selected is in DS */
reg.h.dh = 0;                         /*entry point       */
reg.h.dl = ABIOScall;                 /*call function #   */
reg.x.es = 0;                         /*must be zero      */

err = CDevHelp(preg);                 /*make call         */
```

Setting up the DMA Transfer

To initiate a transfer, you must set the DMA count to one less than the actual number of words or byte to transfer, because the DMA controller terminates when the count changes from 0 to -1. You need to indicate the physical memory address to transfer to and the I/O port address on the board to transfer from:

```
ab.blocklen = sizeof(abios_DMA_IO); /*set block size     */
ab.logid = LID;                      /*logical IO         */
ab.unit = 0;                         /*no units involved  */
ab.function = 0x11;                  /*read IO write memory */
ab.retcode = 0xffff;                 /*initialize         */
ab.timeout = 0;                      /*no timeout         */
ab.count = buffercount -1;           /*set to count -1    */
ab.memoryadd = physptr;              /*physical memory add */
ab.IOaddr = BoardIOPort;             /*your board's IO port */
ab.arblevel = arblevel;              /*your board's arb level*/
ab.mode = 0x4;                       /*programmed IO, no init*/
ab.control1 = 0x1;                   /*increment- word size */
ab.control2 = 0x1;                   /*word size          */

reg.x.ax = LID;                      /*set logical id     */
reg.x.si = LOUSHORT(ab);             /*offset to request blk */
reg.h.dh = 0;                        /*entry point        */
reg.h.dl = ABIOSCall;                /*function number    */
reg.x.es = 0                         /*must be 0          */

err = CDevHelp(preg);                /*call DevHelp       */
```

Under current versions of OS/2, the DMA controller does not set the board I/O port address, so you must also do this directly with calls to **outp**.

```
outp(0x18, 0x7);              /*DMA controller I/O address */
outp(0x1a,
     LOBYTE(BoardIOPort); /*low byte of Board I/O port */
outp(0x1a,
     HIBYTE(BoardIOPort); /*high byte of Board I/O port*/
```

Deallocating the Arbitration Level

Once your device driver completes data acquisition, you should deallocate the arbitration level you are using. This is done exact as shown above for allocating it, except for the function number in the call:

```
struct abios_DMA_IO ab;

ab.blocklen = sizeof(abios_request);    /*set packet size*/
ab.logid = LID;                  /*set logical id      */
ab.unit = 0;                     /*unit=0              */
ab.function = 0xc;               /*deallocate arb level */
ab.retcode = 0xffff;             /*must initialize     */
ab.timeout = 0;                  /*timeout             */
ab.res1 = 0;
ab.arblevel = arblevel;          /*from POS on board   */

reg.x.ax = LID;                  /*set logical ID      */
reg.x.si = LOUSHORT(ab);         /*offset of packet    */
                                 /*selected is in DS   */
reg.h.dh = 0;                    /*entry point         */
reg.h.dl = ABIOScall;            /*call function #     */
reg.x.es = 0;                    /*must be zero        */

err = CDevHelp(preg);            /*make call           */
```

Index